新航道雅思考试（I

IELTS

雅思考试

高分作文

胡 敏 主编
Mark Griffiths 著
李行燕 黄晓波 译

中国广播电视出版社

图书在版编目(CIP)数据

雅思考试（IELTS）高分作文 / （英）格里菲斯（Griffiths, M.）著. —北京：中国广播电视出版社，2004.9

(新航道雅思考试（IELTS）培训系列教材 / 胡敏主编)

ISBN 7-5043-4358-7

Ⅰ. 雅… Ⅱ. 格… Ⅲ. 英语—写作—高等学校—入学考试，国外—自学参考资料 Ⅳ. H315

中国版本图书馆 CIP 数据核字（2004）第 096844 号

雅思考试（IELTS）高分作文

主　　编	胡　敏
作　　者	Mark Griffiths
翻　　译	李行燕　黄晓波
责任编辑	杨　凡
监　　印	赵　宁
出版发行	中国广播电视出版社
电　　话	86093580　86093583
社　　址	北京市西城区真武庙二条 9 号　邮政编码：100045
经　　销	各地新华书店和外文书店
印　　刷	三河市东方印刷厂
开　　本	787 × 1092 毫米 1/16
印　　张	13.25
字　　数	260（千）字
版　　次	2004 年 9 月第 1 版　2004 年 9 月第 1 次印刷
书　　号	ISBN 7-5043-4358-7/H · 181
定　　价	29.00 元

雅思风暴

（丛书序）

胡　敏

1999年留学热潮席卷国内，雅思考试悄然兴起，它的中文全称是“国际英语水平测试系统”，英文缩写为“IELTS”，专为留学与移民英联邦国家的申请者设置。这一年恰恰是我在新东方最忙碌的一年，主讲托福阅读，创办四、六级和考研英语培训项目，还要面对大量的教学与管理工作。在这种情况下，校领导多次找我，希望我能把雅思做起来，因为这项考试注重综合能力，要研发它必须有多年的学术底蕴和教学经验，他们认为我是最佳人选。

经过考虑，我接下了这个项目。当时国内雅思培训刚刚起步，第一个培训班开课时，根本没有可以信赖的教材，基本上是边上课边编教材。两个月培训结束，第一套内部教材也基本搞定，教学效果还算不错。

为了更进一步了解雅思，保证培训质量，我决定到位于英国伦敦的雅思考试主管机构——英国文化委员会走一趟。经过调研，我了解到英国文化委员会雅思总裁名叫肖恩·海德，通过国际友人的引荐，肖恩·海德接见了我。坐在他对面，我把事先准备好的问题提了出来，他一一作答，聊到托福考试时，肖恩·海德说了一句话：“TOEFL is an empire.（托福是一个帝国。）”言下之意雅思无法与之抗衡。

我则充满信心地说：“雅思考试具备巨大的市场潜力，肯定会异军突起。”

听了我的话，肖恩·海德开心地笑了。

之后我访问了剑桥大学考试委员会，走遍了几乎所有相关书店，购买了大量雅思考试类书籍。当我离开英国时，知道自己已经尽了最大努力，拿到了雅思的核心资源，可以把培训做得更好了。

归国航程9个小时，我没有休息，而是抓紧时间学习带回来的书。回国后，第1件事就是着手研发国内第1套真正意义上的雅思教材。由于客观条件及时间限制，它借鉴了国外雅思教材的部分内容，但我相信，假以时日，我肯定会研发出完全本土化的雅思教材。

教材开发完成，我开始全国巡回演讲。根据我对雅思的理解，我总结了4句话概括雅思：留学新途径、移民直通车、外企通行证、英语大课堂。演讲中我反复说明雅思考试的科学性：能够全面评估应试者的语言能力和水平，参加有些语言考试可能会高分低能，但参加雅思考试一定是高分高能。这次巡回演讲，我的足迹踏遍大江南北，先后举办了数十场免费演讲，使国人对雅思有了更多的了解，同时为英语培训开辟了一个新的领域，在国内掀起了第1场雅思风暴。

2001年，在充分准备之后，我认为研发拥有自主知识产权的雅思教材的时机已经成熟，经过我领导下的研发团队夜以继日的努力，终于完成了第2代雅思教材的编写。这套教材共17本，经测试，题目的仿真度达到85%以上，仅这一点就是许多国内外培训机构至今未能达到的。这套教材因其独创性、可操作性和高效性，很快在学员当中赢得了巨大的知名度，许多已经在国外学习的学员，也回国求购这套教材。与此同时，雅思成绩先后受到多个国家的承认，这种内外呼应的结果是，雅思考试如日中天，考生对雅思学习的热情一浪高过一浪。也就是在这个时候，学员和同行开始称呼我为“胡雅思”，这可以说是我在雅思领域制造的第2场风暴。

2002年澳大利亚宣布根据雅思成绩录取留学生，受这个消息的鼓舞，6月我亲赴澳大利亚，到各个学府与同行深入交流，广泛接触中国留学生。接触中我发现，留澳学生年龄普遍偏小，语言基础薄弱。回国后，我马上设计并建立了全国第1个雅思基础班培训基地，全面解决低龄学员的学习问题。第1期招生就爆满，2个月里招了近千名学生，在业内引起巨大轰动，许多培训机构争相模仿这种教学模式。同时我的第3代雅思教材也被隆重推入市场，由此全国各地雅思培训进入爆发期，仅新东方暑期雅思培训就达3万人，许多海外学子纷纷回国接受培训，其他雅思培训机构也出现了前所未有的井喷。

雅思风暴三度抢滩成功，一举成为培训业的宠儿。各大报刊争相刊登我在雅思培训方面的言论，一家主流媒体甚至刊登了一篇题为《雅思风暴，胡敏制造》的文章来形容当时的学习热潮。最近出版的《中国民办教育生存报告》说：“在过去的几年里，这个长着细长眼睛和高高额头的家伙旋风般地成为雅思考试的代名词。”那段时间，我每次参加网上举办的对话活动，短短一两个小时就会有成千上万的问题涌入聊天室，学员们的学习热情使我深受感动。曾经有个年轻人在学校找了我十多天，把他的雅思听力理解教材拿出来给我看，里面做满了各种记号，笔迹力透纸背，把书都划破了。而在此之前他一句英语都不懂，一个单词没学过，完全是靠毅力和信念的支撑，最大程度地信任了我所教授的方法，在3个月内使自己的雅思成绩达到了5.5分。我一辈子都不会忘记这个年轻人，从表面上看，是我总结出来的学习方法让他获益良多，在我看来，是他的积极向上、永不服输让我再一次感受到了功夫不负有心人。

时至今日，雅思考试在全国建立了25个考点，每年举办35次考试，已经有了与托福平分秋色的态势。而在英联邦留学的人员当中有70%以上参加过我主持的雅思培训，绝大部分雅思考生学习过我主编的教材。回想我制造的一场又一场雅思风暴，再看看自己接受的一次又一次洗礼，我深深体会到了弄潮人的快乐与幸福。

2004年9月于北京

Preface

Having taught IELTS preparation courses in China for four years, I am familiar with the main problems students face when preparing to take the writing module. This book aims to help students deal with these problems. Chapter 1 examines the format of the writing module, the assessment criteria, and the common problems that students face. Chapter 2 looks at the requirements of the writing module in terms of the use of grammar and various parts of speech. The next three chapters demonstrate how to write reports, letters, and essays for the IELTS writing module. They also contain sample answers with critiques, as well as model answers, for each type of writing task.

One thing that students often say to me is that they do not know what to write about in Task 2. I believe this is often a result of a lack of extensive reading. Students need to take responsibility for finding out what is going on in the world and why things are happening. I have met many students who are studying, or want to study, international trade, yet know hardly anything about how WTO membership will affect China. People living in Chinese cities often complain about traffic problems, but the only solution they offer is to use cars less, without thinking how this could actually be achieved. Students need to read newspapers and find information on the Internet, which could help them with the issues they may have to write about in Task 2. Remember that the ideas and vocabulary in this book need to be supplemented with others.

It is clear to me that students usually leave things until the last minute. Students do not give themselves sufficient time to prepare for the test. Also, they often do not practise enough by writing reports, letters, and essays. Unless you are using your English every day to do a variety of writing tasks, you can't improve your English by much in less than three months. UCLES, which developed the IELTS test, says that it takes *3 months of study, in an English-speaking environment,* to improve by *one* band score. If going abroad is so important, you need to devote more time to actually preparing for IELTS in an intelligent manner.

Students find it so easy to blame others or complain about their difficult situation when they have problems preparing for the IELTS test. Students love to get online after their tests and complain about the cruel examiners. They need to remember that *ultimately* the responsibility lies with *the student*. Get out and meet people and start *using* your English rather than blaming everyone and everything else for your inability to do well. If you don't want, or don't like, to go out and use your English, then it is clear that you need to rethink your plans to go to live and study abroad.

Introduction for Teachers
(Students should read this, too!)

As a teacher myself, I was eager to produce a book which would be 'teacher-friendly'. The book is laid out in such a way that teachers will probably be happy to work through the contents of the book in the same order that they are presented.

All the structures that students need for the IELTS writing module are presented in the second chapter of the book. Remember that this is not a grammar book and that the grammar and structures contained in that section are really designed to serve as a reminder for students. Students who cannot manage the structures to a reasonable standard simply shouldn't be in the class!

Deal comprehensively with the test format and criteria so that students know exactly what they are facing. The first chapter (hopefully!) contains the answers to any questions students may have. The pages devoted to grammar and structures are designed to ensure that students know what level of English is expected of them in the test. As I mentioned above, students who struggle with these pages shouldn't be in the class.

The three chapters dealing with report, letter, and essay writing approach the task from the standpoint of a student sitting the examination – from understanding the question through to writing the conclusion.

Encourage students to be imaginative and thoughtful. The Task 2 topics give students plenty of scope for original, highly individual answers. Writing in class gives students the feel of working in a controlled environment, whereas working at home allows them to explore new ideas and check new vocabulary. Students should also be encouraged to debate issues. Debating issues before meeting them in the test allows students to test ideas and arguments.

Acknowledgements

Thanks to everyone who helped with the sample essays. It doesn't matter if the essays were good or bad – they have all helped!

I'd also like to thank John at New Channel for making the publishing of this book possible, Jared, Steve, and Simon for their support here in Beijing, and my father for his close support, even though he's several thousand miles away.

The opinions expressed in the sample answers and model answers are not necessarily my own or even similar to my own.

Good luck to all the students who truly wish to learn English and help promote international relations through educational and cultural exchange!

Mark Griffiths

前言

我在中国教授雅思备考课程已有4年时间，因此对于中国学生在准备雅思写作时所面临的主要问题十分熟悉。本书旨在帮助学生解决这些问题。第1章讲述了雅思写作的考试形式、评分标准以及学生普遍面临的问题；第2章讲述了雅思写作在语法和用词方面的具体要求；接下来3章则讲述了如何撰写雅思写作部分的报告、书信和议论文。此外，每一类写作任务都有带评语的例文和范文。

学生常常对我讲他们不知道Task 2应该写些什么，我想这主要是因为他们阅读面太窄。学生必须独立自主地去了解国际时事以及背后的种种原因。我遇到的学生中有许多人在学习（或者想去学）国际贸易，却连入世对中国的影响都说不上来。居住在中国各大城市的人常常抱怨交通问题，可他们能提出来的解决方案只有一个，即减少汽车使用量，从不思考这一方案在现实中该如何实现。学生必须阅读报纸，在英特网上查找信息，这样才能有效完成Task 2的写作。请记住：光靠本书中的观点和词汇还不够，必须多读多记。

学生通常都喜欢“临时抱佛脚”，这一点我非常清楚。他们不会拿出充分的时间来备考，而且练习报告、书信和议论文写作的次数也不够。除非你每天会练习各种各样的英文写作任务，否则就无法在短短三个月内显著提高英文水平。雅思考试的设计者剑桥大学地方考试委员会（UCLES）这样说：雅思分数要增加1分，考生就需要在讲英语的环境中连续学习3个月。如果出国如此重要，你就必须拿出更多的时间踏踏实实地准备雅思考试，而且要勤动脑筋。

学生在备考中遇到问题时，很容易将责任推给别人，或是抱怨自己处境不佳。学生在考试结束后喜欢上网抱怨考官多么多么残酷。但学生必须记住：最终的责任都在自己身上。走出去，与他人会面，开始用英语交流；不要因为自己英语不佳而埋怨所有人或是抱怨所有问题。如果你不想或是不喜欢大胆地使用英语，那么显然，对于出国生活学习的计划你应该三思而后行。

教师必读
（学生也应该读！）

我本人就是教师，因此十分盼望能出版一本方便教师使用的书。本书的章节安排正是如此，教师上课时依次讲解书中内容即可，不用调整章节顺序。

学生在雅思写作考试中会用到的所有句子结构已在第 2 章中罗列出来。请记住：本书不是语法书，第 2 章中总结的语法和句子结构其实是为提醒学生注意而设计。学生如果未能掌握好各类句子结构，干脆不用来上课。

书中全面讲述了雅思写作的考试形式和评分标准，这样学生就能准确把握雅思写作考试。第 1 章回答了雅思考生的所有疑惑（希望如此）。语法与句子结构一章旨在确保学生了解雅思考试所要求的英语水平。正如我之前提到的，在这一章上有困难的学生不具备参加雅思备考班的条件。

接下来 3 章从雅思考生的角度讲述了报告、书信和议论文的写作方法 —— 从审题到写结论。

教师应鼓励学生发挥想像力，并深入思考。Task 2 的话题让学生有充分的空间写出新颖、有个性的文章。通过练习课堂写作，学生可以体会到受控环境下的写作过程；而在家里练习写作，则可以开拓新观点，查找新词汇。教师还应当鼓励学生就各类问题展开辩论。在写作考试前先就考试话题展开辩论，学生便能检验自己的观点和论断是否确凿有力。

鸣 谢

感谢所有在例文编写中给予我帮助的人。不论文章好与否，他们都伸出了援助之手！

我还要感谢新航道的 John，正是他使得这本书的出版成为可能；感谢 Jared, Steve 和 Simon 在北京给予我的支持；感谢我的父亲，尽管他远在千里，却给予了我密切的关怀与支持。

例文和范文中的观点非本人观点，与本人观点也不尽相同。

向所有真心想学好英语并希望通过学术文化交流来改善国际关系的学生道一声：好运！

Mark Griffiths

Contents

目 录

Chapter 1

The Writing Module

雅思写作考试概述

1.1 The Format of the Writing Module 雅思写作考试的形式

The format of the writing module is actually very simple. The module lasts for 60 minutes. It is strongly recommended that you spend 20 minutes on Task 1 and 40 minutes on Task 2. You may do Task 1 first or Task 2 first – the choice is yours. The most important thing is to pay attention to the time remaining. Remember that this time includes time for preparation and time for checking your work.
雅思写作考试的形式其实非常简单。这一部分共 60 分钟。强烈建议用 20 分钟时间完成 Task 1，用 40 分钟时间完成 Task 2。你可以先做 Task 1，也可以先做 Task 2，这由你自己选择。最重要的事情是注意还剩多长时间。请记住：在这段时间里不仅要构思写作，还要检查整篇文章。

Time is not the only factor you must bear in mind. Task 1 must be *at least* 150 words long. Task 2 must be *at least* 250 words long. These are the minimum lengths stated by UCLES, who developed the test.
你要牢记在心的事情不仅是时间。Task 1 文章至少要写 150 字，Task 2 至少 250 字。这是雅思考试的设计者 —— 剑桥大学地方考试委员会规定的最低字数。

When I was teaching IELTS writing classes, I knew many students who believed that 150 and 250 words were the maximum rather than the minimum. This is completely incorrect! Based on what students produced in class and for homework, I believe that a Task 1 report or letter should be at least around 180 words long, whilst a well-developed Task 2 essay should be at least around 300 words long.
我在上雅思写作课时，发现许多学生都以为 150 字和 250 字是最高字数要求，而不是最低要求。这是完全错误的！从学生课上和课下的写作情况来看，我想 Task 1 的报告或书信至少会有 180 字，而一篇论证充分的 Task 2 议论文则至少有 300 字。

Each candidate receives a four-page answer sheet. Pages 1 and 2 (the front page and left inside page) are for Task 1, whilst pages 3 and 4 (right inside page and back page) are for Task 2. Candidates have to write some information (name, candidate number, test centre, date, and module) on page 1 before the test begins.
每个考生会拿到 4 页答题纸。第 1 页和第 2 页（即正面和里侧左页）用来写 Task 1 文章，第 3 页和第 4 页（即里侧右页和反面）用来写 Task 2 文章。考试开始前，考生还必须在第 1 页上填写相关信息（姓名、考号、考试中心、日期和考试类别）。

Frequently Asked Questions about the Format of the Writing Module
有关雅思写作考试形式的常见问题解答

Can I ask the examiner if I don't understand the question(s) in the writing test?

Several candidates report trying this and every time they have not been helped at all by the invigilators (= the people who hand out and collect the test papers). Note that these invigilators may not even be examiners!

如果我不理解写作题目，可以问考官吗？

有几名考生表示曾尝试过这一作法，但每次监考人员（即发试卷和收试卷的人）都没有出手相助。请注意监考人员不一定就是考官！

What should I do if I need extra pencils and/or paper?

Raise your hand and ask an invigilator. Do not disturb others by asking aloud.

如果我需要额外的铅笔和/或纸，该怎么办？

举手问监考人员。不要大声询问，以免打扰别人。

Can I use some paper for making notes?

You can use the question paper. You are not permitted to write on any paper, except the question paper and the answer sheet. If you do – or if you try to – you may be considered to be cheating.

我可以在纸上作笔记吗？

你可以在试卷纸上作笔记。你只能在试卷纸和答题纸上写字，其他纸一律不允许。如果你在其他纸上写字（或试图在其他纸上写字），可能会以作弊论处。

What happens if I write less than the minimum number of words?

You can expect to receive a lower score than if you had written the minimum. Presumably, UCLES have investigated how many words would be required to write a reasonably developed answer for Task 1 and for Task 2. If your answer is shorter than that minimum, you have probably not developed the data into a report (or information into a letter) (Task 1) or not included sufficient arguments, ideas and evidence (Task 2).

如果字数不够会怎样？

字数不够的文章一定会比达到最低字数的文章得分低。可以设想，剑桥大学地方考试委员会一定调查过写一篇内容充实的 Task 1 和 Task 2 文章大概需要多长的篇幅。如果你的文章字数达不到最低要求，就 Task 1 而言，你可能没有将所有数据写入报告，或者没有将所有信息写入书信；就 Task 2 而言，可能是论点、观点和论据不足。

1.2 Interpreting the Band Scores 雅思写作考试评分等级说明

UCLES publishes the meanings of the overall band scores given to students who take IELTS. These are available, for example, on the official IELTS website. (For a list of this and other useful websites, see Appendix 2). In the listening and reading modules, the band score is determined purely by the number of correct answers. UCLES does not publicly specify what the criteria are for the writing and speaking modules, but it is possible to get a general idea by examining the overall band scores. Whilst it is possible to receive a half band score for the listening and reading modules and also for the overall result, writing and speaking scores are given as whole bands only.

雅思总分的含义由剑桥大学地方考试委员会公布，可以在雅思官方网站和其他网站上查到（相关网址请参见附录2）。在听力和阅读部分的考试中，得分完全由正确答案的数量来确定。剑桥大学地方考试委员会没有公布写作和口语部分的具体标准，但通过研究总分的含义，还是可以获得一个大致的印象。听力和阅读部分有0.5分，写作和口语部分则没有。

Band 9 — Expert User 9分—专家级语言能力

"Has fully operational command of the language: appropriate, accurate and fluent with complete understanding."

"能够自如地运用语言；得体、准确、流利、理解无误。"

A candidate will score band 9 for the writing module if the English they produce fulfils the required task completely. The writing will basically be perfect in terms of organization, method of expression, grammar and/or vocabulary, and it will get the message across extremely fluently, appropriately and accurately, throughout the entirety of the two tasks.

考生写出的英语如果完全能够满足写作要求，可获9分。其文章在组织结构、表达方式、语法和词汇上基本完美，而且在两部分的写作中，考生自始至终都能极其流畅、恰当并准确地传达信息。

Band 8 — Very Good User 8分—语言能力很好

"Has fully operational command of the language with only occasional unsystematic inaccuracies and inappropriacies. Misunderstandings may occur in unfamiliar situations. Handles complex detailed argumentation well."

"能够自如地运用语言，只是偶尔在语言上不准确或不得体（并非习惯性）。理解偏误可能出现在不熟悉的场合。能够表达复杂、详细的观点。"

A candidate will score band 8 for the writing module if the English they produce fulfils the required tasks at a very high level. The writing will be almost perfect in terms of organization,

method of expression, grammar and/or vocabulary, and it will get the message across very clearly and with a very high degree of accuracy, even when the candidate uses complex written English. Task 2 will be very well developed and reasoned.
考生写出的英语如果能够以相当高的水准完成写作要求，可获8分。其文章在组织结构、表达方式、语法和词汇上近乎完美，而且考生能够清楚明白地传达信息，准确性相当高，即便是写十分复杂的书面语也是这样。Task 2论证充分，条理清晰。

Band 7 — Good User 7分—语言能力好

"Has operational command of the language, though with occasional inaccuracies, inappropriacies and misunderstandings in some situations. Generally handles complex language well and understands detailed reasoning."
"能运用语言，但在某些情况下偶有不准确、不得体和理解偏差。总的来说能运用复杂的语言，理解详尽的推理。"

A student should score band 7 for the writing module if the English they produce is clearly sufficient to provide developed answers to the questions in Task 1 and Task 2 of the module. The student will probably make occasional mistakes, particularly with complex language. The student should be able to express his/her ideas reasonably clearly and fluently, using a wide range of vocabulary and grammatical structures.
考生写出的英语如果足以回答Task 1和Task 2中的问题，可获7分。考生可能偶尔会出错，写复杂句时尤其如此。考生应当能够比较清楚、流畅地阐述观点，遣词造句有多样性。

Band 6 — Competent User 6分—有运用语言的能力

"Has generally effective command of the language despite some inaccuracies, inappropriacies and misunderstandings. Can use and understand fairly complex language, particularly in familiar situations."
"大致可以有效地运用语言，但有些语言欠准确，欠得体，有时有理解偏差。能够运用和理解较复杂的语言，尤其在自己熟悉的领域。"

A candidate should score band 6 for the writing module if the English they produce fulfils the required task at a reasonable level. The writing will not be of high quality in terms of organization, method of expression, grammar and/or vocabulary, but it will be sufficient to get the message across clearly and with a certain degree of accuracy. The candidate will be able to use complex written English.
考生写出的英语如果基本完成写作要求，可获6分。其文章在组织结构、表达方式、语法和词汇上质量不高，但足以清楚地传达信息，并达到一定程度的准确性。考生能够使用复杂的书面语。

Band 5 — Modest User 5 分—语言能力一般

"Has partial command of the language, coping with overall meaning in most situations, though is likely to make many mistakes. Should be able to handle basic communication in own field."
"对语言的掌握不全面，多数情况下可表达大意，可能犯很多错误。但在自己熟悉的领域交流起来基本上无问题。"

A student should score band 5 for the writing module if the English they produce is sufficient to express general meaning to answer the questions in Task 1 and Task 2. However, the written English will probably contain many mistakes. Unfamiliar topics (such as the candidate may meet in Task 2) may present problems because the student may lack the necessary vocabulary to develop answers beyond an overall meaning.
考生写出的英语如果总体上能够达意，并足以回答 Task 1 和 Task 2 中的问题，可获 5 分。但语言错误很多。对于不熟悉的话题（如 Task 2 中考生可能遇到的话题），考生可能感到十分棘手，因为除传达基本意思以外，考生可能缺乏必备的词汇量进行充分论证。

Band 4 — Limited User 4 分—语言能力有限

"Basic competence is limited to familiar situations. Has frequent problems in understanding and expression. Is not able to use complex language."
"语言能力仅限于基本表述熟知的内容。理解和表述屡屡出错。不能使用复杂语言。"

A student may score band 4 for the writing module if they are only able to express basic meaning using written English. The student's written English may often be hard to understand, particularly when discussing unfamiliar topics, such as they might meet in Task 2. This may be due to a limited vocabulary and/or poor grammar. It could also be a result of an inability to understand the question. The student may not be able to communicate when using complex grammatical structures.
考生只能用书面语传达基本的意思，即得 4 分。其书面语令人费解，谈论不熟悉的话题时尤其如此（如 Task 2 中考生可能遇到的话题）。这可能是因为考生词汇量有限，语法掌握得不好；也可能是因为考生没能理解题目。考生写出的复杂句式可能无法达意。

Band 3 — Extremely Limited User 3 分—语言能力极其有限

"Conveys and understands only general meaning in very familiar situations. Frequent breakdowns in communication occur."
"仅可表达、理解所熟悉领域的大致意思。交流经常中断。"

A student may score band 3 for the writing module if they are only able to produce a limited amount of written English. The student will probably not be able to answer questions on unfamiliar topics, such as they might meet in Task 2. Even when discussing familiar topics, the student may only be able to express basic meaning. The student's written English will probably

be hard to understand, or even impossible to understand, possibly because of a limited vocabulary and/or poor grammar.
考生如果只能写出有限篇幅的书面语，即得3分。考生可能无法回答不熟悉的话题（如Task 2中考生可能遇到的话题）。即便是谈论熟悉的话题，考生也许只能表达基本意思。也许是因为考生词汇量有限或语法掌握得不好或两者兼有，其书面语令人费解，或者根本无法理解。

Band 2 — Intermittent User 2分—基本不能使用语言

"No real communication is possible except for the most basic information using isolated words or short formulae in familiar situations and to meet immediate needs. Has great difficulty understanding spoken and written English."
"不能进行真正交流。仅能在自己熟悉领域用互不连贯的词、句表达最基本的信息和满足最直接的要求。口头和书面英语的理解均非常困难。"

A student will score band 2 for the writing module if they are only able to produce a very limited amount of original written English, using very basic vocabulary and phrases. The student will probably have problems understanding the questions in the written test questions.
考生如果只能写出有限、简短的书面英语，使用非常基础的词汇和短语，即得2分。考生可能在理解写作考题上有问题。

Band 1 — Non User 1分—不能运用语言

"Essentially has no ability to use the language beyond possibly a few isolated words."
"除可能会用几个互不关联的单词外，实际上无法运用语言。"

A student will score band 1 for the writing module if they only write a few words of original written English.
考生只写一两句英文，获1分的写作成绩。

Band 0 — Did not attempt the test 0分—没有参加考试

"No assessable information."
"无可供评分的信息。"

A student will score band 0 for the writing module if they do not produce any original written English or do not even attempt to answer the questions. Candidates who write answers copied or plagiarised from other sources will score band 0.
考生如果没有写下任何英文，甚至白卷一张，就是0分。考生如果抄袭其他渠道的文章也是0分。

1.3 The Assessment Criteria 雅思写作考试评分标准

Criteria for Task 1 Task 1 的评分标准

The examiner will assess Task 1 on the basis of three criteria – **Task Fulfilment, Coherence and Cohesion, and Vocabulary and Sentence Structure.**
考官将根据 3 项标准对 Task 1 文章打分：任务完成；连贯与衔接；词汇与句子结构。

Task Fulfilment (TF) refers to how well the candidate completes the required task. The examiner will see whether all the required information is included in the report or letter and whether that information is sufficiently developed. The examiner will check the accuracy, appropriacy, and relevance of the information included in the answer.
任务完成（TF）衡量考生在多大程度上完成了所要求的写作任务。考官将考察报告或书信中是否包含所有必备信息，且信息内容是否充分。考官将考核文章语言的准确性和恰当性以及文中信息的相关性。

Coherence and Cohesion (CC) refers to how easily and how well the message of the report or letter can be understood by the reader. The examiner will check to see that the report or letter has a suitable layout and logical ordering of points. Using correct connectives to link points will aid Coherence and Cohesion.
连贯与衔接（CC）衡量报告或书信中的信息是否清楚易懂。考官将考察报告或书信的行文安排是否合适，逻辑关系是否连贯。正确使用连接词将各层意思连接起来，将有助于考生在连贯与衔接一项上拿高分。

Vocabulary and Sentence Structure (VSS) refers to the range, appropriacy, and accuracy of vocabulary, spelling, tenses, and sentence structures. The examiner will assess the ability of the candidate to use a variety of tenses correctly, a range of vocabulary appropriately, spell words accurately, and use vocabulary and grammar to express points.
词汇与句子结构（VSS）衡量词汇、拼写、时态和句子结构是否多样、恰当且准确。考官将考察考生能否正确使用各种时态和词汇，准确拼写单词，并使用各类词汇和语法结构来表达意思。

Criteria for Task 2 Task 2 的评分标准

The examiner will assess Task 2 on the basis of three criteria – Arguments, Ideas, and Evidence, Communicative Quality, and Vocabulary and Sentence Structure.
考官将根据 3 项标准对 Task 2 文章打分：论点、观点与论据；交流质量；词汇与句子结构。

Arguments, Ideas, and Evidence (AIE) refers to whether a point of view is clearly expressed, developed and supported. A good candidate will be able to assess opposing points of view as well as support his/her argument with suitable evidence. The examiner will check the accuracy, appropriacy, and relevance of the information included in the answer.

论点、观点与论据（AIE）衡量考生能否清楚地表达、阐述并支持自己的观点。一名优秀的考生将能够评判对方的观点，并使用恰当的论据来支持自己的论点。考官将考核文章语言的准确性和恰当性以及文中信息的相关性。

Communicative Quality (CQ) is very similar to Coherence and Cohesion in Task 1 and refers to how easily and how well the message of the essay can be understood by the reader. The examiner will check to see that the essay communicates clearly, has a suitable layout and has a logical ordering of points. Using correct connectives to link points will aid Communicative Quality.

交流质量（CQ）类似Task 1中的"连贯与衔接"一项，衡量论证的观点是否清楚易懂。考官将考核该议论文能否清楚地传达信息，行文安排是否合适，逻辑关系是否清晰。正确使用连接词将各层意思连接起来，将有助于考生在交流质量一项上拿高分。

Vocabulary and Sentence Structure (VSS) refers to the range, appropriacy, and accuracy of vocabulary, spelling, tenses, and sentence structures. The examiner assess the ability of the candidate to use a variety of tenses correctly, a range of vocabulary appropriately, spell words correctly, and use vocabulary and grammar to express points.

词汇与句子结构（VSS）衡量词汇、拼写、时态和句子结构是否多样、恰当且准确。考官将考察考生能否正确使用各种时态，恰当使用各类词汇，准确拼写单词，并使用各类词汇和语法结构来表达意思。

1.4 Common Mistakes Made by Students 学生常犯的错误

Task 1 — Academic Task 1 — 学术类

In Task 1 of the Academic Module, candidates are required to write a report of not less than 150 words describing data or information presented in the form of charts, tables and/or graphs. If more than one chart, table, or graph is presented, candidates are usually also expected to make comparisons between them.
按照学术类 Task 1 的写作要求，考生必须写出一篇至少 150 字的报告，描述图表数据或信息。如果题中有多个图表，考生除描述数据或信息外，通常还需要对比几个图表间的关系。

The most common mistakes that students make are as follows.
学生最常犯的错误如下：

1. **Not including sufficient information** drawn from the material presented. Students may not be *required* to include all of the figures presented to them in their answers, but including at least the most noticeable ones serves to improve the clarity of the answer. (See Task Fulfilment)
未能充分囊括材料中的信息。尽管 Task 1 不要求考生列出图表中的所有数字，但考生至少应该描述最明显的几个数字，从而使文章清晰明确。（见“任务完成”）

2. **Giving reasons** for the data and/or information. Task 1 is simply about data transfer, not opinions or reasons for the data. (See Task Fulfilment)
讲述数据 / 信息背后的原因。Task 1 写作只需要考生传达数据，不必就数据发表观点或罗列出数据背后的原因。（见“任务完成”）

3. **Not developing answers sufficiently.** This is a particular problem in short answers, i.e. ones of less than the required 150 words. It could also mean that a student has not seen an obvious trend or connection. (See Task Fulfilment)
文章内容不够充实。字数不足 150 字的文章尤其会犯这类错误，这也可能是是考生未能看出一个明显的趋势或联系。（见“任务完成”）

4. **Presenting answers in an unclear form,** particularly by either not using connectives to link sentences and points or by not using correct paragraphing and logical ordering of points. (See Coherence and Cohesion)
文章条理混乱。具体来讲，要么不使用连接词来连接句子和段落，要么分段错误，逻辑关系混乱。（见“连贯与衔接”）

5. **Making basic grammatical and spelling mistakes.** If a student is making basic mistakes throughout Task 1, that student is giving a poor impression of their English. (See Vocabulary

and Sentence Structure)
出现基础的语法和拼写错误。如果 Task 1 文章从头到尾都有基础错误，那么考官的印象就是该考生英文基础很差。（见“词汇与句子结构”）

6. **Making mistakes,** usually in more complex sentences and structures, **which make points difficult for the reader to understand**. These are called intrusive mistakes. You will certainly make grammatical mistakes, but keep them non-intrusive and the effect on your score should be minimal. (See Vocabulary and sentence Structure)
出现语法错误，导致读者难以理解作者观点。这类错误多见于复杂句和复杂的语法结构中，叫做“干扰型”错误。犯语法错误当然难免，但考生应尽量避免所犯的语法错误干扰读者理解，这样才能尽可能降低语法错误对写作成绩的影响。（见“词汇与句子结构”）

Task 1 – General Training Task 1 – 普通培训类

In Task 1 of the General Training Module, candidates are required to write a letter of not less than 150 words, usually associated with living or working in a foreign country or with an everyday problem that any ordinary person could encounter.
按照普通培训类 Task 1 的写作要求，考生必须写一篇至少 150 字的书信，话题通常涉及海外生活或工作，或是任何普通人可能遇到的日常问题。

The most common mistakes that students make are as follows.
学生最常犯的错误如下：

1. **Not including all of the information required.** This information is included on the task card, usually in the form of bullet points. Students are *required* to include at least all of these points. Further relevant points may also be included if they serve to develop the answer in an appropriate manner. (See Task Fulfilment)
未能阐述所有必要信息。这些信息通常分项列在试卷卡上。考生必须至少写出这些信息；如果其他信息有助于充实文章，也可以适当加以阐述。（见“任务完成”）

2. **Including irrelevant information in answers.** Stick with the bullet points and *appropriate* further development of the letter. (See Task Fulfilment)
文章中包含不相关的信息。信中只阐述试卷卡分项列出的信息和其他适当的信息。（见“任务完成”）

3. **Not developing answers sufficiently.** This is a particular problem in short answers, i.e. ones of less than the required 150 words. (See Task Fulfilment).
文章内容不够充实。字数不足 150 字的文章尤其会犯这类错误。（见“任务完成”）

4. **Presenting answers in an unclear form,** particularly by either not using connectives to link sentences and points or by not using correct paragraphing and logical ordering of points. (See

Coherence and Cohesion)
文章条理混乱。具体来讲，要么不使用连接词来连接句子和段落，要么分段错误，逻辑关系混乱。（见“连贯与衔接”）

5. **Making basic grammatical and spelling mistakes.** If a student is making basic mistakes throughout Task 1, that student is giving a poor impression of their English. (See Vocabulary and Sentence Structure)
出现基础的语法和拼写错误。如果 Task 1 文章从头到尾都有这类基础错误，那么考官的印象就是该考生英文基础很差。（见“词汇与句子结构”）

6. **Making mistakes,** usually in more complex sentences and structures, **which make points difficult for the reader to understand.** These are called intrusive mistakes. You will certainly make grammatical mistakes, but keep them non-intrusive and the effect on your score should be minimal. (See Vocabulary and Sentence Structure)
出现语法错误，导致读者难以理解作者观点。这类错误多见于复杂句和复杂的语法结构中，叫做“干扰型”错误。犯语法错误当然难免，但考生应尽量避免所犯的语法错误干扰读者理解，这样才能尽可能降低语法错误对写作成绩的影响。（见“词汇与句子结构”）

Task 2 – Academic and General Training Task 2 – 学术类和普通培训类

In Task 2 of both the Academic and General Training Modules, candidates are required to write an essay of not less than 250 words discussing and expressing an opinion on a topic usually associated with a social issue. Some plans are included near the end of this book to help you see how to organize your ideas.
按照学术类和普通培训类 Task 2 的写作要求，考生必须写一篇至少 250 字的议论文，通常就某个社会话题展开论述。本书附有一些方法，可帮助你组织论点。

The most common mistakes that students make are as follows.
学生最常犯的错误：

1. **Not answering the question.** Read the question carefully. A question asking candidates to discuss whether children should learn to use computers from an early age is not asking students to list the advantages and disadvantages of computers. Be careful to **focus on the entire question, not on one or two words** from the question. Sometimes there may even be two related questions. (See Arguments, Ideas, and Evidence)
答非所问。仔细读题，例如，按照题目要求，考生应探讨儿童是否应从小开始学习电脑操作，那么考生就不应该只探讨电脑本身的利弊。请注意：应把握整个问题，而不是问题中的一两个词。有时候，题目中还会列出两个相互关联的问题。（见“论点、观点和论据”）

2. **Including irrelevant and/or confusing information in answers.** Stay with the question and appropriate essay development. (See Arguments, Ideas, and Evidence)

文中包含不相关/不清楚的信息。紧扣题目，并适当阐述观点。（见“论点、观点和论据”）

3. **Not developing answers sufficiently and/or not including support for points and opinions.** This is a particular problem in short answers, i.e. ones of less than the required 250 words, but also occurs in longer essays where the student superficially lists points rather than including evidence or support. (See Arguments, Ideas, and Evidence)
论证不充分，或未能给出充分的论据来支持观点。字数不足 250 字的文章尤其会犯这类错误；即便是篇幅较长的文章，考生也只是轻描淡写地罗列几个观点，没有给出论据加以支持。（见“论点、观点和论据”）

4. **Presenting answers in an unclear form,** particularly by either not using appropriate connectives to link sentences and points or by not using correct paragraphing and logical ordering of points. (See Communicative Quality)
文章条理混乱。具体来讲，要么不使用连接词来连接句子和段落，要么分段错误，逻辑关系混乱。（见“交流质量”）

5. **Making basic grammatical and spelling mistakes.** If a student is making basic mistakes throughout Task 2, that student is giving a poor impression of their English. (See Vocabulary and Sentence Structure)
出现基础的语法和拼写错误。如果 Task 1 文章从头到尾都有这类基础错误，那么考官的印象就是该考生英文基础很差。（见“词汇与句子结构”）

6. **Making mistakes,** usually in more complex sentences and structures, **which make points difficult for the examiner to understand.** These are called intrusive mistakes. You will certainly make grammatical mistakes, but keep them non-intrusive and the effect on your score will be minimal. (See Vocabulary and Sentence Structure and Communicative Quality)
出现语法错误，导致读者难以理解作者观点。这类错误多见于复杂句和复杂的语法结构中，叫做“干扰型”错误。犯语法错误当然难免，但考生应尽量避免所犯的语法错误干扰读者理解，这样才能尽可能降低语法错误对写作成绩的影响。（见“词汇与句子结构”和“交流质量”）

7. **Using inappropriate words, phrases, and proverbs.** Students with low level English often try to give the impression that their English is better than it actually is by mixing certain words, phrases, and proverbs into their essays (and also into their oral English during the Speaking Module). This is a strategy recommended by numerous schools and textbooks as a way to improve scores quickly without much effort. In fact, this strategy has completely the opposite effect because the student cannot use the words, phrases, and proverbs appropriately. (See Vocabulary and Sentence Structure and Communicative Quality)
单词、短语或谚语使用不当。英文水平不高的考生常常在议论文中滥用单词、短语或谚语（在口语考试中也这样做），试图掩盖自己英文不佳的事实。众多培训学校和雅思教材纷纷推荐这一策略，以帮助考生轻松提高分数。实际上，这一策略是弄巧成拙，因为考生未能正确使用这些单词、短语或谚语。（见“词汇与句子结构”和“交流质量”）

1.5 Test Preparation 雅思写作考试备考

Here are some ideas on how to prepare for the writing module of the IELTS test. Remember that most students perform worse on the ‘active’ parts of the test (speaking and writing) and so should focus on using English actively as much as possible.

以下就如何准备雅思写作考试提出一些建议。请记住：多数考生都是“主动”部分（即口语和写作）的成绩不如“被动”部分（即听力和阅读）理想，因此考生应集中精力，积极主动地使用英语，而且用得越多越好。

1. **Practice discussing issues** with a partner or as part of a small group. *Try to find people who have a similar level of English as yourself.* If your English is much better than the others’, they will not be able to express their ideas clearly. You will not learn from them and they may get disheartened. If your English is worse, you will remain passive and may disrupt the flow of the conversation by interrupting and asking for words or translations. The others may also regard you as a ‘hanger on’ – a person who is there, but doesn’t contribute anything. *Discuss a wide range of issues.* Topics like ‘your studies’, ‘your family’, and ‘your hobbies’ will not be in the writing test! You cannot predict exactly which questions you will get in the test, so you must be ready for anything reasonable!

练习讨论问题。可以跟一个同伴或者一个小组开展讨论。尽量找同你英文水平相当的人。如果你的英语远比其他人好，而他们又无法清楚地表述自己的观点，你就无法从他们身上学到东西，他们也会失去信心。相反，如果你的英语比别人差，你就会相对被动，还可能因为你打断别人、请求别人解释单词或翻译句子而导致讨论中断。其他人甚至会觉得你是个“累赘”——一个只坐着却不做任何贡献的人。讨论各类话题。学习、家庭和嗜好之类的话题根本不会在写作考试中出现！你无法准确估计考试题目，因此任何合理的话题你都必须准备！

2. **Read newspapers and magazines** which have articles about a variety of topics, particularly social issues and recent developments, which are often asked about in Task Two of the writing module. The English language newspaper ‘*21st Century*’ (published in China) is particularly useful, not only because of the range of topics, but also because many words used in the articles are translated into Chinese and explained.

阅读报刊杂志。其中的文章会涉及各类话题，尤其是社会问题和最新动态，这些问题经常在雅思写作的 Task 2 部分出现。中国出版的英文报纸《21 世纪报》尤其有用，不仅因为这份报纸涵盖方方面面的话题，更是因为其文章中的许多单词都有中文译文和解释。

3. **Watch English news and documentary programmes or listen to English language radio.** Unfortunately, you may find the English to be too fast. However, you will learn a lot and discover some useful vocabulary. With DVD’s or VCD’s, you can rewind and listen again if you wish, and you can usually see the subtitles in Chinese and English.

看英语新闻和纪录片节目，或者听英语广播。不幸的是，你可能会觉得里面的英文语速太快，但你还是会学到很多东西，并发现一些有用的词汇。如果是观看DVD和VCD，你就能倒回去再听一遍，而且通常都能看到中文字幕和英文字幕。

4. **Get on the Internet!** It is interesting how so many students talk about using the Internet to find information, but never actually use it for this purpose!

(i) Find English language chat rooms, where you can discuss the issues you need to know about for the IELTS writing module.

(ii) Visit websites which contain news and informative stories. These will help you in the same way as newspapers and magazines.

(iii) Be wary of IELTS related websites. They often have good topics, sometimes have good questions, but rarely provide decent sample answers. Use the topics and questions in your practice sessions. Do not copy the 'model answers', but use some of the vocabulary as appropriate.

上网！不少学生都说应该上网查资料，但他们上网从来都没正经查过资料：真是怪哉！

(i) 找到英语聊天室，探讨准备雅思写作必须了解的话题。

(ii) 拜访有英语新闻和详细报道的网站，这跟阅读报刊杂志的效果一样。

(iii)谨慎对待与雅思有关的网站。这些网站上往往会有一些比较好的话题，甚至会有一些比较好的考题，但很少会提供优秀的例文。你可以自行练习这些话题和考题。不要照搬所谓的"标准答案"，但可以适当使用"标准答案"中的部分词汇。

5. **Practice writing essays.** At first, write in your own time to get used to it, but as you get closer to your test date, do so in the time limit you will have to work under during the actual test. Compare your essays with those by other people. Correct mistakes in them and advise each other on layout, content, and cohesion.

练习写议论文。一开始，先拿出自己的时间熟悉议论文写作；临近考试时，可模拟实际考试在规定的时间内练习议论文写作。比较自己的作文和他人的作文。纠正作文中的错误，并就行文、内容和衔接等问题相互提供意见和建议。

6. **Keep a vocabulary notebook.** Organise the vocabulary by topic and include both the translation into Chinese and the correct pronunciation. You can also include phrases, prepositions, and collocations (= words that often go together) under each entry in your notebook.

准备一个词汇本。按话题对词汇进行分类，并写上中文翻译和正确的读音。你还可以在每一个词条后写上相关的短语、介词和搭配（即经常连在一起使用的词）。

7. **Become confident when you use English.** This should be your aim, because when you are confident that your English is good, you will spend less time worrying about it and more time relaxing and writing a coherent answer. Of course, you will be more confident if you have prepared and practiced thoroughly.

对自己的英语有信心。这应该是你的目标，因为如果你自信自己的英文不错，就会用更少的时间担心语言，用更多的时间轻松自如地写作。当然，如果你经过了充分的准备和练习，就会变得加倍自信。

Frequently Asked Questions about Test Preparation 备考常见问题解答

What is the most difficult part of the IELTS writing test?

Different students have different strengths and weaknesses, but generally students do not do as well on the "active" parts of the test (speaking and writing) compared to the "passive" parts of the test (reading and listening). Within the writing module, most candidates report that they find Task 2 the most difficult, which is not surprising, because it is designed to be more demanding.

雅思写作考试哪部分最难？

不同的考生有不同的优势和劣势，但多半考生都是“主动”部分（即口语和写作）的成绩不如“被动”部分（即阅读和听力）理想。就写作部分而言，大多数考生都反映 Task 2 最难。这也难怪，因为考试机构原本就将 Task 2 设计为难度最高的考题。

Should I take an IELTS preparation course before taking the test?

An IELTS preparation course at a good school with teachers who are truly informed about IELTS will provide you gain the information and skills you need in order to make the most of your English during the test. This can certainly help improve your band score, usually by one band. However, an IELTS course is not a substitute for a general English course. If you do not have a reasonable knowledge of English when you begin the course, the IELTS course will be virtually useless to you.

考雅思之前，我应该学习雅思培训课程吗？

如果是一所优秀的英语学校，而且学校教师对雅思考试把握透彻，那么在这样的学校学习雅思培训课程就能让你获得必备的信息和技能，从而在考试中最大限度地运用英语。学习雅思培训课程通常能将雅思成绩提高 1 分。然而，雅思培训还是无法替代基础的英语课程。如果在雅思培训课程开始前你就缺乏一定的英语基础，那么雅思培训课程对你就没有太多帮助。

How can I decide if a school is good or not before I enrol?

Find out something about the teachers and their experience. A teacher who is not a native speaker should have already taken the test and received at least a band 7. If they cannot get a good score, how can they teach you to do it? A good school will also send its teachers to take the test so that they know exactly how it is conducted. Alternatively, the school may be an IELTS test centre. Do not focus too much on whether a school is a new one or an old one. Be very cautious of schools which "guarantee" you a certain score.

在报名之前我如何判断一所英语学校的好坏？

了解一下学校师资情况，看看其教师是否经验丰富。一名英语为非母语的教师应该参加过雅思考试，分数至少达到 7 分。如果他们分数不高，又怎么能教雅思呢？一所优秀的英语学校还会派教师去参加雅思考试，这样教师就能亲身体验雅思考试的全过程。或者，这所学校本身就是雅思考试中心。不要过于关注一所学校成立的时间长短。有些学校“担保”你拿到一定的雅思分数，对于这类学校，你要格外小心。

Is it a good idea to memorise some answers from books before the test?

Memorising answers for the test is not a recommended strategy, because the examiner may notice this and not give you any credit for the answer. Remember that examiners also have access to IELTS preparation materials, so noticing a copied answer is not too difficult. An examiner would certainly get suspicious if (s)he saw an average Task 1 answer followed by a perfect Task 2 answer! The candidate rules now clearly state that copied answers will receive band 0.

考试前是否需要强记书本上的一些文章？

在考试中照搬答案绝不是明智的做法，因为考官一旦发现，就不会给你评高分。请记住：考官同样能获得雅思备考资料，所以发现考生抄袭答案并不是件难事。如果考官看到一篇语言平平的 Task 1 文章后紧跟着一篇完美无暇的 Task 2 文章，自然会起疑心。目前的考试规定明确提出，凡抄袭的答案一律记 0 分。

Student's Notes:

Chapter 2

Sentence Structures and Parts of Speech

句子结构和词性

2.1 Tenses 时态

In this section, we will briefly look at the variety of tenses that a student may need to use in the IELTS writing module. First, let's look at the verb tenses.
本章将简要探讨学生在雅思写作中可能会用到的各种时态。首先，让我们看看动词的各种时态。

Past simple	Present simple	Future simple
一般过去时	一般现在时	一般将来时
Past perfect	Present perfect	Future perfect
过去完成时	现在完成时	将来完成时
Past continuous	Present continuous	Future continuous
过去进行时	现在进行时	将来进行时
Past perfect continuous	Present perfect continuous	Future perfect continuous
过去完成进行时	现在完成进行时	将来完成进行时

Present Simple 一般现在时

This tense is used for:
(i) statements that are always true. "Cars **create** pollution."
(ii) states. "I **prefer** email to other forms of communication."
(iii) regular activities. "My parents **drive** to work.." Do not use 'will' in this situation!
You can use the present simple with words that say **how often** something happens (e.g. rarely, sometimes, often, always).
(iv) scheduled events in the future, particularly with transport and timetables. "The plane arrives at 8 o'clock."
Remember to use '**do**' in **negative** sentences. "People **don't** want to create pollution."
Remember to add '**s**' or '**es**' for he/she/it sentences. "Solar power **doesn't** create pollution." "She **likes** wearing fashionable clothes."
'Do' can be used in positive sentences to emphasise a statement. "You don't like chocolate!" "I **do** like chocolate!"
一般现在时用于描述：
(i) 永远正确的事实，如：Cars create pollution.
(ii) 状态，如：I prefer email to other forms of communication.
(iii) 频繁发生的活动，如：My parents drive to work. 这种情况不要用将来时中的 will。
你可以在一般现在时中运用表示事情发生频率的副词，如：rarely，sometimes，often，always 等。
(iv) 按计划将要发生的事件，尤其用于交通和时间表，如：The plane arrives at 8 o'clock.
记住在否定句中用 do，如：People don't want to create pollution.

记住第三人称单数 he/she 要加 s/es，如：Solar power doesn't create pollution. / She likes wearing fashionable clothes.
在肯定句中可以用 do 表示强调，如："You don't like chocolate!" / "I do like chocolate!"

Present Continuous 现在进行时

This tense is used for:
(i) things that are happening at the time of speaking (or around the time of speaking). **"I'm reading** an interesting book on the subject." It can be used to describe trends, which is very useful in Task 1 for describing data ("Africa's population **is increasing** rapidly.") and in Task 2 for describing developments ("China **is developing** quickly.")
(ii) talking about future plans that have already been made. "**I'm planning** to research this topic **next semester**." Notice that in this situation, a word or phrase referring to the future should be included. If not the sentence will look the same as in point (i).
In negative sentences, 'not' is placed between the auxiliary verb ('be') and the action verb. "We **are not reducing** the amount of waste at an acceptable rate."
Remember that the continuous tenses are used with action verbs. They are **not** used with many common verbs such as 'want' ('I **want** a better world' **not** 'I am wanting a better world'). Here is a list of common verbs not used with continuous tenses.
现在进行时用于描述：
(i) 说话时（或说话前后）发生的事情，如：I'm reading an interesting book on the subject. 这种时态可用来描述趋势，比如在 Task 1 中描述数据（Africa's population is increasing rapidly.），在 Task 2 中描写发展（China is developing quickly.）
(ii) 已经确定的未来计划，如：I'm planning to research this topic next semester. 注意：在这种情况下，句子中应该有一个表示未来的单词或短语，否则该句就跟（i）中的句子完全一样了。
在否定句中，not 放在助动词 be 和行为动词之间，如：We are not eating reducing the amount of waste at an acceptable rate.。
记住：进行时是用于行为动词的时态，许多动词（如 want）不能用于进行时态，比如：要说 I want a better world.不能说 I am wanting a better world.

以下是不能用于进行时的常用动词列表：

appear	believe	belong	concern	consist	contain
depend	hate	hear	imagine	involve	know
like	love	matter	mean	need	owe
own	possess	prefer	realise	recognize	remember
resemble	see	seem	suppose	understand	want
wish					

We can illustrate the difference between 'action' verbs and the verbs on the above list quite simply. 'See' and 'hear' (both on the list above) are things you do automatically, but 'watch' and 'listen' are things you must actively do. You may *hear* a boring lecturer, but not be *listening* to him (trying to understand what he is saying). You might *see* some people far away, but not be *watching* them (observing their actions).

区别行为动词和以上列表中的动词也很简单。see 和 hear（见上表）是你自发完成的动作，而 watch 和 listen 是你必须积极主动去做的动作。比方说，老师讲课很乏味，你会听到他说话（hear），却没有认真听他说话的内容（listen）。你可以看到远处有一些人（see），却没有观察他们在做些什么（watch）。

Exercise 1

Put the verbs into the correct forms — present simple or present continuous.

将下列动词变成正确的形式：一般现在时或现在进行时。

1. The needle of a compass [point] North.
2. She [prefer] tea to coffee.
3. My father [watch] the TV news every evening.
4. Wait a minute. I [do] my homework.
5. I [visit] my grandmother at the weekend.
6. Water [not boil] at 30 degrees centigrade.
7. Switch off the TV. I [not watch] it.
8. Some people [say] you are as old as you [feel].
9. I [read] a good book at the moment.
10. I [not understand] you now.

Present Perfect 现在完成时

This tense is used for talking about:

(i) experience. "I have seen many examples of this." (Sometime in my life.)

(ii) change. "The price of oil has increased." (Before, it was cheaper than now.)

(iii) a continuing situation. "I have lived here for two years." (I **came** here two years ago and I am **still** here.)

Remember to use the third form of the verb – the past participle – when you make the present perfect.

You can use 'for' and 'since' with the present perfect. Use 'for' with a period of time (two years, three days, an hour) and 'since' with a specific time (2002, Tuesday, 2 o'clock).

In negative sentences, 'not' is placed between the auxiliary verb ('have') and the main verb. "We **have not seen** any evidence against this assertion."

现在完成时用于描述：

(i) 经历，如：I have seen many examples of this.(我曾经历过。)
(ii) 变化，如：The price of oil has increased.(过去更便宜。)
(iii) 持续的状况，如：I have lived here for two years.(我 2 年前来这里，现在还在这儿。)
记住：现在完成时应使用动词的第三种形式，即过去分词。
现在完成时可以用 for 和 since 来表示时间：for 表示时间段（2 年、3 年、1 小时），since 表示时间点（2002、星期二、2 点钟）。
在否定句中，not 放在助动词 have 和主动词之间，如：We have not seen any evidence against this assertion.

Present Perfect Continuous 现在完成进行时

This tense is used for talking about:
(i) an action continuing up to now. "I have been playing computer games."
(ii) an action which has just finished. There is usually a result arising from that action. "I have been researching this issue for several weeks."
Remember to use 'have' + 'been' + the gerund ('-ing') when you make the present perfect continuous.
'For' and 'since' are often used with the present perfect continuous. Use 'for' with a period of time (two years, three days, an hour) and 'since' with a specific time (2002, Tuesday, 2 o'clock).
In negative sentences, 'not' is placed between the auxiliary verb ('have') and 'been'. "The new procedures **have not been working** effectively."
现在完成进行时用于描述：
(i) 过去发生并持续到现在的动作，如：I have been playing computer games.
(ii) 刚刚结束的动作，该动作通常会产生一定结果，如：I have been researching this issue for several weeks.
记住：现在完成进行时的结构是 have +been+ 动名词 (-ing)。
现在完成进行时常常用 for 和 since 来表示时间：for 表示时间段（2 年、3 年、1 小时），since 表示时间点（2002、星期二、2 点钟）。
在否定句中，not 放在助动词 have 和 been 之间，如：The new procedures have not been working effectively.

Past Simple 一般过去时

This tense is used for completed actions which happened in the past. It doesn't matter how long the event lasted. "My grandfather never smoked and lived for 100 years."
Remember to use **'didn't'** in **negative** sentences. "I **didn't** understand these reasons."
一般过去时用于描述过去发生且已经完成的动作，不论该事件持续了多长时间，如：My grandfather never smoked and lived for 100 years.
记住：否定句中用 didn't，如：I didn't understand these reasons.

Exercise 2

Put the verbs into the correct present or past forms.
将下列动词变成正确的现在时或过去时形式。

1. They [write] that book for months.
2. She [not be] there yesterday.
3. My father [watch] the football all afternoon.
4. I [do] my homework. I [want] to go out now.
5. Cars [use] for transport for over 100 years.
6. The water [not boil] yet.
7. I often [go] there.
8. We [walk] for two hours. Where is the restaurant?
9. I [read] a good book recently.
10. People [not read] many books nowadays.

Past Continuous 过去进行时

This tense is used for:

(i) actions that happened at a particular moment in the past. These actions had begun, but were not finished. "I **was reading** a book on alternative energy."

(ii) setting the scene in stories. "It was a typical summer afternoon in Beijing. The sun **was shining** and the birds **were singing**." Notice that in this situation, the past continuous is used to describe the 'background' not the main focus of the story. In other words, the story is not about the sun and the birds – they are just there as the story happens.

Remember that the past continuous (like the present continuous) is used with action verbs. It is **not** used with verbs such as 'believe', 'want', 'like', 'prefer', and 'hate' ('I **wanted** to understand the situation' **not** 'I was wanting to understand the situation').

In negative sentences, 'not' is placed between the auxiliary verb ('be') and the action verb. "We **were not using** our resources efficiently."

过去进行时用于描述：

(i) 过去某时间发生的动作。这些动作在过去开始，但当时没有结束，如：I was reading a book on alternative energy.

(ii) 铺垫故事情景，如：It was a typical summer afternoon in Beijing. The sun was shining and the birds were singing. 注意：在这种情况下，过去进行时用于描述背景，而不是故事主题。换言之，例句不是讲太阳和小鸟，它们只是故事发生时的背景。

记住：跟现在进行时一样，过去进行时也是用于行为动词的时态，而不与believe、want、like、prefer和hate之类的动词连用，比如：要说I wanted to understand the situation.不能说I was wanting to understand the situation.

在否定句中，not放在助动词be和行为动词之间，如：We were not using our resources

efficiently.

The past continuous is often used together with the past simple to discuss two actions. One action must be long and the other short. Use the past continuous for the long action and the past simple for the short action. We use 'while' and 'when' to join two actions into one sentence. Use 'while' before the long action (past continuous). Use 'when' before the short action (past simple). Notice that there are four possible combinations if you use 'while' and 'when'.
过去进行时常常与一般过去时连用，表示两个动作。一个动作必须时间长，用过去进行时；一个动作时间短，用一般过去时。我们用 while 或 when 将两个动作连接起来：时间长的动作前用 while（过去进行时），时间短的动作前用 when（一般过去时）。注意：使用 while 和 when 时共有以下 4 种组合。

The economy suffered problems while the government was reforming it.
While the government was reforming it, the economy suffered problems.
The government was reforming the economy when it suffered problems.
When the economy suffered problems, the government was reforming it.

Past Perfect 过去完成时

This tense is used for talking about an action in the past, which happens before another action in the past. The past simple is used for the other, later, action. "The problem had ended when the legislation was introduced." (The legislation was introduced after the problem had ended.")
Remember to use the third form of the verb – the past participle – when you make the past perfect.
You can use 'for' and 'since' with the past perfect. Use 'for' with a period of time (two years, three days, an hour) and 'since' with a specific time (2002, Tuesday, 2 o'clock).
"I had worked there for ten years (since 1994) when I retired."
In negative sentences, 'not' is placed between the auxiliary verb ('have') and the main verb.
"We **had not realised** the severity of the problem before you told us about it."
过去完成时用于描述在过去一个动作之前发生的动作，晚一些发生的那个动作则用一般过去时，如：The problem had ended when the legislation was introduced.（这句话意思是"在问题发生后法律才被制定。"）
记住：过去完成时要求使用动词的第三种形式，即过去分词。
过去完成时可用 for 和 since 来表示时间：for 表示时间段（2 年、3 年、1 小时），since 表示时间点（2002、星期二、2 点钟），如：I had worked there for ten years (since 1994) when I retired.
在否定句中，not 放在助动词 have 和主动词之间，如：We had not realised the severity of the problem before you told us about it.

Past Perfect Continuous 过去完成进行时

This tense is similar to the past perfect, but is used for talking about longer, continuous actions in the past, which happen before another action in the past. The past simple is used for the other, later, action. "He had been working in Britain for five years when he decided to move to Canada." ("He decided to move to Canada after he had been working in Britain for five years.")
You can use 'for' and 'since' with the past perfect. Use 'for' with a period of time (two years, three days, an hour) and 'since' with a specific time (2002, Tuesday, 2 o'clock).
"I had been working there for ten years (since 1994) when I retired."
In negative sentences, 'not' is placed between the auxiliary verb ('have') and 'been'. "We **had not been playing** football."
过去完成进行时类似于过去完成时，用来讲述时间更长、在过去一个动作之前发生的持续动作。晚一些发生的那个动作则用一般过去时，如：He had been working in Britain for five years when he decided to move to Canada. (相当于:He decided to move to Canada after he had been working in Britain for five years.)
过去完成进行时可用for和since来表示时间：for表示时间段（2年、3年、1小时），since表示时间点（2002、星期二、2点钟），如：I had worked there for ten years (since 1994) when I retired.
在否定句中，not放在助动词have和been之间，如：We had not been playing football.

Exercise 3

Put the verbs into the correct past tense forms.
将下列动词变成正确的过去时形式。

1. We [play] football for 20 minutes when the rain [start].
2. They [not hear] of him before you [mention] him.
3. It [snow] when we [arrive].
4. The phone [ring] while I [cook] dinner.
5. The man [watch] us when we [go] into the shop.

Future Using 'will' 使用will的一般将来时

'Will' is used for:
(i) talking about the future when there is no prior fixed plan. Usually, the decision is made just before we speak. "Wait a minute. I'll help you."
The exception here is when we use 'be'. 'Be' can be used even if the plan is fixed. "I'll be in Beijing on Wednesday."
We often use 'think' in these situations. "I think I'll suggest that solution at the next meeting in August."

Many students use 'will' instead of the present simple. "What do you do in your office?" "I will make sure the computers are working properly." In these cases, 'will' is always incorrect.
(ii) predictions. "Men will walk on Mars before the year 2020." We often use 'think' in these situations, too. "I think men will walk on Mars before 2020."
Although formal writing doesn't usually contain many contractions, you can use 'will not' or 'won't' for negatives in the IELTS test.
will 用于描述：
(i) 事先没有计划的未来事情。通常，这个决定是在讲话前刚刚作出，如：Wait a minute. I'll help you. be 是一个例外，即使计划已经确定，也可以用 be，如：I'll be in Beijing on Wednesday.
在这种情况下，我们常常会用 think，如：I think I'll suggest that solution at the next meeting in August.
许多学生滥用 will，来代替一般现在时，如：What do you do in your office? / I will make sure the computers are working properly. 这种情况统统不用 will。
(ii) 预测，如：Men will walk on Mars before the year 2020. 在这种情况下，我们常常也会用 think，如：I think men will walk on Mars before 2020.
尽管正式的书面语很少用缩写，但在雅思考试中，否定句可用 will not，也可用 won't。

Future Using 'be going to' 使用 be going to 的一般将来时

This is used when we are talking about fixed (certain) future plans. "She is going to study in America next September." It *can* also be used with 'think', so it often doesn't appear to be different to 'will'. The difference is in the attitude of the speaker.
Remember to use the correct form of 'be' (am, is, are).
be going to 用于讲述未来确定的计划，如：She is going to study in America next September. 可与 think 连用，所以似乎与 will 区别不大。区别就在于讲话者的态度。
记住：要使用 be 动词的正确形式（am，is，are）

Future Continuous 将来进行时

We use the future continuous to talk about particular times in the future. An action will start before that moment, but will not have finished. It will be continuing at that moment. "The chart suggests that next year Chinese people will be eating more hamburgers."
In negative sentences, 'not' is between 'will' and 'be'. "The chart suggests that next year Chinese people **will not be eating** more hamburgers."
该时态用于描述未来具体的时间点。动作在将来某时间点之前发生，但到那时还在继续，如：The chart suggests that next year Chinese people will be eating more hamburgers.
在否定句中，not 放在 will 和 be 之间，如：The chart suggests that next year Chinese people

will not be eating more hamburgers.

Future Perfect 将来完成时

This is used to talk about an action in the future before another action in the future. Study the following situation. You will be old in 40 years time. China will be a developed country in 30 years. "When I am old, China **will have become** a developed country."
In negative sentences, 'not' is between 'will' and 'have'. "When I am old, China **will not have become** a developed country."
该时态用于讲述将来另一个动作之前发生的动作。例如这种情形：40 年后，你将会变老；30年后，中国将成为一个发达国家。你就可以这样说：When I am old, China will have become a developed country.
在否定句中，not 放在 will 和 have 之间。

Future Perfect Continuous 将来完成进行时

We use this to talk about a long action before a point in the future. "Next year, our factory **will have been using** clean energy for ten years."
In negative sentences, 'not' is between 'will' and 'have'. "On Tuesday, they will not have been working for one month."
该时态用于讲述未来时间点之前持续较长时间的动作，如：Next year, our factory will have been using clean energy for ten years.
在否定句中，not 放在 will 和 have 之间。如：On Tuesday, they will not have been working for one month.

Exercise 4

Put the verbs into the correct future forms.
将下列动词变成正确的将来时形式。

1. I [probably visit] my aunt tomorrow.
2. She [not sleep] for a long time when she arrives.
3. Call me at midnight. I [not sleep].
4. They [built] the stadium by 2008.
5. Soon, she [work] here for 20 years.

Simple 一般时	Present 一般现在时	It **is** + past participle of main verb It **is** + 谓语动词的过去分词
	Past 一般过去时	It **was** + past participle of main verb It **was** + 谓语动词的过去分词
	Future 一般将来时	It **will be** + past participle of main verb It **will be** + 谓语动词的过去分词
Continuous 进行时	Present 现在进行时	It **is being** + past participle of main verb It **is being** + 谓语动词的过去分词
	Past 过去进行时	It **was being** + past participle of main verb It **was being** + 谓语动词的过去分词
	Future 将来进行时	It **will be being** + past participle of main verb It **will be being** + 谓语动词的过去分词
perfect simple 一般完成时	Present 现在完成时	It **has been** + past participle of main verb It **has been** + 谓语动词的过去分词
	Past 过去完成时	It **had been** + past participle of main verb It **had been** + 谓语动词的过去分词
	Future 将来完成时	It **will have been** + past participle of main verb It **will have been** + 谓语动词的过去分词
perfect continuous 完成进行时	Present 现在完成进行时	It **has been being** + past participle of main verb It **has been being** + 谓语动词的过去分词
	Past 过去完成进行时	It **had been being** + past participle of main verb It **had been being** + 谓语动词的过去分词
	Future 将来完成进行时	It **will have been being** + past participle of main verb It **will have been being** + 谓语动词的过去分词

Passive Voice 被动语态

In active voice, the object receives the action of the verb. "Dogs [subject] eat [verb] meat [object]." In passive voice, the subject receives the action of the verb. "Meat [subject] is eaten [verb] by dogs [object]." The object of the active verb becomes the subject of the verb, and vice versa. Notice that the main verb is always in its past participle form.

We use the passive in two situations:

(i) when we want to make the passive object more important. "**Our GDP was increased** by those reforms." I am more concerned about the GDP than the reasons for the growth.

Notice that we use 'by' to introduce the active object. We can use 'with' to introduce an instrument used by an active object. "The laws were introduced **by** the government **with** the support of the people."

(ii) when we do not know the active subject. "Our GDP **was increased**." I don't know how it was increased.

在主动语态中，接受被动事物，如：Dogs [主语] eat [动词] meat [宾语].

在被动语态中，接受动作的主体是主语，如：Meat [主语] is eaten [动词] by dogs [宾语].

主动语态中的宾语变成被动语态中的主语，反之亦然。

注意：谓语动词总是过去分词形式。

被动语态用于两种情况：

(i) 想强调被动事物，如：Our GDP was increased by those reforms. (我更关注 GDP，而不太关注 GDP 增长的原因。)

注意：被动语态中，我们用 by 来引出动作的施动者，可用 with 来引出动作的施动者所使用的工具，如：The laws were introduced by the government with the support of the people.

(ii) 不清楚动作的施动者，如：Our GDP was increased. (我不清楚 GDP 增长的原因。)

Conditionals 条件从句

The **first conditional** is used for possible **future** actions that depend on the result of another future action. The conditions will probably be met. Use 'if' + present simple + will. "**If** the number of cars **drops**, there **will** be less pollution."

第一类条件句用于将来可能发生的动作，该动作的发生以另一个动作的发生为条件。该条件可能可以实现。结构是：if+ 一般现在时 +will，如：If the number of cars drops, there will be less pollution.

The **second conditional** is also used for possible **future** actions that depend on the result of another future action. However, the conditions will probably **not** be met. Use 'if' + past simple + would + base form of verb. "**If** the number of cars **dropped**, there **would be** less pollution."

第二类条件句也用于表示将来可能发生的动作，该动作的发生以将来另一个动作的发生为条件。然而该条件可能无法实现。结构是：if+ 过去式 +would+ 动词原形，如：If the number of cars dropped, there would be less pollution.

The **second conditional** can also be used for imaginary **present** actions where the conditions are **not** actually being met. "If people worked less, they would be more relaxed." In other words, people are working too much and are not relaxed.
第二类条件句还可用来表示事实上在目前不能实现的条件下的虚拟的现在的动作，如：If people worked less, they would be more relaxed. 换言之，人们现在还是工作太多，休息太少。

The **third conditional** is used for **past** actions that did **not** happen because the conditions were not met. Use 'if' + past perfect + would have + past participle. "If the government had reduced the number of cars, the pollution problem would have been resolved." In other words, the government did not reduce the number of cars and so the pollution problem still exists.
第三类条件句用于表示在过去不能实现的条件下，过去不会发生的动作。结构是：if+过去完成时+would have+过去分词，如：If the government had reduced the number of cars, the pollution problem would have been resolved. 换言之，政府当时没有减少汽车数量，因此污染问题依然存在。

The **zero conditional** is used for actions that are **always** true if the conditions are met. Use 'if' + present simple + present simple. "If you reduce the number of cars, the amount of pollution drops."
零条件句用以表示如果条件能够实现，那么结果总是跟着出现，结构是 if + 一般现在时 + 一般现在时，如：If you reduce the number of cars, the amount of pollution drops.

Modal Verbs 情态动词

'**Can**' is used to refer to ability ("The government can make new laws."), requests ("Can we have more controls on pollution, please?"), and permission ("You can reduce the number of cars, if you wish.").
'**Could'** is used to refer to past ability ("The previous government could change policies quickly"), requests (Could you pass me the salt?"), and possibilities ("The government could introduce new laws.").
can 表示能力（The government can make new laws.）、请求（Can we have more controls on pollution, please?）、和允许（You can reduce the number of cars, if you wish.）
could 表示过去的能力（The previous government could change policies quickly.）、请求（Could you pass me the salt?）和可能性（The government could introduce new laws.）

'**Be able to**' is not a modal verb, but it can be used instead of 'can' and 'could'. It is also often used in formal writing and may be useful for expressing ideas in Task 2. The meaning of 'able' is clearly associated with ability. You can change the form of 'be' to suit the tense you wish to

use, e.g. “The government **has been** able to …”
be able to 不是情态动词，但可以替代 can 和 could。常用于正式的书面语，也可用于表述 Task 2 中的观点。able 的含义显然与能力直接挂钩。可根据具体时态改变 be 动词的形式，如：The government has been able to …

‘**Have to**’ is objective. It is actually not a modal verb, but is often included with modals for convenience. It is used to express an **impersonal obligation** – rules that must generally be obeyed. “Foreigners **have to** have a visa to enter China.” The past of ‘have to’ is ‘had to’.
‘**Must**’ is usually subjective. It is used to express a **personal obligation** – something the speaker believes is necessary. “I **must** leave the office before 7.”
‘**Must not**’ is used to express what is not permitted. It can be used objectively or subjectively. “You must not carry dangerous objects on passenger aircraft.”
‘Must’ (and therefore ‘must not’) have no past tense, so you have to use ‘had to’ for past actions.
have to 表示客观。have to 其实不是情态动词，但为方便起见，常常也算作情态动词。have to 表示并非出自个人意愿的责任，即大家必须共同遵守的规则，如：Foreigners have to have a visa to enter China.
have to 的过去时形式是 had to。
must 通常表示主观，表示出自个人意愿的责任，即讲话者认为必要的事情，如：I must leave the office before 7.
must not 用来表示不允许发生的事情，既可以表示客观，也可以表示主观，如：You must not cross carry dangerous objects on passenger aircraft.跟 have to 不同，must 和 must not 没有过去时形式。如果是过去时态，要用 had to 代替。

‘**May**’ and ‘**might**’ are used to express possibilities. Usually these possibilities are not likely or viewed as unlikely by the speaker or writer. They can be used interchangeably.
may 和 might 用来表示可能性。通常，（讲话者或作者认为）这些可能性不太可能变成现实。二者可相互替换。

2.2 Verbs—Synonyms and Antonyms 动词 — 近义词和反义词

Writing for IELTS involves expressing your exact meaning. To do this well, it is necessary to use a variety of verbs. Using a variety of them shows the examiner your wide vocabulary.
雅思写作要求你准确表达自己的意思。要做好这一点，就必须使用多种多样的动词，这样才能向考官展示你丰富的词汇量。

Exercise 5

1 In the following two sets, there are eight pairs of verbs. Join the verbs that have **opposite** meanings from each other.
以下有 8 对动词，请将反义词连接起来。

Set A.

agree	accept
challenge	contradict
compare	contrast
criticise	decrease
divide	fail
increase	join
strengthen	praise
succeed	weaken

Set B.

admit	wake
damage	borrow
extend	deny
lend	heal
permit	prohibit
present	receive
produce	reduce
tire	use

Set C.

double	contract
expand	cool
free	fall
heat	halve
leave	limit
move	oppose
rise	remain
support	stop

Set D.

continue	force
inform	generalise
interfere	hide
notice	leave
retain	mislead
show	miss
specify	reform
volunteer	stop

2 In the following two sets, there are eight pairs of verbs. Join the verbs that have **similar** meanings to each other.
以下有 8 对动词，请将近义词连接起来。

Set E.		Set F.	
choose	defend	abandon	attack
decrease	happen	accelerate	follow
divide	lower	answer	hasten
emphasise	raise	assume	leave
increase	recommend	criticise	permit
justify	select	exchange	respond
occur	split	facilitate	think
suggest	stress	pursue	trade

2.3 Connectives (Linking Words) 连接词

As with tenses, an average to good student will be expected to demonstrate an ability to use these words and phrases both regularly and correctly. The following is a list of connectives and linking phrases, according to function, which students can include in their sentences or use to link them.

Notice the verb patterns used with different connectives!

跟时态一样，英文水平为中上等的学生理应表现出自己有能力频繁并且正确地使用连接词和连接短语。下面列出各种连接词和连接短语，并按功能分类，供学生参考使用。注意动词短语与不同连接词的搭配！

Time and Sequence 时间和顺序

When students relate events that occur over a period of time, they can make what they say clearer by including phrases such as the following ones in their answers.

学生在讲述一段时间内发生的事情时，可在行文中使用下列短语，让叙述更加清晰。

before / prior to/ until / after / after that / afterwards / then

It is necessary to prepare well **before (prior to)** taking the IELTS examination.

Before (Prior to) tak**ing** the IELTS examination, it is necessary to prepare well.

We cannot deal with the problem **until** people recognise that one exists.

We must demonstrate to people that this is a real problem. **After that,** we can convince the government to introduce legislation to deal with it.'

After discuss**ing** the issue, we reached some conclusions.

Afterwards (Then), we presented these to leading figures in the community.

eventually / finally / in the end

(These are used when something happens after a lot of time and/or many problems)（用于连接

经历很长时间和/或各种问题后才发生的事情）

After discussing the issue for two years, the committee **eventually (finally)** found that we were right.

In the end, the committee found that we were right.

as soon as

(Two actions immediately follow each other) （后一个动作紧跟着前一个动作）

The problem will be solved **as soon as** these laws are introduced.

As soon as these laws are introduced, the problem will be solved.

when / once

(two actions follow each other, but the time between them is not specific) （两个动作接连发生，但不确定两个动作间间隔的时间）

When / Once these actions are taken, the situation will improve dramatically

The situation will improve dramatically **when / once** these actions are taken.

while (whilst, when, as) / just as / meanwhile / throughout / during

(Things happen at the same time) （事情同时发生）

I told him **while (whilst / when / as)** we were having dinner. (Notice we use the past tense for the shorter action and the past continuous for the longer one!)

The education reforms were introduced **just as** the course began. (Two short actions)

The local government did nothing. **Meanwhile**, the situation deteriorated.

They argued **throughout** the conference. (From the beginning to the end)

They argued **during** the conference. (It is not clear exactly when or how long)

(Notice that 'throughout' and 'during' are followed by nouns.)

first(ly), second(ly), … / for one thing … (and) for another / (and) besides / (and) anyway

(Giving a sequence of reasons) （逐个列举原因）

First(ly), (because) the government hasn't made any laws and **second(ly)** (because) business leaders are opposed to the idea.

For one thing, the government hasn't made any laws **and for another** business leaders are opposed to the idea.

Giving Examples 举例

Most students can use **for example**. You can demonstrate a little variety by also using **for instance** and **such as**. The phrase **in particular** is usually used to give an example that is distinctive in some way. In formal writing, you can also use the phrase **'A case in point** is …' The word **namely** is usually used when listing (naming) a given number of examples. 'The

United Kingdom is made up of four countries, **namely** England, Scotland, Wales, and Northern Ireland.'

大多数学生都会使用 for example 一词。你还可以用 for instance 和 such as 来表示举例，从而显示出一定的用词多样性。in particular 这个短语通常用来表示某个特殊的例子。在正式的书面语中，你还可以使用短语 A case in point is ...namely 一词通常用来列举给定数量的例子。

Contrast 对比

although / though / even though / in spite of (the fact that) / despite (the fact that)

Although / Though / Even though the arguments against are quite strong, I (still) believe we should go ahead with the scheme.

We should (still) go ahead with the scheme, **although / though / even though** the arguments against are quite strong.

We should (still) go ahead with the scheme **in spite of / despite** there **being** strong arguments against it.

We should (still) go ahead with the scheme **in spite of the fact that / despite the fact that** there are strong arguments against it.

The word **still** is used to emphasise the contrast. It is usually stressed in spoken English or underlined in informal writing.

用 still 一词来强调对比。在口语中通常用重音表示强调，在非正式文章中则用下划线表示强调。

however / on the other hand

I don't like playing sports. **However (On the other hand)**, I enjoy watching them.

whereas / on the other hand

Many people disagree with the proposals **whereas** others agree with them.

Many people agree with the proposals. **On the other hand,** others disagree with them.

nonetheless / yet

I don't believe that this idea will work. **Nonetheless,** we should give it a try.

I don't believe that this idea will work, **yet** we should give it a try. (formal)

compare / contrast

Britain is a small **country compared with (in comparison with)** China.

Comparing Britain with China, we can see that Britain is much smaller.

The birth rate in many European countries has dropped. **In contrast**, the birth rate in some African countries has risen.

The birth rate in European countries has dropped, **contrasting with** the birth rates in some African countries, which have risen.

Similarities 类比

similar to / both / neither

Britain is **similar to** the United Sates in many ways. For example, **both** believe in free enterprise. **Neither** of these countries has a large state-controlled economy.

Reason 原因

because / since / as

Because / Since / As I am Chinese and I love sport, I am very pleased that Beijing will host the Olympics in 2008.

I am very pleased that Beijing will host the Olympics in 2008 **because / since / as** I am Chinese and I love sport.

because of / owing to / due to

The factory had to close **because of / owing to / due to** a lack of orders for its products. (Note that **due to** and **owing to** are more formal and more common in written English.)

（注意：due to 和 owing to 通常用于比较正式的书面语。）

Purpose 目的

the purpose of / so (that) / in order to / to*

The purpose of introducing the death penalty was to reduce violent crime.

The death penalty was introduced **so that** violent crime would be reduced.

The death penalty was introduced **in order to** reduce violent crime.

The death penalty was introduced **to** reduce violent crime.*

*The use of **to** in this way is called the 'infinitive of purpose'.

Consequence 结果

The goods had to be sent at once. **As a result / Therefore / Consequently**, there was no time to check them properly.

There is a chance that my English will not be good enough. **In that case**, I will take an intensive course before trying again.

Addition (Giving extra information or reasons) 附加内容（给出额外信息或原因）

in addition (to) / (but) also / as well (as) / not only (but also) / what's more

In addition to being fun, playing sport **also** keeps you fit.
Playing sport is fun, **as well as** keeping you fit.
Not only is playing sport fun, **but** it **also** keeps you fit.
Playing sport is fun and it keeps you fit **as well**.
Playing sport is fun. **What's more**, it keeps you fit.
furthermore / Besides / Moreover
I think the death penalty is morally wrong. **Furthermore (Besides / Moreover)**, there is no evidence that it is effective in discouraging crime.

Summary 总结

Most students use **in conclusion** to end or summarise an argument. You can also use **in summary** and **to conclude**. In spoken English, you can also use **to sum up** and **in short**, though these are probably a little colloquial for the English required in the IELTS writing module.
大多数学生会用 in conclusion 来结束或总结一段论证。你还可以用 in summary 和 to conclude 来替换。在口语中，你还可以用 to sum up 和 in short，但这两个词相对雅思写作所要求的英语可能稍显口语化。

Preference 偏好

Rather than / instead of

We should reduce the demand for drugs **rather than** control the supply.
We should control the supply of drugs **instead of** focussing on the demand for them.

Rather / Instead

You can use these two words interchangeably at the beginning of a sentence. The sentence before will usually be a negative one, dismissing an idea or concept ('Many people argue that **we shouldn't conduct animal experiments**.'). The sentence following 'rather' or 'instead' should contain the suggested idea or concept ('**Rather, / Instead, we should use pieces of animal tissue,** specially grown in laboratories.').
这两个词在句首可换用。之前的一个句子通常是否定句，否定某个观点或概念，(如：Many people argue that we shouldn't conduct animal experiments.) rather 和 instead 所连接的句子应提出供参考的观点或概念，(如：Rather, / Instead, we should use pieces of animal tissue, specially grown in laboratories.)

Alternatives 其他选择

alternatively / on the other hand

People should pay for their own health care. **On the other hand**, companies should help employees who have problems with the high costs involved.

The government could ban the use of cars in cities. **Alternatively,** they could charge people large sums of money to use cars there.

Condition 条件

provided (that) / providing (that) / so long as / as long as

These new laws are acceptable **provided** (**that**) / **providing** (**that**) / **so long as / as long as** there are safeguards.

'if' conditionals if 条件句

Notice the different **grammar structures used with 'if'** conditionals according to the situation. (注意：根据不同的情景下的 if 条件，使用不同的语法结构。)

If you **drive** (present tense), there is always the chance of an accident (present tense) (If you do something, there is always a result.)

If you **drive** (present tense) a lot, you **will see** (future tense with 'will') accidents on the road.'(You do something, there will probably be a result.)

If you **drove** (past tense) badly, you **would** have (would + infinitive without 'to') an accident. (Something unlikely happens, a likely result would be …)

If it **hadn't been** (past perfect) foggy, we **wouldn't have crashed**. (would + present perfect) (Something would or would not have happened in the past if the conditions had been different.)

unless/ whether … or not / otherwise

We must do something, **unless** the situation changes by itself.

We need to do something, **whether** the majority of people support us **or not**.

We had to introduce the open-door policy, **otherwise** our economy would have collapsed.

depend(ing) on / It depends

The government can introduce the laws at different times in different cities, **depending on** the circumstances.

The government can introduce the laws at different times in different cities. It **depends on** the circumstances.

The government can introduce the laws at different times in different cities. **It depends**. (A reason may not be given.)

in case

We should prepare a second alternative **in case** the first **doesn't** work. (**not** in case it **won't** work!)

Exceptions 例外

except

All the companies agreed to cut pollution levels **except** the largest ones.

except (for) / apart from

Everyone, **except for (apart from)** Mr. Wang, agreed with the proposal.

'Except for' and 'apart from' are always followed by nouns or noun phrases.
except for 和 apart from 永远连接名词或名词短语。

with the exception of

This phrase is used in exactly the same way as 'except for' and 'apart from'.
该短语用法跟 except for 和 apart from 完全相同。

Exercise 6

Practice your linking words.
连接词练习。

1. They decided to walk to the shop (afterwards / after) lunch.
2. (Prior / Before) going to work, he put on his tie.
3. We can't begin (until / prior) to he arrives.
4. I'll give him the present (as soon as / eventually) I see him.
5. (After that / After) playing computer games, I was tired.

6. The door opened just (as / meanwhile) I sat on the chair.
7. She watched TV (throughout / while) we cooked dinner.
8. He drank some tea. (Meanwhile / When) I made some sandwiches.
9. I watched him (as / throughout) he walked across the street.
10. He told us some stories just (as / whilst) we were having dinner.

11. They are criminals. (Not only / Moreover) they are violent criminals.

12. (In addition / As well as) being healthy, this food tastes great!
13. The house is beautiful. (As well / In addition) it is in a quiet neighbourhood.
14. My father loves rugby. He (also / furthermore) likes football.
15. I like beef, but I like pork (as well as / too).

16. He didn't pass the test (in spite of / even though) he worked hard.
17. (Although / Despite) she spoke slowly, I couldn't understood the foreign teacher.
18. (In spite of that / In spite of) I still love him.
19. The streets are jammed, (despite / although) having fewer cars on them.
20. She did badly on the test. I think she is still the best student (despite / though).

21. My sister likes swimming (whereas / on the other hand) I like basketball.
22. It is risky. (On the other hand / Comparing) you could make a lot of money.
23. Mary did a lot of housework. (Contrasting with / In contrast) Jenny did none.
24. He is brave, (yet / whereas) he is foolish.
25. We lost the money. (In contrast / Nonetheless) we are not bankrupt.

26. We will go on the picnic (provided that / unless) it rains.
27. We will hold the concert indoors (in case / depending on) it rains.
28. Luckily, I saved it on a CD. (Otherwise / In case) it would have been lost.
29. Let's drive – in case it (rains / will rain).
30. We may hold the concert indoors, (depending on / provided that) the weather.

31. We couldn't talk in the disco (because / because of) the noise.
32. The company had problems (due to / because) customers not paying their bills.
33. I am good at computer games (since / because of) I play a lot of them.
34. I can swim every day, (as / owing to) there is a swimming pool very near my home.
35. He lost his job (because / because of) he was lazy.

36. He has many skills. (For example / Namely) he can repair TV's.
37. (In conclusion, / To sum), this project is waste of time.
38. We should have employed the older man (rather / instead of) the younger one.
39. We spent a lot of time and money on the project, but (eventually / once) it was finished.
40. She felt ill (as / meanwhile) she was travelling on the bus.

41. Travelling can be relaxing. (Besides / Not only) it can be educational.
42. (Although / However) she is young, she has a lot of experience.
43. (Whereas / Nonetheless) you are more experienced, she is more energetic.
44. I have a similar opinion (to / with) yours.

45. I want to study abroad, (whether / otherwise) you like it or not!

46. There is a lot of construction work in Beijing, (due to / since) the 2008 Olympics.
47. I went to the bakery (to / so to) buy some bread.
48. I failed the test. (In case / Therefore) I will take it again next month.
49. We all went to the wedding, (apart / except) Wendy.
50. The telephone rang (while / during) we were chatting.

2.4 Adverbs of Frequency and Degree 频率副词和程度副词

These words are very useful, because things rarely happen all the time or never. You need to be able to express exactly *how* often and *how* much.
事情很少总是发生和从不发生，所以频率副词和程度副词作用很大。我们需要学会准确地表示频率和程度。

Adverbs of Frequency 频率副词

Adverbs of frequency indicate 'how often'. Be careful about using the word always. 'I **always** go swimming' suggests that you swim all the time, every day. One alternative is to add a time phrase. Say 'I go swimming whenever I have time' or 'I go swimming every Saturday morning'. Another is to say **almost always**.
频率副词表示"有多么频繁"。使用always（总是）时要注意。I always go swimming.表示你总是每天都去游泳。另一种说法是加上时间频率副词，比如I go swimming whenever I have time.或者I go swimming every Saturday morning. 另一种选择是说almost always（几乎总是）。

Used in an answer, **have ever** has no meaning. Say either 'I have (been/heard/etc.)' in positive sentences or 'I have **never** (been/heard/etc.)' in negative ones.
have ever 在句子中没有任何意义。肯定句中可以说I have（been/ heard 等），否定句中可以说I have never (been/heard 等)。

Use the following words to indicate how often you do something: **(almost) always, frequently, (quite) often, regularly, sometimes, occasionally, seldom, hardly ever, (very) rarely.**
请使用下列词语来表示你所做事情的频率: (almost) always, frequently, (quite) often, regularly, sometimes, occasionally, seldom, hardly ever, (very) rarely

Exercise 7

Complete the following sentences using your own ideas.
用自己的观点完成下列句子。

1. … almost always results in …
2. … frequently causes …
3. … is often caused by …
4. … occasionally changes the way …
5. … seldom affects …
6. … demonstrates that … hardly ever …
7. … rarely improves …
8. Creating … never …

Adverbs of frequency go before the main verb, except when the main verb is 'to be', in which case they go after it. 'Sometimes', 'occasionally' and 'often' can also go at the beginning or end of a sentence.
频率副词位于主要动词之前，除非主要动词是 to be，在这种情况下，频率副词跟在 to be 之后。Sometimes，occasionally 和 often 可以放在句首和句尾。

Adverbs of Degree 程度副词

Adverbs of degree indicate 'how much'. Use the following words to indicate how good, big, interesting or expensive something is: **incredibly, extremely, very, pretty, quite, fairly, somewhat.** The words **a little**, **a bit** and **slightly** are often used in negative situations. 'The situation was **a little** dangerous.' 'The measures were **a bit** expensive.' 'It decreased GDP **slightly**.
程度副词表示"有多……"。下列副词可用来表示某物有多好，多大，多有趣和多昂贵：incredibly, extremely, very, pretty, quite, fairly, somewhat。a little, a bit 和 slightly 常用于否定句中，例如：The situation was a little dangerous. / The measures were a bit expensive. / It decreased GDP slightly.

Exercise 8

Think of things that …
想一想哪些事情适合用下列程度副词来表示。

1. are incredibly successful.
2. were extremely unlikely, but happened.
3. would be very useful.
4. are pretty expensive.
5. were quite hard to make 10 years ago.
6. would be fairly hard without computers.
7. are somewhat difficult to buy.
8. were a bit hard to find 20 years ago.

2.5 Expressing Probability 表达可能性

Certainty 肯定

The ability to express probability is essential for communicating your exact meaning in Task 2. Use the following words and phrases to help you.
表达可能性的能力对于在 task2 中传达你的确切含义非常重要。请使用下面词汇。

Foreigners in Beijing who speak Chinese **clearly / obviously** have an advantage over those who don't.
These measures will **undoubtedly** / **definitely** resolve the problem.
There will **certainly** be problems if these proposals are adopted.
I'm **certain** / **sure** there will be difficulties.
There will be difficulties **for sure**.
Without a doubt there will be difficulties. There will be difficulties **without a doubt**.

Very Likely 非常可能

This legislation will **almost certainly** be introduced next year.
It is **almost certain** this legislation will be introduced next year.

Likely 可能

There's a good chance this will solve the problem.
Chances are this will solve the problem. (Informal)
This will **probably** lead to a reduction in costs in the long term.

Possibly 可能

This **may** / **might** / **could** (**possibly**) result in some dissatisfaction from car users.
Perhaps this measure will not be as effective as many experts believe.
I **think** the situation will improve, but I'm **not sure**.
Maybe / **Perhaps** these measures will help.

Unlikely 不可能

It **probably won't** lead to a reduction in costs immediately.
I doubt **very much (that)** the situation will improve much over the next few months.
There's **not much chance (that)** we will see a reduction in traffic accidents.

Certainly Not 肯定不会

I'm **sure** this problem **not** getting the attention it deserves.

I will **certainly / definitely not** accept their argument without something to support it.

Exercise 9

In your opinion, how probable is it that … (Remember to answer using full sentences!)
在你看来，下列事情发生的可能性有多大？（请用完整的句子回答。）

the Chinese women's football team will be world champions next year?
you will get the job you most want to do when you finish your studies?
you will have at least one child before you are thirty years old?
Pandas will become extinct in the next 20 years?
no-one in China will use cash by the year 2020?
you will live to be 100 years old?

2.6 Clauses 从句

There are several types of clauses. A clause is a part of a sentence that usually contains a subject and a verb. The clause is usually connected to the rest of the sentence using a conjunction. A clause cannot be a complete sentence on its own.
从句有几种。从句是全句的一部分，通常包含一个主语和一个动词，由关联词与主句联系起来。从句不能独立成句。

The words **which, where, who, whose, when,** and **that** are conjunctions that can be useful for linking a clause to the main part of the sentence.
连接从句和主句的常用连词包括 which, where, who, whose, when, that。

'**Which**' is used for objects. "People should choose cars **which** (**that**) are environmentally friendly."
Use '**by / through which**' to indicate ***how*** something may happen or be done.
'These are the ways **by / through which** we can solve the problem.'
Which 用来指物，如：People should choose cars which (that) are environmentally friendly.
by / through which 表示某件事情发生或完成的方式，如：These are the ways by / through which we can solve the problem.
'**Where**' is used for places. "This is the country **where** death rates are the highest."
Where 用来指地点，如：This is the country where death rates are the highest.

'Who' is used for people. "These are the same people **who** (**that**) argue that we need to spend more money on education."
Who 用来指人，如：These are the same people who (that) argue that we need to spend more money on education.

'Whose' is used for things that belong to people. "Mr. Li is the businessman **whose** company developed new technologies for dealing with this problem." 'Whose' can also be used with people to describe relationships. "That's the woman **whose** husband owns a factory in the city."
whose 用来指所属，如：Mr. Li is the businessman whose company developed new technologies for dealing with this problem. whose 还用来表示关系，如：That's the woman **whose** husband owns a factory in the city.

'**When**' is used with time clauses. "October 1 is **when** Chinese people celebrate their National Day."
when 用来指时间，如：October 1 is when Chinese people celebrate their National Day.

'That' can be used instead of the conjunctions 'which', 'where', and 'who', but be careful using 'that' with places! Usually, a preposition is required, e.g. "This is the hotel **that** I stayed **at** on my last visit."
that 可用来代替 which,where 和 who,一定要小心，that 指代地点时，介词不能省去，如：This is the hotel that I stayed at on my last visit.

However, the information following 'that' must be essential to the sentence, e.g. 'This is the issue **that must be dealt with first**." 'That' can replace 'which' because the information following must be given so that the sentence has meaning. (For grammar lovers, this is called a '**defining** relative clause'!)
但that后面的信息必须是句子的核心内容，如：This is the issue that must be dealt with first. that 可以代替 which，因为如果缺少后面的信息，句子就失去了意义。（语法中叫做"限定性定语从句"）

Look at this sentence. 'Mrs. Bolton, **who I met last week**, is head of the company.' In this sentence, 'who' cannot be replaced with 'that' because the fact that I met Mrs. Bolton last week is not required for you to understand the main idea of the sentence. (For grammar lovers, this is called a '**non-defining** relative clause'!)
请看例句：Mrs. Bolton, who I met last week, is head of the company. 在这句话中，who 不能用that来替换，去掉"我上周遇到了博尔坦"这句话也不会影响到对全句意义的理解。（这类分句被语法爱好者称为"非限定性定语从句"。）

Exercise 10

1 Choose the correct conjunction(s) to make relative clauses.
选择正确的连词填空。

1. This is the mobile phone _____ she bought last week.
2. She is one of the best people _____ I have ever worked for.
3. He must be the businessman _____ wallet I took by mistake.
4. The disco _____ we went dancing was wonderful.
5. Are they the people _____ missed the bus?
6. February 14th is the day _____ people celebrate Valentine's Day.
7. I was listening to the radio _____ I heard the cars crash.
8. Here's the report _____ I prepared yesterday.
9. There's the professor _____ I met on the campus last month.
10. That's the kindergarten _____ I used to go to _____ I was a child.

Using words like 'before' and 'after', you can create **adverbial clauses of time**.
before 和 after 这类词用于连接时间状语从句。

Before you go to study abroad, you need to prepare carefully for life there.
After you return from studying abroad, you should find a job quite easily.

2 Make similar sentences of your own for the following situations.
根据下列情景造句。

1. Before and after a person gets married.
2. Before and after you take an examination.
3. Before and after going to university.
4. Before and after purchasing a computer.
5. Before and after a couple have a child.

You can use phrases of purpose (such as 'to', 'in order to', 'for', 'in order for') to create **infinitive phrases**.
to, in order to, for, in order for 等表目的的短语用于连接不定式短语。

3 Match the information on the left with the information on the right to create sentences. Notice how the phrases of purpose can be in the middle of sentences or at the beginning.
将左右两边的信息匹配起来造句。请注意：目的短语既可以放在句中，也可以放在句首。

1. A person needs to be strong	to operate a successful business.
2. You need good people working for you	in order to attract customers.
3. An athlete must train hard	in order to succeed in the world.
4. People should eat the right food	for success in the Olympics.
5. A bar requires something special	to maintain good health.
6. In order for the police to check your identity,	you need to prepare well.
7. In order to ensure security,	you need a mobile phone.
8. To keep children happy at a party,	they may take your fingerprints.
9. For success in IELTS,	there should be some cameras.
10. In order for us to contact you anytime,	make sure there is entertainment.

2.7 Expressing Opinions 表达观点

Task 2 of the writing module specifically requires you to state your opinion on the given topic. In your essay, you will almost certainly need to refer to the opinions of others. There are also a few ways to express your opinion indirectly, by using "It is …"

雅思写作部分的Task 2明确要求你就所给话题阐明自己的观点。在作文中，你又不可避免地会提到其他人的观点。此外，还有几种间接表达自己观点的说法，均使用It is。

Giving Your Opinion 给出自己的观点

(Personally,) I think / don't think cars are a good way to travel in cities.

It might / may be better to invest more money in education.

It might / may be better if we invest**ed** more money in education.

In my opinion, we need to change the way we think about this issue.

As far as I'm concerned, they can do what they like – it's their country.

I doubt (that) the situation will improve in the next few weeks. (= I don't believe)

I agree entirely with what you say.

I disagree strongly with what you say.

Giving the Opinion of Others 给出他人的观点

According to the latest government figures, inflation is rising. (Note that we cannot say '*according to me*'.)

It is said that he killed his wife. (People think this, but it is not proven.)

It **is /has been reported** that there has been an accident at a factory in Shanghai. (used with the media)

Many (most, a lot of, a few) young Chinese people often (sometimes, frequently) **say / think / believe / agree / suggest** that something should be done about this issue.

Style – An Important Reminder 文体——一个重要提示

When expressing your opinions, try not to be dogmatic. If you make statements like "It is *undeniable* that …", "It is *absolutely obvious* that …", or "It is impossible to believe that …", then it must be *perfectly clear* that the facts are on your side and *cannot* be reasonably interpreted otherwise. In IELTS Writing Task 2, this is probably not going to be the case. Questions for Task 2 are chosen partly *because* there are several different ways to answer them and several possible viewpoints and opinions.
表达自己观点时，千万不可固执己见。如果说出 It is undeniable that …, It is absolutely obvious that … 或者 It is impossible to believe that … 之类的话，那么毫无疑问，事实就站在你这边，不可能有其他的说法。在 Task 2 的写作中，可能不会出现这种情况。Task 2 的问题正是因为会有多种回答，属于"仁者见仁，智者见智"的问题，所以才被用作考题。

Adding words to such sentences can make them appear less dogmatic and sound more reasonable. For example, you could write, "It is *difficult* to deny that …", "It is *reasonably* obvious that …", and "It is *hard* to believe that …" instead.
可以在这类句子中加入几个词，缓和语气，使得句子听起来更加合理。例如，可以将比较绝对的说法换成 It is difficult to deny that …, It is reasonably obvious that …, It is hard to believe that … 等。

2.8 Adjectives 形容词

Antonyms and Synonyms 反义词和近义词

Writing involves presenting images to readers. To do this, it is necessary to use adjectives to describe things, places, or people. Try to use a variety of them to show the examiner your wide vocabulary. Below is the order of adjectives coming before a noun in English. Of course, there are cases where the order is not followed. The basic sequence is from subjective to objective.
凡文章都要在读者脑海中形成某种印象。要做到这一点，就必须用形容词来描述事物、场所和人。通过使用多种多样的形容词，便可以向考官展现你丰富的词汇量。以下是英文中修饰名词的形容词顺序，基本顺序是从主观到客观。当然，也存在不遵循这一顺序的情况。

opinion	size	age	shape	colour	origin	material	purpose	+
e.g. good	e.g. big	e.g. old	e.g. square	e.g. blue	e.g. English	e.g. metal	e.g. writing	noun

Exercise 11

1 In the following two sets, there are ten pairs of adjectives. Join the adjectives that have **opposite** meanings from each other.
以下共有 10 对形容词。请将意思相反的形容词连接起来。

Set A.		Set B.	
active	constant	mainstream	common
brave	constructive	novel	fair
changeable	cowardly	omnipotent	incompetent
destructive	imprudent	potent	interesting
enticing	modest	reliable	marginal
foreseeable	passive	skilful	mature
grandiose	repulsive	tedious	powerless
icy	unpredictable	unjust	uncertain
judicious	unprofitable	worthy	unsuitable
lucrative	warm	young	weak

2 In the following two sets, there are ten pairs of adjectives. Join the adjectives that have **similar** meanings to each other.
以下共有 10 对形容词。请将意思相近的形容词连接起来。

Set C.		Set D.	
acceptable	agreeable	ludicrous	absurd
blunt	appropriate	mistaken	clear
clumsy	awkward	necessary	coordinated
decent	forbidden	organised	entire
economical	imaginary	permanent	inappropriate
fictitious	outspoken	rapid	indispensable
grave	passionate	sensible	lasting
heated	sagacious	transparent	misinformed
illicit	serious	unsuitable	rational
keen	thrifty	whole	swift

Comparatives and Superlatives 比较级和最高级

Finally, let's take a look at an aspect of English that is really quite simple, yet often overlooked by students. The IELTS test requires students to be able to compare and contrast. It is quite shocking how few students are able to do this effectively. Even using such basic comparative phrases as '**bigger than', 'much smaller than', 'about the same price as**', and **'a little more expensive than**' will indicate to the examiner that you are able to compare and contrast.
最后，让我们来看看英语中比较简单但又常常被考生忽略的一部分内容。雅思考试对学生进行比较和对比的能力有明确要求，但真正具备这一能力的学生寥寥无几。哪怕是使用非常基础的比较短语（如bigger than, much smaller than, about the same price as和a little more expensive than），考官都能看到你的确会用英语作比较。

Remember that shorter adjectives tend to be made into comparatives and superlatives in the following manner: small, small**er**, **the** smallest; big, bigg**er**, **the** bigg**est;** funny, funn**ier**, **the** funn**iest**.
请记住：较短的形容词通常直接加 -er 和 -est 变成比较级和最高级，如 small, smaller, the smallest; big, bigger, the biggest; funny, funnier, the funniest。

Longer adjectives usually become comparatives and superlatives thus: beautiful, **more** beautiful, **the most** beautiful; modern, **more** modern, **the most** modern.
较长的形容词通常用 more 和 most 变成比较级和最高级，如 beautiful, more beautiful, the most beautiful; modern, more modern, the most modern。

'**More and more**' and '**increasingly more**' mean the same as 'increasingly' and can be used with longer adjectives which use 'more' and 'most' to create comparatives and superlatives. You cannot say 'more and more bigger' or 'increasingly more large' ('bigger and bigger', 'larger and larger' are correct). You can say 'more and more beautiful' and 'increasingly more comfortable'.
more and more，increasingly more 跟 increasingly 意思相同，可以同较长的形容词连用（即使用 more 和 most 变比较级和最高级的形容词）。不能说 more and more bigger 或者 increasingly more large（但 bigger and bigger，larger and larger 是正确的）。你可以说 more and more beautiful，increasingly more comfortable。

Use '**less and less'** to express that something is not as common now as it was before.
less and less 用于表示发生频率比从前少的事情。

You can use 'more and more' with nouns ('more and more cars', 'more and more information'), but 'less and less' can only be used with uncountable nouns ('less and less information'). With countable nouns, you should use 'fewer and fewer' ('fewer and fewer cars').
more and more 可以跟名词连用（如 more and more cars，more and more information）；但

less and less 只能跟不可数名词连用（less and less information）。跟可数名词连用的应该是 fewer and fewer（fewer and fewer cars）。

Exercise 12

Compare and contrast the following pairs. In particular, include comparatives and connectives as often as possible.
对比下列组合，并尽可能多地使用连词和比较级。

China – USA
Chinese food – Western food
men – women
China now – China 20 years ago
table tennis – football
clothes today – clothes 100 years ago
hotels – homes
holiday in China – a holiday abroad
buses - trains
going to a bar – going to a teahouse
teachers – policemen
Spring Festival – May Day holiday
cities – the countryside
paying by credit card – paying in cash
mice - tigers
being single – being married
children – adults
computer games – board games
summer – winter
newspapers – the Internet
English – Chinese
large families – small families
farmers – managers using
email – writing letters

2.9 Use of Impersonal Pronouns in Place of Nouns 用非人称代词代替名词

Paraphrasing 释义

Repetitious use of words is undesirable and therefore students should avoid saying things like, "I like swimming because swimming is very healthy and swimming is fun. I go swimming with my family. We go swimming near our home." This would be better said in the following manner. "I like swimming because it is a very healthy thing to do and it is also fun. I go swimming with my family at a pool near our home." Notice that the last two sentences have been combined. The word 'swimming' has been repeated in the second sentence only to make it clear that the speaker is still talking about the same topic. Using impersonal pronouns in place of nouns like this is called 'paraphrasing'.

一个词翻来覆去地用是不可取的，因此考生应当避免写出这样的句子：I like swimming because swimming is very healthy and swimming is fun. I go swimming with my family. We go swimming near our home. 可以改为：I like swimming because it is a very healthy thing to do and it is also fun. I go swimming with my family at a pool near our home. 可见，后两句被合并为一句。第二句中之所以重复 swimming，是为了表明作者还在谈论同一个话题。像这样用非人称代词代替名词的作法就叫做 "释义"。

Important Uses of "it" it 的重要用途

We can use the pronoun 'it' to mean 'situations'. Look at these examples.

代词 it 可以用来表示情景。请看例句。

I like it when people are open to new ideas. (= I like situations where people are ready to accept new ideas.)

It makes me angry when my children break things and don't tell me. (= Situations where my children act in this way make me angry.)

Notice that we use the singular pronoun 'it', not the plural pronoun 'they', even though we are talking about situations generally.

注意：这里用的是单数 it，而不是复数 they，尽管这里讲的是通常的情况。

Exercise 13

Complete these sentences by joining the information on the left with information on the right. There may be more than one combination for each. Then think of other answers *you* would give. Compare your answers with other people's answers and discuss *why* you gave those particular answers.

匹配左右信息，完成句子，各句可有多种组合。然后自己造句，将自己的句子跟他人对比，并讨论句子背后的原因。

1. I love it when my friends	spit on the street.
2. I hate it when people	stop me doing what I want to do.
3. It makes me angry when I see people	play close to moving cars.
4. It makes me laugh when I see	burp.
5. Children make me nervous when they	study hard, but don’t pass exams.
6. It bothers me when my parents	children playing happily.
7. It’s embarrassing when I	cry.
8. It makes me feel warm inside when people	buy me surprise presents.
9. It makes me feel bad when I see people	pushing to get on buses.
10. It’s surprising when students	help each other for no special reason.

Chapter 3

Academic Task 1

学术类写作 Task 1

3.1 Sample Question 1 样题 1

The table shows the number of foreign visitors (in millions) to 7 countries. Write a report for a university lecturer describing the information shown below. You should write at least 150 words.

Country visited	**Total**	**From the UK**	**From the USA**
Australia	3	0.3	0.3
Canada	15	0.6	12.0
France	53	7.4	0.1
Ireland	4	2.4	0.4
Italy	20	1.2	1.8
Mexico	7	0.1	5.5
Thailand	6	0.3	0.3

3.1.1 Understanding the Material 理解材料

The important things to notice are that:

(i) the figures show the total number of visitors (from all countries) as well as the number of visitors from the UK and the USA.

(ii) the figures show the number of people who went to seven selected countries in the world.

(iii) the figures for visitors from the UK and the USA are included in the total figures.

(iv) the figures do not show the total number of British and American people who travelled abroad — only those who travelled to the seven countries listed on the left.

(v) the figures are given in millions of people.

应当注意的事情如下：

(i)数字表示的是所有国家到访者的总数和英国、美国到访者的数量。

(ii)数字表示的是去到 7 个特定国家到访者的数量。

(iii)英国到访者和美国到访者的数字是包含在总数字里面的。

(iv)数字并不表示到外国旅游的英国到访者和美国到访者的总数，表示的仅仅是到达左边列出的 7 个国家的人数。

(v)数字的单位是百万。

3.1.2 Organising the Report 组织文章

The best way to organise this report is to work down the list of countries visited and look at the total numbers of visitors and the numbers from the UK and the USA. Before doing that, check to see if there are any similarities between any of the countries.

组织这篇报告的最好方法就是写下所到的国家，弄清到访者的总数和来自英国和美国的到访者数量。在此之前，看看各国之间有无相似之处。

There are two main examples of similarities between the countries visited. First, visitors from the USA make up about 80% of the total number of visitors to both Canada and Mexico. Second, the number of visitors from both the UK and the USA to Australia and Thailand are the same (0. 3 million in each case). Therefore it may be appropriate to deal with Canada and Mexico together and Australia and Thailand together.
所到国家之间的相似之处主要有两个例证。第一，加拿大和墨西哥的到访者总数中有 80% 是美国到访者。第二，到澳大利亚和泰国的到访者中，英国到访者的数量和美国到访者的数量是一致的（各有 30 万人）。因此，可以把加拿大和墨西哥一起来处理，澳大利亚和泰国一起处理。

As for the European countries (France, Ireland, and Italy), France and Ireland are similar in that they receive more British visitors than American ones. However the proportions are different.
对于欧洲国家（法国，爱尔兰和意大利）来说，法国和爱尔兰有相似之处，它们接待的英国到访者多于美国到访者。但是，比例上还是有所不同。

So, the report could be organised like this:
因此，这篇报告可以这样来建构：

1. Introduction. 导言
2. Canada and Mexico. 加拿大和墨西哥
3. Australia and Thailand. 澳大利亚和泰国
4. France and Ireland. 法国和爱尔兰
5. Italy. 意大利
6. Conclusion. 结论

3.1.3 Writing the Introduction 开头写作

Introductions to the reports in Academic Task 1 should be quite short — rarely more than 2 sentences. Which introduction do you think is the most suitable for this report? Why are the others unsuitable?
学术类写作 Task 1 中，报告的首段应当简短，尽量不要超过两句话。你认为下面哪一个首段最适合本报告？其它的为什么不合适？

1. "The table shows the total number of visitors to seven countries around the world and details the number of those visitors who came from the UK and the USA. Certain patterns are evident from these figures." (36 words)
2. "The table shows the total number of tourists to countries around the world and the number of

tourists who came from the UK and the USA. We can see some interesting things from the table" (35 words)

3. "The table shows the people who go from some countries to other countries. It is very interesting!" (17 words)

Introduction 1 is the most suitable. It is simple, but clear, and it points out that patterns exist.
Introduction 2 is actually incorrect, because it uses "tourists". The table says "visitors', which includes tourists and others, such as businessmen. The phrase "some interesting things" is not very informative.
Introduction 3 is much too simple – almost childish.
段1最合适，简洁，明了，直接指出的确存在一些模式。
段2事实上是不正确的，这里使用的是tourists(游客)，而表格中使用的是visitors(到访者)，包括游客和其他人，比如商务人士。some interesting things(一些有趣的东西)并没有提供什么有用的信息。
段3则过于简单，近乎幼稚。

3.1.4 Writing a Paragraph （主体）段落写作

You can deal with the countries in any order, but let's follow the organisation model we prepared above. For the paragraph on Canada and Mexico, we need to include the following information:

1. the three figures (in millions of people).
2. the fact that Americans make up about 80% of the visitors to these countries.
3. the fact that British people make up a small proportion of the visitors to these two countries.

当然你可以以任何顺序来排列这些国家，但是我们还是根据上面的组织方式来进行。在关于加拿大和墨西哥的段落里面，我们应当包含下面的信息：

1、三个数字（单位是百万人）。
2、这些国家的到访者中，美国人占80%。
3、这些国家的到访者中，英国人所占的比例很小。

Our paragraph could look something like this:
我们的段落大体上可以这样：

Canada received more than twice as many visitors as Mexico (15 million compared to 7 million), yet the percentage of visitors to those countries from the USA was about the same, 80%. 12 million Americans visited Canada whilst 5.5 million visited Mexico. British visitors to these two countries were much fewer in number, with 0.6 million visiting Canada and 0.1 million visiting Mexico."
(61 words)

For the paragraph on Australia and Thailand, we need to include the following information:

1. the three figures (in millions of people).
2. the fact that British and American visitors are equal in number.

在关于澳大利亚和泰国的段落里面，我们应该包含下面的信息：

1、三个数字（单位是百万人）

2、到访的英国人和美国人数量相同

Our paragraph could look something like this:

我们的段落大体上可以这样：

Australia had half as many visitors as Thailand (3 million compared to 6 million), but the number of visitors to those countries from both the UK and the USA was the same, 0.3 million.

(34 words)

For the paragraph on France and Ireland, we need to include the following information:

1. the three figures (in millions of people).
2. the fact that more British people go there than Americans.
3. France had a higher total number of visitors than any of the other countries on the list.
4. over half of Ireland's visitors came from the UK.

在关于法国和爱尔兰的段落里面，我们应当包含下面的信息：

1、三个数字（单位是百万人）。

2、来自英国的到访者多于美国人。

3、访问法国的总人数超过表中其他任何一个国家。

4、访问爱尔兰的人有半数以上来自英国。

Our paragraph could look something like this:

我们的段落大体上可以这样：

France and Ireland received more visitors from the UK (7.4 million and 2.4 million respectively) than from the USA (0.1 million and 0.4 million respectively). France had a higher total number of visitors than any of the other countries on the list. Over half of Ireland's visitors came from the UK.

(51 words)

Our paragraph on Italy could look like this:

关于意大利的段落可以这样写：

Italy received 20 million visitors, of which 1.2 million were from the UK and 1.8 million were from the USA.

(20 words)

3.1.5 Writing the Conclusion 结论写作

Like introductions, conclusions to the reports in Academic Task 1 should be quite succinct. Which conclusion do you think is the most suitable for this report? Why are the others unsuitable?
就像开头一样，学术类写作 Task 1 中的结论也应该简洁明了。你认为下面的结论中哪一个最适合这篇报告？其他结论为什么不合适？

1. "The table shows the total number of visitors to the seven countries around the world is different, but sometimes the same (Australia and Thailand). Many British people go to France and many Americans go to Canada and Mexico." (38 words)
2. "In conclusion, we can see some countries have similar trends, but Italy doesn't." (13 words)
3. "Although the table shows a limited number of countries, it can be seen that British and American people tend to visit those countries nearest geographically. However, the relationship is not definitive." (31 words)

Conclusion 3 is the best, as it acknowledges the limits of the data, yet points out the most obvious trend.
Conclusions 1 and 2 are not really specific enough.
结论 3 最适合，因为结论 3 承认这些数据的局限性，但是指出了最为明显的趋势。
结论 1 和结论 2 不够具体。

3.1.6 Complete Model Answer 完整的范文

The table shows the total number of visitors to seven countries around the world and details the number of those visitors who came from the UK and the USA. Certain patterns are evident from these figures.

Canada received more than twice as many visitors as Mexico (15 million compared to 7 million), yet the percentage of visitors to those countries from the USA was about the same, 80%. 12 million Americans visited Canada whilst 5.5 million visited Mexico. British visitors to these two countries were much fewer in number, with 0.6 million visiting Canada and 0.1 million visiting Mexico.

Australia had half as many visitors as Thailand (3 million compared to 6 million), but the number of visitors to those countries from both the UK and the USA was the same, 0.3 million.

France and Ireland received more visitors from the UK (7.4 million and 2.4 million respectively) than from the USA (0.1 million and 0.4 million respectively). France had a higher total number of visitors than any of the other countries on the list. Over half of Ireland's visitors came from the UK.

Although the table shows a limited number of countries, it can be seen that British and American people tend to visit those countries nearest geographically. However, the relationship is not definitive.

(215 words)

3.1.7 Sample Answer 1 考生答卷 1

Indications of foreign visitors in seven countries. Australia, Canada, France, Ireland, Italy, Mexico, and Thailand, compiled by our research group reveal the great difference that exist in every country's travel market. According to this table, it can be roughly divide into three group.

The table indicates France is in the top in the ranking. The number of foreign visitors is up to 53 million, which is overwhelmingly greater the the second country and is nearly 18 times as many as the bottom country. There are 7.4 million foreign visitors come from the Unite of Kingdom, respectively, only 0.1 million visitors come from the United Sates.

The second group includ Italy and Canada, The table illustrate their figures of foreign visitors in all is 20 million and 15 million the number of travellers from the U.K to Italy is equal to those from the U.S. However, There are 12 million visitors from the U.S to Canada by contrast with only 0.6 million from the U.K.

The amount of foreign visitors in Mexico, Thailand, Ireland and Australia is only 7.6, 4 and 3 million. They are the last group in our statistics table.

(192 words)

Task Fulfilment: The student has divided the countries into three unsuitable groups. For example, Mexico is closer to Canada than Italy, in terms of these figures. Both countries receive most of their visitors from the USA and relatively few from Britain. The report does not look at all countries evenly. It focuses on a few of them. The student fails to see any trends.
任务完成：该学生将这些国家分成了三组，但是分组方法不当。例如，从数字上来讲，墨西哥比意大利更接近加拿大。两国的访客中，美国人居多，英国人相对要少。该报告没有均衡地对待所有国家，只是谈了几个国家。该学生也没有找出任何发展趋势。
Coherence and Cohesion: The report is fairly easy to follow, even though the student doesn use many connectives.
连贯与衔接：文章尽管没有使用很多连词，还是很容易读懂。
Vocabulary and Sentence Structure: The range and accuracy of both vocabulary and grammar are good. There are some basic mistakes, but nothing very serious. The student should not refer to our [re]search group and should pay attention to spelling.

词汇与句子结构：词汇与语法的广度与精确度都做得很好。存在一些基本性的错误，但无伤大雅。学生应当避免使用 our[re]search group，并且应当注意拼写。

3.1.8 Sample Answer 2 学生答卷 2

It is popular to travell all over the world now. The number of foreign visitors to 7 countries (Austria. Canada. France. Ireland. Italy. Mexico. Thailand) shows the fact. It displays figures of total and also provides details of visitors from the UK and the USA.

The most obvious trend shown by the table is that France receives much more people than any other country, which is 53 million. and fewer people go to Australia (3 million). There are also many people spend their holiday in Italy. Canada and etc Most of the visitors come from the UK and the USA. They all love travelling. However, they have diffrent opinions to have tours so they choose different countries to visit. Most of the American love to visit Canada (12 million) and Englishmen prefer France. In contrast with them, a few Americans go to France, Also Englishman do not love to travel to Mexico because it's too far away and not attractive enough.

(161 words)

Task Fulfilment: The student covers part of the table well, but ignores other parts. There are key factual errors, e.g. most visitors to Italy do not come from the UK and USA. The student should not give reasons in Task 1 ("they have diff[e]rent opinions about tours"). These sentences could be rephrased, e.g. "Englishmen do not love to travel to Mexico because it's too far away and not attractive enough." This sentence shows opinion, not facts. It should read "From the table, we can see that British people travel less to countries which are far away, such as Mexico" This sentence shows facts, not opinion, yet it is essentially the same sentence, based on the same information.
任务完成：该学生对图表的有些部分处理得较好，但是忽略了其他部分。还有一些事实错误，例如，意大利的访客中，多数不是英国人和美国人。学生在 Task 1 中不应该给出原因 "they have diff[e]rent opinions about tours" (他们在旅行问题上观点相左)。这些句子可以重新组织一下，例如，Englishmen do not love to travel to Mexico because it's too far away and not attractive enough. 这句话陈述的是观点，而不是事实。本句应该这样：From the table, we can see that British people travel less to countries which are far away, such as Mexico.这个句子陈述的是事实，而不是观点。从本质上来说，这句话与前一句是同一句话，两句话都是建立在相同的信息上的。
Coherence and Cohesion: The report is easy to follow and the student uses good connectives and discourse markers.
连贯与衔接：文章很好地使用了连词和语篇标记，容易读懂。
Vocabulary and Sentence Structure: The grammar is very good, but the student uses some inappropriate words, e.g. 'love'. The chart does not show where people love to go – it shows where they go. Sure, these may be the same, but we cannot see that from the chart. Stick with facts! 'Travel' and 'different' are spelt incorrectly.
词汇与句子结构：语法很好，但是该学生存在用词不当的现象，例如love（喜欢）一词，图表显示的不是人们喜欢去哪里，而是他们事实上去了哪里。当然，这两个地方可能是同一个地方，但是我们从图表中是看不出来的，要紧紧抓住事实。travel、different 出现了拼写错误。

3.2 Sample Question 2 样题 2

The pie charts below show the area and current population of the seven continents as a percentage of the total. Write a report for a university lecturer describing the information shown below. You should write at least 150 words.

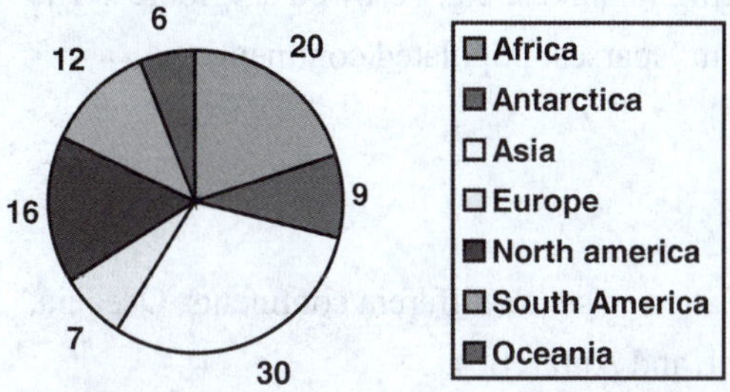

% of world land area

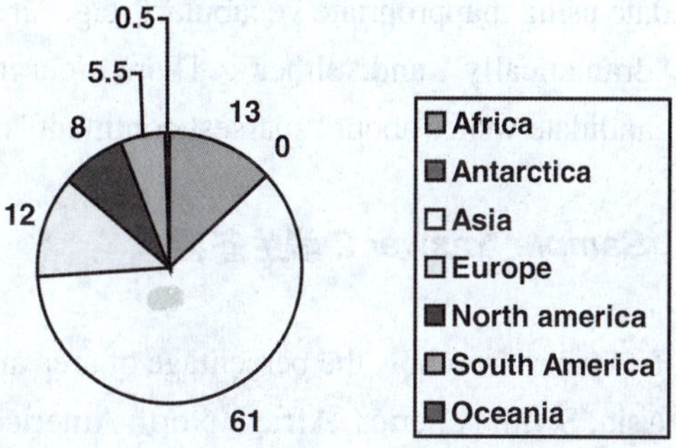

% of world population

Sample Answer 1 学生答卷 1

The pie charts below show the situation of area and populated distribution in the world seven continents.

Obviously, there are two types of continents in the world, the crowed and sparse one. The densest continent is Asia, whose population and area are standing for 61% and 30% respectively. Europe is the second densest continent, occupied 7% of areas and 12% of population in the world.

Each thing has its both sides. While the people in Asia and Europe are living in crowded environment, some other persons are enjoying wider places, except Antarctica do not have inhabitants at all, but stands for 9% of areas. The sparsest continent is Oceania, which has 6% of area and 0.5% of population. The second sparsest continents should be North and South American, which inhabit 8% and 5.5% of the globle population. Dramatically, these two continents take the similar percentage of the earth either, which are 16% and 12% respectively.

(154 words)

Task Fulfilment: The report is sufficient, but not very well developed – notice the number of words. The report does not include all the necessary information, e.g. Africa is not mentioned at all. Other information appears confusing, particularly that regarding North and South America. On the other hand, the candidate gets credit for noticing the main point, i.e. that certain continents are densely populated and others are sparsely populated.

Coherence and Cohesion: The report is a little difficult to understand, particularly as the report is not clearly organized and the candidate does use sufficient appropriate connectives in order to link points and sentences.
Vocabulary and Sentence Structure: There is not one correct sentence in the entire report. There are grammatical mistakes, e.g. "The second sparsest continents should be …" (there is no 'should', the report is based on facts presented to the candidate). There are several instances of the candidate using inappropriate vocabulary, e.g. "are standing for", "persons are enjoying wider places", "dramatically", and "either". There are a few spelling mistakes, e.g. "crowed", "globle". The candidate writes about "sparsest continent" rather than 'sparsest populated continent'.

Sample Answer 2 学生答卷 2

The pie charts show the percentage of area and population in seven different continents, Oceania, Asia, South America, Africa, North America, Europe and Antarctica.

From the table it can be divided into three groups. One owns small area but big population, which including Asia and Europe. It has much larger population than others. Of course, it can be considered densely populated. Asia has the highest portion of the world's population, with 61% of the total, although it owns 30%, the highest portion of the world's area.

On the other hand, the second group has different case from the former. It consists of Oceania and Antarctica, which are very sparsely populated, with the lowest percentage 0.5% and 0%. In addition, compared with other continents but Europe, the portions of areas are quite small with the figures of 6% and 9%.

The third group are gathered South America, Africa and North America. They are relatively sparsely populated. The portions of areas are close twice as high as their population's.

It can be concluded that the distribution of population is not average in seven continents.

(181 words)

Task Fulfilment: The report is of sufficient length, but the inclusion of more figures to illustrate the points being made would be nice. The candidate has noticed that certain continents are densely populated and others are sparsely populated and has divided the continents into three appropriate groups.
Coherence and Cohesion: The candidate has organized the report into paragraphs reasonably well, but has made certain parts difficult to understand through the misuse of connectives.
Vocabulary and Sentence Structure: The sentence structures are reasonable, though there are many grammatical mistakes. There are several instances of the candidate using inappropriate

vocabulary, e.g. "owns small area", "Of course", "has different case", "gathered", and "not average". On the other hand, there are no spelling mistakes and the candidate correctly uses "sparsely populated" and "densely populated".

Sample Answer 3 学生答卷 3

The pie charts show the percentage of the area and current population of the seven continents.

Overall, Asia has the largest percentage of the total land area (30 per cent) and Oceania has the least (6 per cent). Africa has 20 per cent, while North America and South America have the percentage of 16 and 12 respectively. Antarctica and Europe both have a little less than 10 per cent.

Similar to the percentage of the land area, the biggest percentage of total population is in Asia. However, Africa and Europe have nearly the same amount (13 per cent and 12 percent respectively), which are followed by North America (8 per cent) and South America (5.5per cent). It's noticeable that Oceania has only 0.5 per cent of the total, when Antarctica even has 0.

In conclusion, Asia and Africa have the largest area and population percentage in the world, and population density is low in cold weather area such as Antarctica.

(159 words)

Task Fulfilment: The report reads more like a list than a description of the information. The candidate has not noticed that certain continents are densely populated and others are sparsely populated.

Coherence and Cohesion: The report is clearly organised into paragraphs and the candidate has used sufficient connectives, making the writing easy to understand.

Vocabulary and Sentence Structure: The sentence structures are good, though there are some grammar mistakes. The candidate uses some good, though simple, phrases. There are no spelling mistakes.

How to Answer Sample Question 2 怎样写好样题 2

Understanding the Material

Obviously, you must compare the two pie charts. So, look at the two figures for each continent. Sometimes the 'area' figure will be higher (Africa, Antarctica, North America, South America, and Oceania). Sometimes the 'population' figure will be higher (Asia and Europe). Notice that the difference is particularly large with Antarctica and Oceania, so it is a good idea to deal with them separately.

Vocabulary

Nouns – the figure(s), the percentage(s), per cent, continent(s).

Verbs – occupy, take up, compare, distribute.

Adjectives – small, large, low, high, more, less.

(Comparatives and superlatives will be needed!)

Adverbs – sparsely / densely (populated).

Quantities – half, third, twice, (three) times.

Organising the Report

Introduction – Very short. Say what the pie charts show, in your own words as far as possible.

Body – Ideally, three paragraphs (one for each group of continents). In each paragraph, for each continent, you should certainly show the relationship between the 'area' and 'population' figures. This should be your priority. Show differences between individual continents if you need to build up your word total and/or further develop your answer.

Conclusion – The world's population is not evenly distributed. There are sparsely populated and densely populated continents.

Model Answer 范文

The pie charts show the seven continents of the world and the percentage of the total land mass of the globe that they occupy together with the percentage of the world's population they are home to.

The densely populated continents are Asia and Europe, both having about twice the population that could be expected were the global population evenly distributed over the global land mass. Asia is the largest continent in terms of both area (30%) and population (61%). Europe (with 7% of the area and 12% of the population) is the second smallest continent, yet has a population almost as high as that of Africa, a continent which is three times larger in area.

Africa and the Americas are relatively sparsely populated continents. North America (16% of the area and 8% of the population) and South America (12% of the area and 5.5% of the population) have populations equal to about half of what could be expected if the global population were evenly distributed, whilst Africa's population is about a third lower than would be expected in such a situation (20% of the area and 13% of the population).

The smallest continent, Oceania (with 6% of the area and 0.5% of the population), is very sparsely populated, whilst Antarctica has no permanent population despite covering 9% of the global land mass.

The table clearly demonstrates that the people of the world are unevenly distributed across the continents.

(238 words)

3.3 Sample Question 3 样题 3

The pie charts show the amount of oil production and consumption measured in million barrels per day (MB/D) in seven regions in the year 2001. Write a report for a university lecturer describing the information shown below. You should write at least 150 words.

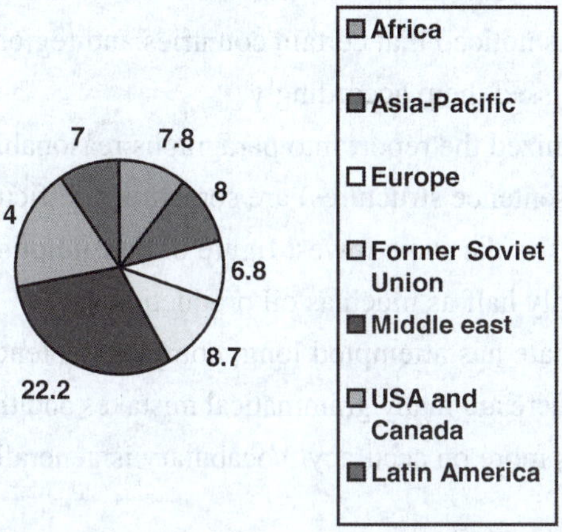

oil production (MB/D)

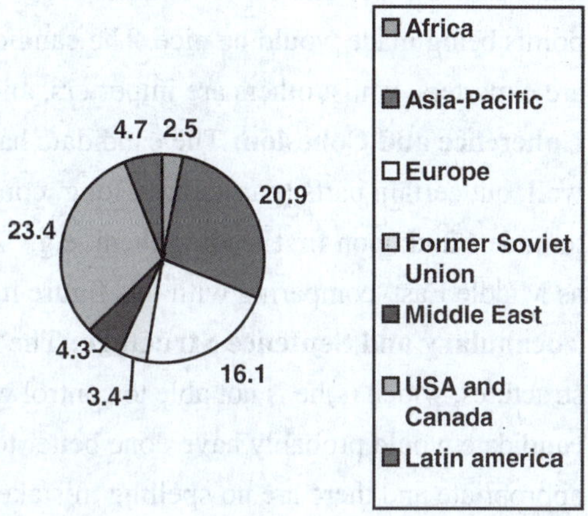

oil consumption (MB/D)

Sample Answer 1 学生答卷 1

The pie charts show a number of oil production and consumption measured in million barrels per day (MB/D) in seven countries or regions.

From the pie charts it can be easily found that it can be divided into two groups. Latin America, Africa and Middle East are gathered into one group, which has higher production than consumption. Middle East has the highest production with 18MB/D, while it has the lowest consumption with 3 million barrels. The production of Latin America is 8 MB/D, which is not only almost equal to their consumption with the number of 7 MB/D, but also combined oil production of Asia and Australia. Africa has the same lowest figure of consumption as Middle East, comparing with this figure it has only half as much as oil production.

The second group consists of the other four countries and regions because of their similar features, that is, consumption is much higher than production. The figure of Europe indicates it has much higher consumption than the others with 25 MB/D. Meanwhile, it has much production with 17MB/D which is second to Middle East only. It can be seen that USA and Canada have much higher consumption with 15MB/D than others except Europe.

It can be seen from the pie charts, there are several export regions, for example, Middle East, whereas there are some import countries of oil such as Europe.

(228 words)

Task Fulfilment: The report is quite long, but the inclusion of more figures to illustrate the points being made would be nice. The candidate has noticed that certain countries and regions are exporters, whilst others are importers, and discussed them accordingly.
Coherence and Cohesion: The candidate has organized the report into paragraphs reasonably well, but certain parts (particularly long, complex sentence structures) are sometimes difficult to understand upon first reading them, e.g. "Africa has the same lowest figure of consumption as Middle East, comparing with this figure it has only half as much as oil production."
Vocabulary and Sentence Structure: The candidate has attempted long, complex sentence structures, which (s)he is not able to control well. There are many grammatical mistakes and the candidate would probably have done better to focus more on accuracy. Vocabulary is generally appropriate and there are no spelling mistakes.

Sample Answer 2 学生答卷 2

The pie charts show the amount of oil production and consumption barrels per day in seven regions in 2001.

In general, the total amount of oil production and consumption were almost equal, which were 74.5 and 75.3 respectively.

It's noticeable that Middle East produced the biggest amount (22.2MB/D) of oil, which was nearly 5 times of the amount of the daily oil consumption. Although Africa only produced 7.8MB per day, it was still three-fold of that of the daily consumption. Former Soviet Union and Latin America were the other two counties who produced more amount of oil than that they consumed, which are 8.7:3.4 and 7.0:4.7 respectively.

Compared with those areas above, the other three areas were reported the opposite situation. All these three areas consumed more amount of oil per day than that they produced. For example, Asia-pacific and Europe both had more than twice the consumptions than productions (8.0:20.9 and 6.8:16.1 respectively), when USA and Canada had a little less than twice (14.0:23.4).

To sum up, Middle East was the biggest oil production area, when Asia-Pacific and America &

Canada were the biggest oil consumption areas.

(187 words)

Task Fulfilment: The candidate has noticed the key point, which is that certain countries and regions are exporters, whilst others are importers. The use of ratios appears a little mathematical, but it is done fairly well.

Coherence and Cohesion: The candidate has organized the report into paragraphs well. The information is clearly presented.

Vocabulary and Sentence Structure: There are grammatical mistakes, but they do not make the writing difficult to understand. Vocabulary is generally appropriate and there are no spelling mistakes. The candidate demonstrates very good use of phrases to compare amounts ("nearly five times …", "a little less than twice …").

Sample Answer 3 学生答卷 3

The pie charts describe the amount of oil production and consumption measured in million barrels per day in Africa, Europe, Middle east and other 4 regions in the year 2001.

As the biggest oil production in million barrels per day in 2001, Middle east produced 22.2 in MB/D, accounting for exactly a third of the total amount of production. However, the oil consumption only is 4.3 in million barrels per day in 2001. In USA and Canada, the oil production is 14 in MB/D and the oil consumption reached a peak of 23.4 in MB/D in 2001. There was a slight change in Latin America about oil production and consumption in MB/D in 2001: decreasing from 7 in MB/D about oil production to 4.7 oil consumption in MB/D.

From the information showed in the chart, it can be seen that the smallest oil production in MB/D in 2001 is Europe, the smallest oil consumption in MB/D in 2001 is Africa (2.5).

(161 words)

Task Fulfilment: The student has not included all the required information and has also failed to notice that there are two groups – net producers (who produce more than they consume) and net consumers (who consume more than they produce). The information that has been included is generally good.

Coherence and Cohesion: The first half of the main paragraph is easy to follow, but the report is hard to follow in a few later places because of inappropriate vocabulary.

Vocabulary and Sentence Structure: The student talks about changes in oil production ('slight change', 'decreasing', 'reached a peak'), which is incorrect as the pie charts only show data from 2001. The grammar and vocabulary in the first half of the main paragraph are good and it is a pity that the student didn't continue with this.

How to Answer Sample Question 3 怎样写好样题3

Understanding the Material

This question is very similar to Sample Question 2. Again, you must compare the two pie charts. So, look at the two figures for each region. Sometimes the 'production' figure will be higher (Africa, the Former Soviet Union, the Middle East, and Latin America). Sometimes the 'consumption' figure will be higher (Asia Pacific, Europe, and the USA and Canada).

Vocabulary

Nouns – the figure(s), region(s), net producer (produces AND consumes, but production is higher than consumption), net consumer (produces AND consumes, but consumption is higher than production).

Verbs – produce, consume, compare, exceed, divide.

Adjectives – small, large, low, high, more, less.

(Comparatives and superlatives will be needed!)

Quantities – half, third, twice, (three) times.

Note – use the abbreviation shown in the pie charts (MB/D). This is much faster than writing 'million barrels per day'.

Organising the Report

Introduction – Very short. Again, say what the pie charts show, in your own words as far as possible.

Body – Clearly, there should be two main paragraphs (one for net producers, one for net consumers). In each paragraph, for each region, you should certainly show the relationship between the 'consumption' and 'production' figures. This should be your priority. Show differences between individual regions if you need to build up your word total and/or further develop your answer.

Conclusion – The world's production and consumption of oil is not evenly distributed. There are sparsely populated and densely populated continents.

Model Answer 范文

The pie charts show the world divided into seven regions and the amount of oil produced and consumed in those regions in MB/D in 2001. In total, the amount of oil consumed exceeded that produced by 0.8 MB/D. The regions can be divided into two groups – one where production outpaces consumption and the other where the reverse is the case.

The former group – the net producers - consists of Africa, the Former Soviet Union, the Middle East, and Latin America. The Middle East is by far the largest producer (22.2 MB/D), but its consumption is relatively low (4.3 MB/D) – just a fifth of what it produces. Africa produces 7.8 MB/D, about three times what it consumes (2.5 MB/D), the Former Soviet Union about 250% more, and Latin America about 150% more.

The other group – the net consumers – consists of the Asia Pacific region, Europe, and the USA and Canada. The USA and Canada is the region which consumes the most oil (23.4 MB/D), though we can see that it is also the second largest producer region (14 MB/D). The Asia Pacific region is the second largest consumer (20.9 MB/D). Europe is the third largest consumer (16.1 MB/D) and the smallest producer (6.8 MB/D).

From the information above, we can see that oil production and consumption are not even around the world.

(206 words)

3.4 Sample Question 4 样题 4

The bar chart shows the sales figures and profits of ABC Electronics in millions of US dollars over the period 1991 to 2000. Write a report for a university lecturer describing the information shown below. You should write at least 150 words.

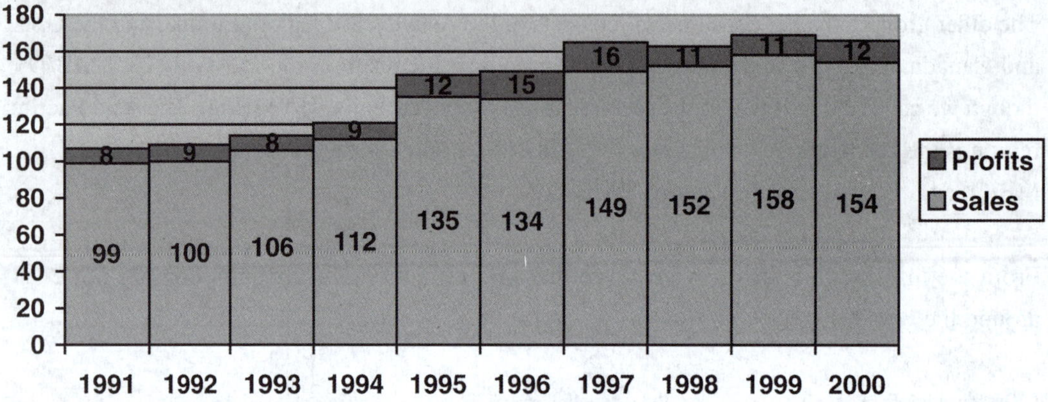

Sample Answer 1 学生答卷 1

The bar chart represents the sales and profits figures of ABC Electronics over the period 1991 to 2000.

It can be seen from the bar chart that the sales in 1991 and 1992 remained steady at 100 million. Then from 1992 to 1999, it increased gradually from 100 million and peaked at a little less than 160 million, except a sharp rise from 110 million to 133 million in 1995. After that, in 2000, the profit decreased slightly to 150 million.

Unlike the trend of sales, the profits were a little bit unsteady during this period. In 1991, the profit was at the lowest point of 8 million, which is followed by 1 million increase in the next year. But it dropped back to 8 in 1993 from which the other 1 million increase appeared again over the next year. Although it showed a gentle climbing trend from 1994 to 1997 (from 9 million to 16 million), it fell rapidly to 11 million in 1998. The situation did not change a lot in the next two years, except a slight rise (1million) in 2000.

In summary, we can see that the profit did not change as steadily as the sales did in ABC Electronics.

(202 words)

Task Fulfilment: The candidate describes the trends reasonably well, with generally appropriate inclusion of figures, though (s)he missed the big jump in sales between 1996 and 1997. A few of the figures are inaccurate. Unfortunately, the candidate did not compare sales and profits.
Coherence and Cohesion: The candidate has organized the report into paragraphs, but has not shown a link between the paragraphs – almost as if the candidate had written two reports, not one. When the candidate does compare the sales and profits, the sentences make no sense ("Unlike the trend of sales, the profits were a little bit unsteady …" and "In summary, we can see that the profit did not change as steadily as the sales …").
Vocabulary and Sentence Structure: Some good vocabulary and phrases have been used to show the change in figures over the years. There are some grammatical mistakes, but they are only serious in the two sentences where sales and profits are compared. There are no spelling mistakes. A noticeable omission was the word 'fluctuate', especially to describe the profits from 1991 to 1994.

Sample Answer 2 学生答卷 2

The diagram illustrates the changes of sales and profits of ABC Electronics in millions of US dollars from 1991 to 2000.

As can be seen from the graph, the whole sales figures and profits fluctuated during the decade. Over the period of the first half of the decade the sales figures had a slight increase from 99 million to 135 million. However, the trend of the sales figures did not go up continuously, the figures in 1996 were 134 million. From then, the number grew all the way from 134 million to 154 million from the year of 1996 to 1999. In 2000 the sales figures, which had a little decreased in contrast to those in the year of 1999, it just was 154 million.

On the other hand, the profits of ABC Elec. Were 8 million and 9 million in 1991 and in 1992, respectively. Then the profits rose from only 8 million in 1993 to 16 million in 1997, which indicated the profits were a dramatic increase. In contrast, there was downward trend in profits from 1998 to 2000. According to the chart, the highest sales figures were 158 million in 1999 while the profits just was 11 million.

In conclusion, it appears from the data that sales figures and profits are in unstable cases.

(217 words)

Task Fulfilment: The student has described the trends reasonably well, but a little more detail would have been good. The student notices that there is no stable trend, but the conclusion could have noted the overall rise in both sales and profits.

Coherence and Cohesion: The student uses many connectives well. The report is reasonably clear and easy to follow.

Vocabulary and Sentence Structure: The vocabulary is good. There are some grammar mistakes, but these do not affect the meaning of the sentences. The student could try using 'increase' and 'decrease' as verbs, e.g. change "had a slight increase" and "had a little decreased" to "increased slightly" and "decreased a little".

How to Answer Sample Question 4 怎样写好样题 4

Understanding the Material

Our last two examples showed two sets of information on two separate charts. This example has the two sets of information shown on one chart. This does not make a difference when you write the report. The key difference with this example is that it also shows how the figures developed over time. Obviously, you should see if there is any relationship between sales and profits, but the development over time is the main focus of your report.

Vocabulary

Nouns – the sales figure(s), sales, profits, an increase, a rise, a fall, a drop, a decrease, a fluctuation.

Verbs – increase, rise, fall, decrease, drop, fluctuate, compare.

Adjectives – small, large, low, high, more, less.

(Comparatives and superlatives may be needed!)

Adverbs – considerably, slightly, noticeably, sharply, relatively.

Note – *an* increase *of*, *to* increase *by*.

Organising the Report

Introduction – Very short. Say what the bar chart shows, in your own words as far as possible.

Body – There are two ways of dealing with the body of the report. The first way is to write one paragraph charting the development of the figures over time (see Model Answer 1). The second way is to see if you can make any general statements about groups of years (see Model Answer 2). In this case, you will be writing a few shorter paragraphs.

Conclusion – Overall, sales and profits rose over the period, but there was little relationship between the sales and profits figures.

Model Answer 1 范文 1

From the bar chart, we can see the sales and profits of ABC Electronics from 1991 to 2000.

The sales show a slight rise from 99 million USD to 112 million USD over the first 4 years.

Profits, however, remain stable at 8-9 million USD per year. Then, in 1995, sales and profits jump to 135 million USD and 12 million USD respectively. Curiously, in 1996, sales drop by a million USD, but profits increase by 3 million USD. The following year, sales rise considerably, to 149 million USD, but profits increase only slightly, to 16 million USD. In 1998 and 1999, sales increase to 152 and 158 million USD, but profits actually fall noticeably to 11 million USD each year. The year 2000 sees profits drop slightly to 154 million USD, but profits rise a little to 12 million USD.

Overall, we can see that sales show an upward trend. Profits, on the other hand, fluctuate until 1993, then increase until 1997, before dropping sharply and remaining relatively stable.

(170 words)

Model Answer 2 范文 2

Between 1991 and 1992, the sales of ABC Electronics grew by only 0.1 million US dollars. However, they increased steadily by 0.6 million per year over each of the next two years. Profits, meanwhile, fluctuated between 0.8 and 0.9 million US dollars.

There was a substantial rise in sales from 11.2 million dollars in 1994 to 13.5 million in 1995, followed by a very slight drop of 0.1 million the next year. On the other hand, profits rose considerably by 0.3 million US dollars per year between 1994 and 1996.

Over the next three years, there was an uneven growth in sales. They rose by 1.5 million dollars between 1996 and 1997. However, profits only increased by 0.1 million. The increase in sales of 0.3 million between 1997 and 1998 corresponded to a dramatic fall in profits from 1.6 million dollars to 1.1 million.

Then, in 1999, sales went up by 0.6 million dollars, to 15.8 million, whilst profits remained stable at 1.1 million. Between 1999 and 2000, profits increased by 0.1 million dollars, even though sales dropped by 0.4 million.

Overall, sales increased over the period by about 55%, whereas profits went up by 50%. In terms of dollar value, the best year for sales was 1999, whilst the best for profits was 1997.

(215 words)

3.5 Sample Question 5 样题 5

The graph shows the unemployment figures (as percentages of the population available for work) for two British cities and the average unemployment figures for Great Britain over the period 1985 to 2001. Write a report for a university lecturer describing the information shown below. You should write at least 150 words.

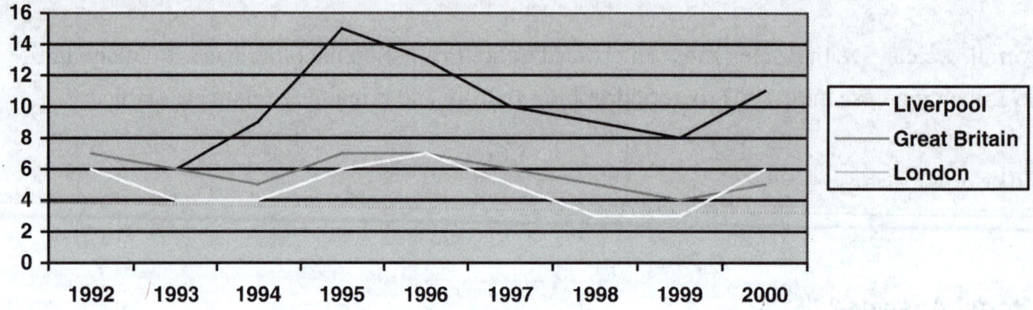

Sample Answer 1 学生答卷 1

This line graph illustrates the fluctuation of the unemployment rates of Great Britain and its other two cities – Liverpool as well as London. from 1992 to 2000.

Concentrated on the line of Liverpool, it arrived at a peak in 1995, which means the rate of unemployment men reached as high as sixteen people in every hundred people. Before that time, the rate almost climbed up gradually, although there was a slight drop to six percent in 1993. After 1995, the trend reversed, its decline lasted for five years, then the number began to soar in 1999.

Compared with the other two lines, beside a tiny difference, they almost keep the similar pace with the Liverpool line. It is obvious that Great Britain's unemployment rate was always above London, the two lines converged in 1996, which the figure is seven percent, however in 1999, London bounded up higher than Great Britain, it attained six percent whereas the other is only five percent.

(161 words)

Task Fulfilment: The student needs to include more details. The report only just crosses the minimum number of words required. As it is, the report does not quite accomplish the task.

Coherence and Cohesion: The report is fairly easy to understand and the student uses connectives and discourse markers well.

Vocabulary and Sentence Structure: The grammar is quite good, with only minor errors. The vocabulary is good and there are no significant inappropriacies.

Sample Answer 2 学生答卷 2

As can be seen from the graph, the three curves reveal the unemployment figures for two cities of Liverpool and London, and the average unemployment figures for Great Britain between 1992and 2001.

From 1992 to about mid 1993, the figures for Liverpool remained constant at 6%. However, the rate started to rise in the mid 1993. And in the late 1994, it rose more rapidly, reaching the peak of approxinatly 155 in the mid 1995. There was a massive drop in the unemployment figures of Liverpool from the mid 1995, when about 15% of the population were available for work, to the mid 1997, when the percentage was 10%. Over the period from mid 1997 to late 1999, the rate of decline slowed down, the figure for the latter year being about 8%. since late 1999, it began to increase again.

Similarly, there was an upward trend in the unemployment figures for London in the period from 1992 to the mid 1996, reaching roughly 7%, however, fluctuated. It was followed by a sharp decrease of 57% until in the mid 1998, it remained constant and rose again since mid 1999.

It can be seen from the line for Great Britain that there was a downward trend between 1992 (6%) and mid 1994 (5%). And from 1994 to 1996, it rose slightly, reaching the peak of 7%. It was followed by a steady fall until 1999 (4%). From then on, there was a gradual increase.

(244 words)

Task Fulfilment: The student describes the line graph well, but misses the key overall trends (the unemployment rates generally follow each other, with Liverpool generally far higher than the other two and London generally just below the national average. The decrease of 57% mentioned in the paragraph on London is clearly an error.)

Coherence and Cohesion: The report is easy to follow and the student uses several good connectives and discourse markers. The report is clearly organised, but lacks a paragraph giving conclusions about the trends.

Vocabulary and Sentence Structure: The vocabulary and grammar are very good. The student uses a wide selection of phrases to describe the trends. The student correctly uses the past tense. Most sentences are complex and there are only minor errors.

How to Answer Sample Question 5 怎样写好样题5

Understanding the Material

Here, you need to compare three lines giving unemployment figures. Many students will be tempted to take the figures for individual years and compare them, then move to the figures for the next year and compare them. This could confuse a reader. It's better to look at the three lines separately, then compare them in the conclusion.

Vocabulary

Nouns – the figure(s), unemployment, per cent, percentage, city, rate, an increase, a rise, a fall, a drop, a decrease, a decline, a fluctuation.
Verbs – increase, rise, fall, decrease, drop, fluctuate, compare, remain.
Adjectives – small, large, low, high, more, less, sharp, slight, gradual.
(Comparatives and superlatives may be needed!)
Adverbs – considerably, slightly, noticeably, sharply, relatively, gradually.
Note – *an* increase *of*, *to* increase *by*.
Quantities – half, third, twice, (three) times.

Organising the Report

Introduction – Very short. Say what the line chart shows, in your own words as far as possible.
Body – There should clearly be three paragraphs (Britain, Liverpool, and London). In each paragraph, you should describe the fluctuation in unemployment rates. You can mention the figures for another place briefly (for example if they are the same at any point, e.g. "In 1996, the unemployment figure for London rose to 6%, the same as the figure for Great Britain." Avoid mixing the figures for two different places as much as possible.
Conclusion – You can compare the figures for the three places, give an overall description of the trends, or (ideally) a combination of both.

Model Answer 范文

The line graph shows the unemployment figures for Liverpool, London, and Great Britain from 1992 to 2000.

The figure for Liverpool remains stable at 6% for 1992 and 1993, before increasing sharply over the next 2 years to 15%. It then falls to 8% in 1999. The decline is marked from 1995 (15%) to 1997 (10%), but less so from 1997 to 1999. At the end of the period, the figure again rises quickly to 11%.

The figure for London begins at the same level as Liverpool's (6%), but afterwards never exceeds Liverpool's. In 1993 and 1994 the figure is 4%, followed by an increase to 7% in 1996. Thereafter, there is a steady decline to 3% in 1998. The figure remains stable at this level in 1999, before doubling to 6% in 2000.

The figure for Great Britain begins at 7% in 1992 and drops to 5% in 1994. Then the figure increases in 1995, back to the 1992 level, and remains at that level in 1996. Between 1996 and 1999, the unemployment figure drops gradually to 4%, prior to rising slightly to 5% in 2000.

From these figures, we can see that the unemployment trend is similar for the two cities and Great Britain as a whole. However, the figures for London and Liverpool fluctuate more than the figures for Great Britain. The unemployment figures for Liverpool significantly exceed the others.

(233 words)

3.6 Sample Question 6 样题 6

The table shows three economic and social indicators for seven American countries for the year 1997. Write a report for a university lecturer describing the information shown below. You should write at least 150 words.

Country	**GDP per capita (USD)**	**Adult illiteracy rate***	**Newspaper sales per 1000 people**
The Bahamas	13000	4.4	99
Argentina	9100	3.6	123
Brazil	4900	16.8	40
Mexico	4300	10.5	97
Surinam	3700	7.0	122
Jamaica	2600	15.2	63
Cuba	2100	4.4	118

Sample Answer 1 学生答卷 1

The graph is the three economic and social indicator which display the figures of GDP per capita, Adult illiteracy and Newspaper Sales per 1000 people for seven American countries. The Bahamas, Argentina, Brazil, Mexico, Surinam, Jamaica and Cuba in 1997.

It can be seen from the table that The Bahamas and Argentina had GDP of $13000 and $9100 per capita, respectively. The figures were overwhelmingly greater than the figures of $2600 in Jamaica and $2100 in Cuba Illiteracy rates among adults. The Bahamas and Cuba both reported illiteracy rates of 4.4 while Brazil, Mexico and Jamaica had a rate more than 10. Argentina has a rate of only 3.6.

The table shows that Another indicators, Newspaper Sales per people have a huge number more than 100 of Argentina Surinam and Cuba. This was fllowed by The Bahamas, 99. Mexico 97. Jamaica 63. and Brazil 40.

(145 words)

Task Fulfilment: The student has not really fulfilled the requirements of the task. Figures tend to be listed and not compared or analysed. Notice that the report is slightly underlength.

Coherence and Cohesion: The student does not use enough connectives and the report is somewhat disjointed, even though it can be followed.

Vocabulary and Sentence Structure: There are few grammar mistakes, but the range is limited, mainly because the material is listed, not examined. The vocabulary is reasonably good. The student has noticeable problems using commas and full stops.

Sample Answer 2 学生答卷 2

Indicators of economic and social conditions in seven countries, The Bahamas, Argentina, Brazil, Mexico, Surinam, Jamaica, Cuba, in 1997, reflect significant differences.

It can be seen from the table that The Bahamas and Argentina had GDP$13000 and $8100 per capita, respectively. These figures were overwhelmingly greater than the corresponding figures of $2600 in Jamaica and $2100 in Cuba. While the middle class was composed by Brazil, Mexico, and Surinam, with their GDP per capita ranging from $4900 to $3700.

However, adult illiteracy rate was not proportional with GDP per capita in those countries. The lowest countries were less than 4.5%, followed by Surinam, 7.0%. The highest one is Brazil, 16. 8%.

Countries with low adult illiteracy had better Newspaper sales. Argentina reported 123 per 1000 people, which is the best, while Brazil claimed only 40.

(134 words)

Task Fulfilment: The report is too short. The paragraph on GDP per capita is well written, but the student has not achieved the same standard with the other two sets of figures. The student has noticed that there is little correlation between GDP per capita and illiteracy and that there is somewhat of a correlation between literacy and newspaper sales.

Coherence and Cohesion: The report is easy to follow and the student uses some connectives appropriately.

Vocabulary and Sentence Structure: The vocabulary is good, with only a few inappropriacies ("the middle class was composed by", "Brazil claimed only 40"). The grammar is fairly good and the student has used the past tense correctly.

How to Answer Sample Question 6 怎样写好样题 6

Understanding the Material

Obviously, you must compare the three sets of information. This is going to be a little difficult for seven countries. As there is a lot of information, you may not need to include all the individual statistics. You may not have time! So, the key thing is to look for trends. The *expected* trend would be that richer countries have lower illiteracy rates (because they have better education systems). Countries with lower illiteracy rates should have higher newspaper sales (because more people can read!). Unfortunately, a quick look at the Bahamas and Cuba seems to indicate that this is not true. The table is confusing, so we should be *extra* careful not to confuse a reader (or get confused ourselves!).

Vocabulary

Nouns – the figure(s), the percentage(s), per cent, country, rate, number, sales, GDP per capita, level.
Verbs – differ, vary, appear, compare.
Adjectives – small, large, low, high, more, less.
(Comparatives and superlatives will be needed!)
Adverbs – considerably, slightly, relatively, surprisingly, generally.
Quantities – half, third, twice, (three) times, double, triple, (nearly / roughly) the same.

Organising the Report

Introduction – Very short. Say what the pie charts show, in your own words as far as possible.
Body – Ideally, three paragraphs (one for each set of figures). In each paragraph, you should *try* to mention each country, though this is not strictly necessary. Try to group countries which have similar figures (relatively high / low, or average) within each set.
Conclusion – There is little relation between the three sets of figures. In particular, the GDP per capita figures bear little relation to the other two sets.

Model Answer 范文

The table shows the GDP per capita, adult illiteracy rates, and newspaper sales per thousand people for seven countries.

We can see that GDP per capita varies substantially from 2100 USD in Cuba to 13000 USD in the Bahamas, with 5 of the 7 countries below 5000 USD per capita GDP.

The illiteracy rates also differ considerably. The highest illiteracy rates are for Brazil (16.8%) and Jamaica (15.2%), whilst Argentina has the lowest rate, at 3.6%. Mexico (at 10.5%) and Surinam (7%) lie in the middle. Surprisingly, the adult illiteracy rate for Cuba and the Bahamas is the same, at 4.4%!

Newspaper sales per thousand people are also diverse. Argentina has the lowest illiteracy rate and the highest newspaper sales per thousand people (123/1000). Surinam (122/1000) and Cuba (118/1000) have similar rates. The Bahamas (99/1000) and Mexico (97/1000) have relatively high levels, too. Jamaica (63/1000) and Brazil (40/1000) have the lowest levels and have the highest illiteracy rates.

From the chart, we can see that there is no relationship between either the adult illiteracy rate, or newspaper sales, and GDP per capita. However, it does appear that the lower the illiteracy rate, the higher the newspaper sales. This can be seen generally, in that the four countries with illiteracy rates of 7% or less have the highest newspaper sales.

(219 words)

3.7 Sample Question 7 样题 7

Look at the diagram of a plant. Write a report for a university lecturer briefly describing the structure of the plant (using the labels on the diagram) and describing the two ways that the plant gets food and energy (through its roots and though its leaves, i.e. photosynthesis). You should write at least 150 words.

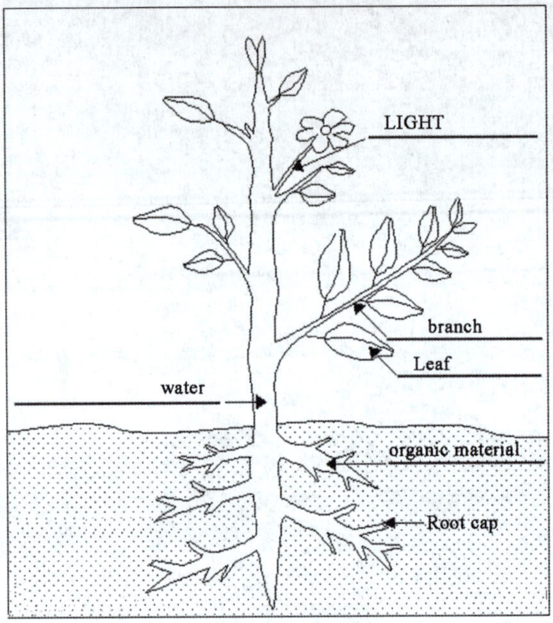

Sample Answer 学生答卷

This diagram reveals the structure of the plant and the process the plant gets food and energy.

According to the figure, the plant can be divided into two part the overground part and the underground part. The line of demarcation is the soil which can be called organic material as well. The plant above this line consists of two organs respectively named branch and leaf. While the organ below this line is the root of the plant. In addition, at the tip of its root is the root cap which is too small to be noted. Besides, there are a great deal of other organs and tissues forming a complete plant, however, those part may be difficult to be observed.

It can be illustrated from the figure that, according to the structure, plant can obtain food and energy in this following ways. Firstly, the root of the plant is able to absorb the water and the nutrition such as phosphorus and potassium from the organic material. Secondly, the leaves makes use of the light to produce energy that is called ATP through photosynthesis in order to maintain the survival of the plant.

(192 words)

Task Fulfilment: The essay fulfils the task well.

Coherence and Cohesion: The report is easy to follow and the student makes very good use of connectives and discourse markers.

Vocabulary and Sentence Structure: There are very few grammar and vocabulary mistakes.

How to Answer Sample Question 7 怎样写好样题7

Understanding the Material

Processes are a lot more visual in IELTS. Even if the diagram were labelled in a language you didn't know at all, you could still see what was happening. This example is a little scientific, but it is basic science that you could be expected to know. In many process diagrams, the cycle is clearly labelled, but in this one it is not, because the process is widely known.

Vocabulary

Nouns – The necessary nouns are already on the diagram. This underlines the fact that IELTS Task 1 is not a vocabulary test, but a test of communicative ability. *If* you know any other useful nouns for parts of plants, feel free to include them. If used appropriately, they will improve your score. However, a candidate who does not use any other nouns is *not* disadvantaged (see the model answer).

Verbs – use, grow, be called, enter, pass, give, get, turn , convert. Remember that for processes, we use the present tense! You can use the 'active' voice and the 'passive' voice. "Plants take in nutrition via their roots." "Nutrition is taken in by plants via their roots."

Adjectives – One of the big differences between 'process-based' tasks and 'chart-based' tasks is that 'chart-based' tasks require more adjectives (and adverbs) whereas 'process-based' tasks require more verbs (and nouns).

Organising the Report

Introduction – Very short. Say what process the diagram shows, in your own words as far as possible.

Body – This task will require two paragraphs (one for nutrition gained via the roots and one for nutrition gained via photosynthesis). The first part of each paragraph should contain the description (of the parts of the plant) and the second part of each paragraph should contain the process (of gaining nutrition).

Conclusion – A conclusion is not strictly necessary for most process-based tasks. The 'conclusion' is implicit in the description of the process.

Model Answer 范文

Plants lie partly above ground and partly below ground. There are two ways for plants to get food and energy, utilising both the components above ground and below.

The parts growing below ground are the roots. The main root, which tends to grow vertically down, is called the 'tap root'. Other roots grow out from this tap root. The ends of the roots draw in water and nutrients from the soil. These nutrients usually enter the soil from decomposing plant and animal matter. Water enters the soil when it rains or when the land is flooded. The nutrients then pass through the root system and the rest of the plant via the stem and branches.

Above ground, the plant has a stem, branches growing out of this stem, and leaves growing on the branches. Plants also use their leaves to turn sunlight into energy. This process is called photosynthesis. Sunlight shines on the leaves, which then channel this energy though the branches and the stem to the rest of the plant.

(171 words)

3.8 Sample Question 8 样题 8

Look at the diagram of a bicycle. Write a report for a university lecturer briefly describing the structure of the bicycle (using the labels on the diagram) and describing the process in which a bicycle can be moved using the pedals (i.e. by pedalling). You should write at least 150 words.

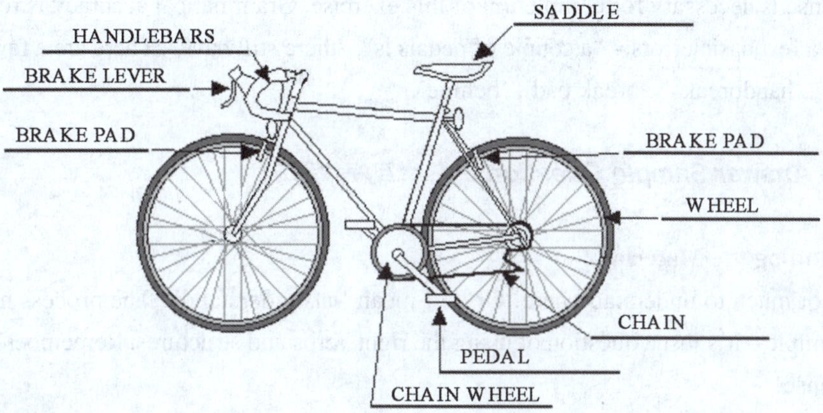

Sample Answer 学生答卷

The diagram indicates the structure of the bicycle.

According to the figure, the bicycle consists of two main parts – the front part and the back part. The former contains a pair of handbreaks with their respective brake levers and a wheel which is laid under the hand breaks. Additionally, it is at the upper part of the wheel that a small break pad is fixed. While the latter primary include a saddle, a chain as well as a wheel. It can be seen from the figure that a couple of pedals is located on each side of the wheel chain which is below the saddle. Moreover, an iron chain is firmly connected between the wheel chain and the wheel behine. Similarly, another break pad has the same location as the one of the wheel in the front part. Besides, there still have a number of important components forming a complete bicycle.

On the basis of the structure of the bicycle. When people ride it, the spin of the pedals is transmited to the back wheel through the chain. so as to make the wheel roll forward. Thus, the bicycle moves.

(190 words)

Task Fulfilment: The student does a reasonably good job of describing the bicycle and how it works, but should have included the functions of some of the parts, e.g. the handlebars are for steering, the brakes are for slowing / stopping the bicycle.
Coherence and Cohesion: The report is clearly laid out and the student uses several appropriate connectives.
Vocabulary and Sentence Structure: The student uses a good range of vocabulary, but there are a few inappropriacies – 'laid', 'latter primary'. The range of grammar is fine – only the present tense is necessary for completion of this exercise. Grammatical accuracy is reasonable. There are a few basic errors – "a couple of pedals is", "there still have". There are a few spelling mistakes – 'handbreaks', 'break pad', 'behine'.

How to Answer Sample Question 8 怎样写好样题 8

Understanding the Material

There's not much to understand here! Or do I mean '*mis*understand'? The process here is extremely simple – it's just a question of using the right verbs and structures. Remember to use the present tense!

Vocabulary

Nouns – As with the previous example, the necessary nouns are already on the diagram.
Verbs – pedal, cycle, brake, slow down, accelerate, speed up, turn, move, sit, connect, support, join, comprise, steer, stop, start.

Organising the Report

Introduction – Very short, perhaps even unnecessary. Say what process the diagram shows, in your own words as far as possible.
Body – This task can be done in one paragraph (describing the bicycle and the process together) or two (one for description, one for the process). Remember to use words such as 'when' or 'if'. If you say "The brakes stop the bicycle", it is more of a statement of fact rather than a description of a process. "When the brakes are used, the bicycle stops" focuses more on the process involved. Use statements of fact to describe the structure of the bicycle. Use 'which' or 'that' to demonstrate relations between parts and actions, e.g. "The cyclist moves the handlebars which steer the bicycle."
Conclusion – A conclusion is not strictly necessary for most process-based tasks. The 'conclusion' is implicit in the description of the process.

Model Answer 范文

A bicycle basically comprises two wheels behind each other. These wheels are joined together and supported by a frame. The frame has a saddle for the cyclist and handlebars to allow the cyclist to steer left and right. When the cyclist sits on the saddle, (s)he places his/her feet on the pedals. These pedals are loosely connected to the frame, so that they can be turned by the movement of the cyclist's feet. This action is called pedalling. The pedals are connected to a chain wheel, which in turn is connected to the rear wheel by a chain. Pedalling moves the chain wheel, which moves the chain, and thus the rear wheel, hence moving the whole bicycle forward. Once in motion, the cyclist moves his/her hands on the handlebars to move in the desired direction. The cyclist can also stop pedalling and use the brakes (one set for each wheel) to bring the bicycle to a stop. When the brakes are used, the brake pads clutch the wheels, stopping them from turning, thus halting the bicycle.

(176 words)

3.9 Useful Words and Phrases 有用的词汇及短语

In Academic Task 1, and perhaps also in the Speaking Module and Writing Task 2, you may need to describe changes which occur over a period of time (see the questions about ABC Electronics and the British unemployment figures and the model answer for the ABC Electronics question). The following words and phrases are particularly useful for discussing changing trends. Remember that trends may be seen in figures that have been presented in different ways – line charts, bar graphs, even pie charts if they are for different years. You should also look at the pages on 'Adverbs of Degree' and 'Comparatives and Superlatives' for suitable language to use when discussing trends.

在学术类写作 Task 1 当中，或者再加上口语面试和学术类写作 Task 2 之中，你可能需要对一段时间内发生的某种变化进行描述（参看A B C电子学的问题、英国失业率的问题以及A B C电子学问题的参考答案）。下面这些词汇和短语对于探讨这样的变化是大有裨益的。应该记住一点，这些发展趋势可能会通过不同的表现方式呈现出来——曲线图，柱状图形，或者饼状图。你也应该参考一下关于程度副词和形容词的比较级与最高级的章节，以寻找合适的语言来讨论这种发展趋势。

Words you can use when you want to say ... 下面的表达方式可以相互替换使用：

increase – rise, grow, soar, climb, go up, get higher, rocket,
decrease – reduce, cut, decline, drop off, fall, plummet, nose-dive, tumble, plunge, drop, dip, slump,
steady – stable, constant, even, flat, gradual, regular,
slight – small, insignificant, minor, slender,
insignificant – immaterial, unimportant, inconsequential,
significant – dramatic, important, considerable, large, major, huge,
fluctuate – vary, rise and fall,
level out – bottom out,
stabilise – even out, become stable, remain steady,
lessen – diminish, reduce, lower, cut,
peak at – reach a height of (in/at), plateau at,
approximately – roughly, around, about, nearly, just under, just over,

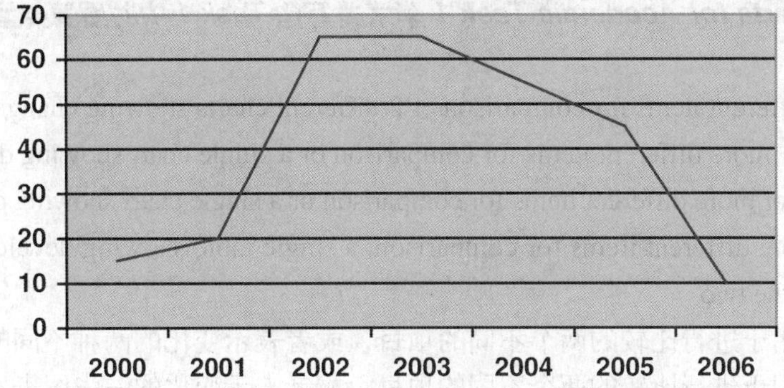

2000 → 2001 – an increase, a rise, a climb, to go up, to increase, to rise, to climb.

2001 → 2002 – a significant increase, a dramatic rise, a huge rise, a massive increase, a sub stantial rise, large growth, considerable growth, soar, rocket, climb rapidly, increase considerably, rise substantially.

2002 → 2003 – plateau, level out, stabilise, remain steady.

2003 → 2005 – a steady fall, a gradual decrease, a steady reduction, a gradual decline, drop off, drop.

2005 → 2006 – a significant decrease, a dramatic fall, a considerable decrease, a large fall, a major fall, a huge decrease, a significant reduction, a considerable decline, plummet, nose-dive, tumble, plunge, slump.

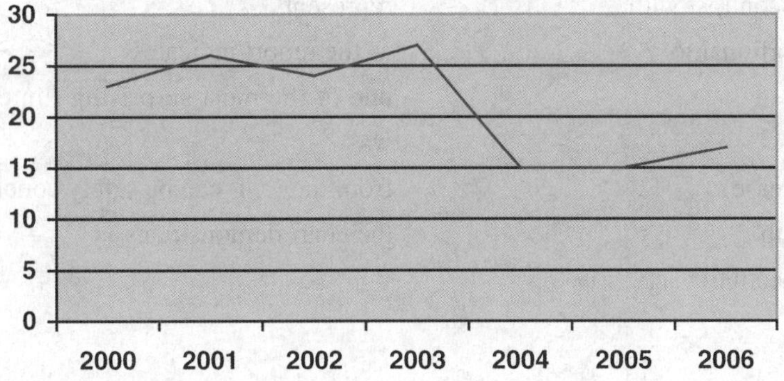

2000 → 2003 – a fluctuation, vary, rise and fall, fluctuate.

2003 – reach a peak, reach a height, achieve a high point.

2003 → 2004 – a decrease, to decrease, a reduction, a decline, to decline, a fall, to fall.

2004 → 2005 – bottom out, level out, stabilise, remain steady.

2005 → 2006 – a slight increase, a small rise, a slender rise, a minor increase, a slight growth, go up slightly, increase somewhat, rise a little.

Types of Charts for Academic Task 1 学术类写作 Task 1 中的图表类型

Pie chart – 2 different items for comparison or 2 different charts showing changes
Bar chart – 2 or more different items for comparison or a single chart showing developments
Line graph – 2 or more different items for comparison or a single chart showing developments
Table – 2 or more different items for comparison, a single table showing developments, or a combination of the two

饼状图形——用于进行比较的两个不同的项目，或者表示变化的两种不同的图表
柱状图形——用于进行比较的两个不同的项目，或者表示变化的一张图表
曲线图形——用于进行比较的两个或多个不同的项目，或者表示变化的一张图表
表　　格——用于进行比较的两个或多个不同的项目，或者表示变化的一张图表，或者是上面两者的集合

Useful phrases for Academic Task 1 用于学术类写作 Task 1 的短语

Identify and discuss the trends
发现发展趋势并进行讨论

The chart indicates / displays (not unfolds!)	a far less (more) significant change (took place)
Indicators … reflect …	the biggest change occurred
The chart compares	… experienced a significant (rise / fall) in …
It can clearly be seen that	a x-fold increase
The graphs provide an overview of	upward / downward trend
A similar / different trend / pattern was seen in	anomalies
This is in stark contrast with	represent
Inversely proportional to	as the report indicates
(remain) ahead of	one of the most surprising / interesting finds was
exceed	from the … it can be safely concluded that
an overall (increase)	the chart demonstrates
corresponds with	
experience a (decline)	

Chapter 4

General Training Task 1

普通培训类写作 Task 1

4.1 Sample Question 1 样题 1

For the General Training module, Task 1 is always a letter. Here is an example.
一般来说，普通培训类写作 Task 1 要求考生写一封书信。例如：

You have read about a scholarship offered by a university and wish to apply.
Write a letter to the university and include the following information:

- **the scholarship you wish to apply for**
- **some details about yourself**
- **your academic suitability for the scholarship**

and any other relevant information.

You should write at least 150 words.
You do not need to write your address.
Begin your letter as follows:
Dear Sir or Madam,

The situation and task are first, followed by what you *must* include in your letter. You may include other information if it is relevant to the development of the letter. Begin your letter as indicated (in this example "Dear Sir or Madam,") and end it with an appropriate complementary closing (in this case "Yours Faithfully,").
首先交待情景和写作要求，然后说明在信中必须包括的要点。与之相关的其他信息也可以写进来。按照指示写开头（比如此样题的 Dear Sir or Madam,），然后以得体的信尾客套语结束（比如此样题的 Yours Faithfully,）。

Let's take this task and write a letter in response.
现在根据以上样题写一封信。

4.1.1 Understanding the Situation 理解情景

Look at sample question 1. You must clearly state which scholarship you are applying for. Scholarships have names. They are normally named after the individuals or organisations who sponsor them. Scholarships can cover tuition only, or the total cost of studying, including accommodation and living expenses.
看一下样题 1。你必须明确地说明你想申请何种奖学金。奖学金是有名称的，通常是以设立该奖学金的个人或组织的名称命名的。奖学金可能只是提供学费，或者提供学生学习所需的所有费用，包括住宿和生活费。

The people and organisations that award scholarships always look at the background of the

students who apply. Whilst they are not particularly bothered whether your mother is a doctor or a police officer, they want to know the kind of family you come from.
提供奖学金的个人和组织往往要对申请者的背景进行审查。虽然他们并不关心你的母亲到底是医生还是警察，他们希望知道你的家庭背景。

Then, you must obviously demonstrate that you are the best student to receive the scholarship, on the basis of your past (and anticipated) academic record. Remember that getting a scholarship is a very competitive affair!
当然，你必须清楚地表明，你是获得奖学金的最佳人选，其根据就是你以前（包括将来的）的学习状况。记住，申请奖学金，竞争可是很激烈的。

Remember that in the General Training Task 1 letter, you must include all the required information.
记住，在普通培训类 Task 1 的信件中，你必须提供所有要求你提供的信息。

4.1.2 Vocabulary 词汇

Before you take the IELTS test, think about the types of letters that could be in Task 1. A list is included at the end of this chapter. Consider topics that might be suitable for each type of letter and the vocabulary that you may need to use. Be particularly careful to note which words are verbs, nouns, adjectives, etc. Here is a list of vocabulary that might be useful for this particular task. Notice that you should also consider useful phrases and collocations.
在雅思考试之前，考虑一下 Task 1 中可能会出现什么类型的信件。本章的末尾附上了一份列表。想一想什么样的主题最适合每种类型，你可能会用到什么样的词汇。尤其要注意词性，哪些是动词，哪些是名词、形容词等等。下面的词汇表对于当前的任务可能很有帮助。同时，你也应该注意一些有用的短语和搭配。

award a scholarship	cover costs	awarded annually
in the field of	background	extra-curricular activities
sports team	competitions	well-rounded person
personality	character	characteristics
qualities	traits	academic achievements
reliable	trustworthy	friendly
active	hard working	diligent
highest grades	grade point average	straight ‘A’ student
recommended	informed	apply
application	confident	accepted

4.1.3 Organising the Letter 组织信件

General Training candidates have a great advantage in Task 1 of the writing module, because the organisation of the letter has already usually been done for them. Just look back at the question!

1. Reason for writing (the scholarship).
2. Something about yourself (background and personality)
3. Your suitability (academic record).

普通培训类考生在写作模块中的 Task 1 上占有很大的优势，原因是信件的组织已经为他们做好了。只需回顾一下问题。

1．写作原因（奖学金）
2．关于你自己的一些信息（背景和个性）
3．为什么你是合适人选（学习成绩）

4.1.4 Writing the Introduction 开头写作

From the sentences below, select the most appropriate for beginning the letter about the scholarship.

从下面的几个句子中选出申请奖学金信件最合适的开头。

1. "My name is John and I'm a student."
2. "I am writing to you regarding the Hunt Scholarship, which is awarded annually to a student of history at your university."
3. "It is with great pleasure and anticipation that I am writing to you concerning that most prestigious of all scholarships, the enchanting and gracious Hunt Scholarship."
4. "I need the scholarship because I am a poor student from China."
5. "Scholarships are very useful, because they allow students who cannot afford to study, the opportunity to get an education."

Sentence 1 is something a child might write. If you want to go to a university, you had better have a more developed mind than a child!

Sentence 4 is equally bad. Scholarships are to help people who have financial difficulties or constraints, but you don't get a scholarship just because of that.

Sentence 5 might be acceptable as the introduction for an essay, but it is unsuitable for a letter as it talks about scholarships in general, not the specific one you want to get.

Sentence 3 is far too poetic. The language is inappropriate. How can a scholarship be 'enchanting and gracious'?

So, you will have guessed by now that sentence 2 is the best. It specifies immediately what you are writing about and orientates the reader by referring to how often it is awarded and to students of which subject. It also clearly indicates to the examiner that you know what the letter has to be about.

句子 1 看上去过于儿童化。如果你想到大学读书的话，最好让自己的智力超过儿童。

句子 4 同样差劲。奖学金是帮助那些有财务困难的人们完成学业的。但是仅仅是因为没钱，你是得不到奖学金的。

句子 5 作为论文的开始还可以勉强接受，但不适合作信件的开头，因为本句在泛泛地谈论奖学金，并没有说你要申请哪个奖学金。

句子 3 过于诗情画意。语言不合适。奖学金怎么可能“迷人且优雅”呢？

那么，到目前为止，你应该猜到句子 2 是最佳选项。本句开门见山地指出你所写的对象，写出奖学金的发放频率和发放对象，读者一目了然。同时你也向评审人员表明，你清楚地知道这封信要涉及什么问题。

Now, what else do you need to do in the introduction? Choose from of the following.

1. Say what a wonderful person you are.
2. Confirm that you are eligible for the scholarship.
3. Mention your hobbies.
4. Write about your parents.
5. Say what a great student you are.
6. State that you would like to apply for the scholarship.

那么到目前为止，在开头里面你还要做些什么呢？从下面选项中选择：

1、说你自己是个如何好的人
2、证明你符合得到奖学金的条件
3、谈谈你的爱好
4、写些关于你父母的东西
5、说说你自己是个怎样优秀的学生
6、声明你自己愿意申请这份奖学金

The answer is that you need to do 2 and 6. Confirming your eligibility tells the reader that you have found out about the scholarship. You will create a very poor impression if you are a history student applying for a scholarship awarded to biology students! Include 6, but just for clarification. Information regarding 1, 3, 4, and 5, should be included later in the letter.

答案是你应当选 2 和 6。证明你符合申请奖学金的资格可以让你的读者知道你已经了解了该奖学金。如果你是学历史的，却在申请颁发给学生物的学生的奖学金，你会给人留下很差的印象。要把 6 也包含进去。1,3,4,5 相关的信息应该在信件后面的部分里出现。

Your introductory paragraph will now look something like this:

现在你开头的段落大体上应该是这个样子：

I am writing to you regarding the Hunt Scholarship, which is awarded annually to a student of history at your university. I am currently in the first year of my B.A. in History at your university. I would like to apply for this scholarship due to unforeseen financial constraints which may otherwise force me to abandon my studies.

(Total number of words = 58.)

4.1.5 Writing a Paragraph （主体）段落写作

Next, the task requires you to include some details about yourself and why you deserve the scholarship. In this letter, you could deal with them in either order. Either way, you need to make it clear what you are writing about in the first sentence. Let's give some personal details first. Which sentence is best for opening this paragraph?

下面，你的任务是给出一些你的个人信息以及为什么你应该得到这份奖学金。在这封信里，你可以以任何一种顺序来安排它们。不论采用哪种方式，你都要弄清自己在第一句话里要写些什么。我们先给出点个人信息吧。下面哪句话最适合作为段落的开头呢？

1. "I really deserve this scholarship because I'm a wonderful person to all my friends."
2. "I need the scholarship because I am a poor student from China."
3. "I am sure you will agree that I have contributed to extra-curricular activities at this university."
4. "I play on the university football team."

If you chose sentence 2 as the most suitable, you need to go right back to the beginning of this chapter and start again. You don't get a scholarship simply because you are a poor foreign student!

Sentence 1 is inappropriate, because it links your personality and the scholarship too directly. You get a scholarship as a result of many factors, not only because you are nice to your friends.

The last sentence (4) would be reasonable in the paragraph, but not as the opening line.

Sentence 3 is appropriate. Notice how it doesn't contain any subjective words ('wonderful', 'poor'). It leaves the reader interested in knowing exactly how you have contributed. It is also reasonably assertive ("I am sure you will agree ..."), not begging. This indicates you are confident about yourself and don't need to resort to emotions to win your case.

如果你的选择是2的话，你就得从本章的开头重新开始。仅仅因为你是一个外国的穷学生，你是得不到奖学金的。

句子1不合适，因为它把你的个性和奖学金联系得过于直接。你能获得奖学金，原因是多方面的，仅仅因为你够朋友，对朋友好，是得不到奖学金的。

句子4可以作为本段的内容，但是作开头不合适。

句子3最合适。注意，该句没有包含任何主观的词语（好，差等等）。读者会产生兴趣，希望了解你是怎样做出贡献的。语气上也很自信（I am sure you will agree... 我相信您会同意……），而不是在乞求。这一点表明你充满自信，不需要动之以情也可以赢得别人的同意。

What other information is it appropriate to include in this paragraph? Select one or more of the following:

本段中还可以包含哪些信息？从下面的选项中选择。

1. Your parents died in a car accident last year.
2. Your sporting achievements.

3. Your academic achievements.
4. Your hobbies.
5. Your hometown.
6. You are a poor Chinese student.

1、你的父母在去年的一次车祸中不幸身亡
2、你在体育上的成就
3、你的学习成绩
4、你的爱好
5、你的家乡
6、你是个中国穷学生

I seriously hope you didn't choose 6! By the way, did you check whether foreign students are eligible for the scholarship? Some are only for domestic students!

Information regarding 1 isn't really relevant and 3 will be dealt with in the next paragraph, so don't include it yet.

You certainly need to include information relating to 2. Mentioning 4 is acceptable. You might mention your hometown (5), but it is not something will affect the outcome.

我希望你没有选择最后一个选项。顺便说一下，你有没有查清楚外国学生是否可以申请该奖学金？有些奖学金是只面向本国学生的。

选项1所包含的信息事实上是不切题的，选项3应该出现在下一段中，而不是本段。

你当然应该把选项2所包含的信息加进去。选项4可以接受。你也可以顺便提一下你的家乡(5)，但这不会有什么太多帮助。

The paragraph may look something like this:

本段大体可以这样：

"I am sure you will agree that I have contributed to extra-curricular activities at this university. I play on the football team which got to the final of the University Cup this season. I also run Marathons and will represent the university in this event at the forthcoming University Athletics Meeting."

(Total number of words so far = 109.)

Are you a good enough student? Certainly!

你是个足够优秀的学生么？当然是！

"I have performed well academically, with very good grades so far (five grade 'A's and one grade 'B'). I admit that it will be hard to maintain that standard next year, but I am confident in my ability to deal with the workload. As you can see from the enclosed reports, my tutors share my confidence."

(Total number of words so far = 165.)

Notice how the applicant always refers to facts, not emotions. He doesn't boast or compare himself to others. This style is very important. It's about the student and the scholarship. The student doesn't 'promise to make the 'B' an 'A' next year – (s)he just promises to do what (s)he can and demonstrates that experienced tutors believe (s)he has the ability and support the application.

注意，申请者总是涉及事实，而不是情绪。他不会自我吹嘘，也不会拿自己和别人比较。这种风格尤为重要。涉及的是学生和奖学金。学生不会承诺将现在的B转变成明年的A，学生只是保证做到自己力所能及的，并且表明，经验丰富的老师相信她 / 他是有能力的并且会支持这一申请。

4.1.6 Writing the Conclusion 结论写作

Conclusions to letters are often short. The reason is that here is no need to repeat information that the reader read seconds ago. Which sentence is best for concluding this letter?

信件的结尾通常是很简短的。理由是没有必要重复读者数秒钟前阅读过的信息。下面哪句话最适合作这封信的结尾？

1. "I am sure you will agree that I really deserve this scholarship because of my special situation."
2. "I need the scholarship because I am a poor student from China."
3. "I am sure you will give my application due consideration. I look forward to hearing from you in the near future."
4. "Thanks for reading my letter and I will be happy to clear up any issues at a face-to-face meeting."
5. "Thank you for looking at my application."
6. "I hope I can get the scholarship."

If you choose 2, you need to repeat this whole chapter!

No "special situation" was mentioned in the letter, so 1 is inappropriate.

Similarly, there shouldn't be any "issues", so 4 is wrong.

The last sentence (6) is practically meaningless. You are writing because you hope to get the scholarship.

Sentence 5 is suitable, but too simple.

Sentence 3 is properly developed and has the correct tone (level of politeness and formality, without 'begging').

如果你选择的是2的话，你还是再把本章重新读一遍吧。

这封信没有提及任何"特殊情况"，所以选项1不合适。

同样，不应该存在什么"问题"，所以选项4错误。

最后一项几乎毫无意义。你写信的直接原因是你想得到奖学金。

选项5可以入选，但是过于简单。

选项3最合适，语气也很正确（礼貌，正式，没有"卑躬屈膝"）。

(Total number of words = 186.)

4.1.7 Complete Model Answer 完整的范文

Dear Sir or Madam,

I am writing to you regarding the Hunt Scholarship, which is awarded annually to a student of history at your university. . I am currently in the first year of my B.A. in History at your university. I would like to apply for this scholarship due to unforeseen financial constraints which may otherwise force me to abandon my studies.

I am sure you will agree that I have contributed to extra-curricular activities at this university. I play on the football team which got to the final of the University Cup this season. I also run Marathons and will represent the university in this event at the forthcoming University Athletics Meeting.

I have performed well academically, with very good grades so far (five grade 'A's and one grade 'B'). I admit that it will be hard to maintain that standard next year, but I am confident in my ability to deal with the workload. As you can see from the enclosed reports, my tutors share my confidence.

I am sure you will give my application due consideration. I look forward to hearing from you in the near future.

Yours faithfully,
Andrew Scott

4.1.8 Alternative Model Answer 其他范文

Dear Sir or Madam,

I recently read about the 'Magnus Scholarship' in your university prospectus and wish to be considered for the award.

I understand that the scholarship is available to students under the age of 26 taking a Master's degree in the field of natural science. I am 25 and last month I was accepted onto the M.Sc. Microbiology course at your institution.

I completed my B.A. (with first class honours) in biology at Blakesley University in July 1998 and since then have been working in London in the microbiological research department of the Swiss-based company ABC. I am a member of the Royal Biology Society and have made presentations to the American Biology Society on the subjects of cell structure and cellular interaction.

In addition to my academic achievements and work, I play scrum-half for London Scottish and have been selected for the Scottish team trials prior to the next Six Nations Rugby Tournament.

I sincerely hope that you will give my application due consideration. I hereby enclose my detailed CV, a copy of my university degree, and two letters of reference, one from my employer, the other from my personal tutor at Blakesley.

Yours faithfully,
Andrew Scott

(201 words)

4.1.9 Sample Answer 1 学生答卷 1

Dear Sir or Madam,

I'm interested in your university. I'm attracted by its high quality of education. It's my dream to study in your university. So when I know the message that your university will supply us with scholarship, I feel very excited from the bottom of my heart.

I'm an active girl who have many interests, such as swimming, singing, dancing and so on. When I communicate with other people, nearly everyone will give a good impression on me, because I'm an easy-going person. And I have the ability to organize many activities. When I was in my university, I'm the leader of the EEC community (The full name is English Extra Club). I have organized many big activities which is enjoyed by many students and teachers. I'm so prond of it.

I'm also good at study. I have good mark in every subject, especially in mathematics and insurance. (insurance is my major, and I like it very much.) and I think I'm fit for the scholarship. If I have the chance to get the scholarship, I'll try my best to prove myself. I'm looking forward to your supply.

(190 words)

Task Fulfilment: The opening paragraph is totally inappropriate, however, the other two paragraphs are quite good. The student does not mention exactly which scholarship she wants to apply for. This could cause problems for the reader.

任务完成：开头段完全不合适，但是其余两段写得很好。该学生没有提及自己想要得到何种奖学金，这就容易给读者带来问题。

Coherence and Cohesion: The letter is easy to follow, even though the student uses few connectives.

连贯与衔接：文章虽然很少使用连词，还是很容易读懂。

Vocabulary and Sentence Structure: There are some examples of inappropriate vocabulary – "will supply us with scholarship", "from the bottom of my heart", "give a good impression", "big activities", "fit for the scholarship", "looking forward to your supply". There are some basic mistakes – "girl who have", "when I was … I'm the leader", "I have good mark". However, the student does try some complex sentences and achieves reasonable accuracy.

词汇与句子结构：有些用词不当的地方，例如：will supply us with scholarship, from the bottom of my heart, give a good impression, big activities, fit for the scholarship, looking forward to your supply。还有一些很基本的错误，如：girl who have, when I was … I'm the leader, I have good mark。虽然如此，该学生还是使用了一些复合句，精确度也比较高。

4.1.10 Sample Answer 2 学生答卷 2

Dear Sir or Madam,

I have read the notice about the scholarship of the Rockwell. So I wish to apply to get this exhibition.

The Rockwell's Price is the famous scholarship that is offered to the student who makes up in the field of engineering coure. In other words, It is the dream of the students engineering.

As your main idea, I am a student of your university. And Double E is my major course. The average of my achievement is about B. I have entered the Robot Match. I am also interested in some information about every kinds of machine and other fields.

Like other students, this price is my dream too. I hope to receive your reply.

(119 words)

Task Fulfilment: The letter does not create a good impression. It is shorter than the required 150 words, contains minimal academic information and no personal information. The key question for this letter is "Would you consider giving this student the scholarship?" Here, the answer must be "No!"

任务完成：这封信没有给人留下好印象。字数没有达到 150 字的最低字数要求，包含的关于学习情况的信息极少，没有任何个人信息。这封信的主要问题在于：你会考虑把奖学金给这个学生吗？答案一定是“不会”！

Coherence and Cohesion: The sentences are easy to understand, but they are not well connected.

连贯与衔接：各个句子都很容易理解，但是它们之间没有很好地衔接起来。

Vocabulary and Sentence Structure: The range of vocabulary is very limited. There are some cases of inappropriacy – “get this exhibition”, “makes up”, “the dream of the students engineering”, “As your main idea”. In such a letter, you would not use “Double E” (slang), nor would you say you are “interested in … every kind[s] of machine and other fields” (too general). ‘Prize’ is spelt incorrectly twice. Your grade average is “about B”? What is the “Robot Match”? The range of grammar is very limited – almost always the present tense. Accuracy is high, however.

词汇与句子结构：词汇量相当有限。也存在用词不当的现象：get this exhibition, makes up, the dream of the students engineering, As your main idea. 在这样的信件里面，要避免使用Double E（俚语），也不应说你interested in … every kind[s] of machine and other fields（过于宽泛）。Prize在这里出现了两次拼写错误。你的得分等级是接近B？“机器人比赛”具体指什么？语法的使用也很有限，几乎全是现在时态。但是精确度很高。

4.2 Sample Question 2 样题 2

You recently bought a laptop computer. A few days later the laptop stopped working. When you took it back to the shop, they refused to deal with the problem.

Write a letter to the customer service department at the company's head office including the following information:

- **the problem with the laptop**
- **what exactly happened when you returned to the shop**
- **what you would like the customer service department to do**

and any other relevant information.

You should write at least 150 words.

You do not need to write your address.

Begin your letter as follows:

Dear Sir or Madam,

Sample Answer 1 学生答卷 1

Dear Sir or Madam,

As a customer of your company, I'm writing this letter for your assistance.

A few days ago I bought a laptop computer of your company from XXX shop. The type is C600. I paid $2000 dollars for it. But it stopped work 3 days ago. I could not open Window 98 on it. I thought it must be something wrong with the software. Then I tried to install several time but failed. It shows no words on the screen but a bright short line. All these show/indicate my computer is broken.

I went to the shop for changing another computer. The worker refused me. Then I just asked for mend it. he told me there was no one could fix it until 3 weeks later.

I will be very appreciating if you can help me on the problem. Since I have to use the laptop to finish my paper in two weeks, it's really important to me.

I consider you will give me response and handle this issue in high efficiency. You could contact me via my mobile phone xxxx. You also can reply a letter to me. My address is No. XXX, XXX Street, B.C.

Yours sincerely,

(202 words)

Task Fulfilment: The letter very clearly deals with the problem. The student includes necessary details such as the name of the shop, the type of computer, and his mobile phone number. It's probably better to invent the name of a shop, give a fake phone number, etc., rather than using "xxxx", but that is a very minor issue.
Coherence and Cohesion: The letter is well paragraphed and extremely easy to understand. The student doesn't use many connectives, but the sentences flow well.
Vocabulary and Sentence Structure: The vocabulary is generally appropriate with only a few errors ('refused', 'high efficiency', 'give me response'). The letter only contains grammatical errors that do not prevent expression of the message ('for changing', "I will be very appreciating …", "asked for mend it"). The sentence structures are a little simple, but effective.

Sample Answer 2 学生答卷 2

Dear Sir or Madam,

I'm sorry to write this letter to you. There are something wrong with my laptop which bought from your agency. There main problem of the notebook is the hard-disk always running, but the screen is blank all the time.

It's must be some quality trouble, so I returned it to the shop and want to settle the problem. However, the manager of the shop refused to change it or even repair it. He said it must be used in the wrong way which means man-made mistaken. I'm very depressing about the answer.

I'd like you – the customer service department – to help me to work it out. You should take seriously attention to my application. The shabby laptop already influenced my daily work. A lot of important data may lost! Your company must responsible for your products and your customer. I want to change a new notebook or return the money to me.

Hope you to give me an answer as soon as possible. If you want more information about the laptop, please contact with me.

(179 words)

Task Fulfilment: The student answers the bullet points, but could be more specific, e.g. if the screen is blank all the time, how did (s)he get data onto the computer? Which brand and type is the laptop? Which shop is (s)he referring to?
Coherence and Cohesion: The letter is quite clear and the student uses a reasonable tone. The letter is paragraphed well.

Vocabulary and Sentence Structure: The vocabulary is reasonably good. Occasionally, the student uses the wrong form of the word, e.g. 'mistaken' should be 'mistake', 'depressing' should be 'depressed', and 'take seriously' should be 'pay serious'. There are many minor grammatical errors, but these do not prevent meaning coming across.

How to Answer General Sample Question 2 怎样写好样题2

Understanding the Material

In General Training Task 1, the situation should be very clear. Here, you must write a *letter of complaint*, referring to the problem with the laptop, a narrative of what happened when you complained to the shop, and an explanation of what you want done. Students often assume that because they have not created the problem and the fault is clearly with the other side (which is true), they can use very strong language to *demand* what they want (which is false). Remember that you can often get people to do things *better* and *faster* if you are nice and polite. Hostility *may* become necessary if they *still* do not respond, but shouldn't be your first reaction. Therefore, think about the tone you will use in the letter. Be polite (this situation is not your fault personally), but firm (however, you should be committed to selling quality products and providing a reasonable service).

Vocabulary

Nouns – You will obviously need a few nouns associated with parts of a laptop (screen, keyboard, keys, battery, cover, processor, disc drive).

Verbs – complain, return, buy, purchase, use, switch on/off, save (data), make a noise, (not) work, break, function, experience, claim, refund, exchange, contact, telephone, visit, deliver.

Adjectives – rude, impolite, unhelpful, uninformed, careful.

Time phrases – soon, recently, immediately, in/within a few days, last/next (week), as soon as possible.

Organising the Letter

The organisation of a General Training Task 1 letter is often clear from the question. For this letter, the first paragraph should be about the problem, the second should be regarding what happened at the shop, and the third should be about what you want done.

Paragraph 1 – You should certainly mention the brand of laptop and the shop. You can be more specific and mention the model number, serial number, and address of the shop, if you wish. Your decision will be based on how many words you expect to write in the rest of the letter. If you have plenty to say, leave out these extra details. If you are worried that you will not reach 150 words, put the extra details in.

Paragraph 2 – Explain what happened when you tried to return the faulty laptop or have it checked at the shop. Here you need to mention the poor service, but remember, do so in a polite manner. In paragraph 3 you are going to ask the reader to help you! Try to keep the information factual, without too much 'emotional' language. This is certainly not the time to use those 'special' phrases you learnt in bars!

Paragraph 3 – Explain what you want done. Aim high, but be reasonable. Put yourself in the reader's position. What would a customer service manager consider reasonable? A refund? Sure, if you wish. An exchange? Better – they still make sale. A free computer game? Many reputable retailers would do this anyway. A 20% discount? Very unlikely!

Signing off – 'Yours faithfully' is most appropriate here. The situation is quite formal and you have never met the person you are writing to.

Model Answer 范文

Dear Sir or Madam,

I recently bought a Komputa 2000 laptop computer at your Henley branch. However, within a few days, I began to experience problems with it. The main problems were that a few of the programs installed on it ceased to function and that the laptop refused to accept any discs, even though these discs are accepted by both my desktop computer and my friend's Toshiba 2000.

When I returned to the shop to claim a replacement or a refund under the terms of the warranty provided by your shop, I was informed that I am not entitled to either as the warranty card is invalid. The reason why the warranty card is invalid was not explained to me. When I asked for an explanation, the staff refused to give me one. Whilst the staff were not rude as such, they were rather abrupt.

As a result, I am writing to you in order to sort the situation out. I believe the warranty card to be complete and valid. I enclose a photocopy for you to check. I would like to arrange for my faulty laptop to be exchanged or for my money to be refunded. Please contact me when you have looked into the matter. I may be contacted by telephone on (0237) 657483.

Yours faithfully,

Andrew Scott

(221 words)

4.3 Sample Question 3 样题 3

You have received a bank statement showing that the bank has deducted some money from your account. You *think* that they have made a mistake.
Write a letter to the bank including the following information:

- **your account details and the *possible* problem with the statement**
- **what you think may have happened to cause the mistake**
- **what you would like the bank to do**

and any other relevant information.

You should write at least 150 words.
You do not need to write your address.
Begin your letter as follows:
Dear Sir or Madam,

Sample answer 学生答卷 1

Dear Sir or Madam,

When I saw your given me a bank statement. I found a problem about that my account has some money was been deducted. I cannot understand it.

My account is US account (account number is 12137828). In the account, original sum of money is US$6,000 from 27/June/2003 to 27/July/2004 that interest is 13/16% per year. So I will get US.$6045 finally. But why your deducate US$100 from my account this time? However, donot including taxes and serives fees in this $100. Whether your adding more than one serives for me, or you got mistake about my account. I really want to know US$100 what's going to. Could your give me a reason about it. Thank you so much!

(118 words)

Task Fulfilment: The letter is fairly clear and covers all the bullet points. The student includes essential details such as the account number, currency, dates, and amounts. Unfortunately, the letter is still shorter than the required number of words, indicating that it has not been developed.
Coherence and Cohesion: The letter is not very well organised – one short introductory paragraph and then a long one. The student uses a few connectives.
Vocabulary and Sentence Structure: The vocabulary is reasonable, but the language is too sharp – almost rude – near the end of the letter. The grammar is poor, particularly with regard to question forms in the latter part of the letter. The student misspells 'services' ('serives') and writes 'donot' instead of 'do not'.

How to Answer Sample Question 3 怎样写好样题3

Understanding the Material

In this task, a key thing to remember is that you are not absolutely *sure* about the mistake – you are asking the bank to *check*. You could have four paragraphs in your letter: (i) your account details, (ii) the possible problem, (iii) how the problem may have occurred, and (iv) what you want done. However, you could combine two items to reduce the number of paragraphs to three (see model answer). As with the last question, remember that you can often get people to do things *better* and *faster* if you are nice and polite. Hostility *may* become necessary if they *still* do not respond, but shouldn't be your first reaction. Therefore, think about the tone you will use in the letter. Be polite (this situation is not your fault personally), but firm (however, it is important to get things right with money). The use of modal verbs – could, would, should, might, may – in your letter will help you to do this well.

Vocabulary

Nouns – statement, bank account, error, credit card, cheque, bank, branch, withdrawal, deposit.
Verbs – check, deposit, withdraw, investigate, claim, return, notice, add, credit, debit, inform, contact, telephone, receive, believe, find (a mistake), make (a mistake).
Adjectives – quickly, immediately, carefully.

Organising the Letter

The organisation of a General Training Task 1 letter is often clear from the question. As was mentioned above, it might be possible to combine paragraphs, e.g. the bank account details and the problem with the statement, or the problem and the cause of the problem. Let's work on the basis of four paragraphs, whilst remembering that the final version may differ slightly from this.

Paragraph 1 (account details) – You should certainly mention the account number and branch (though obviously you should be writing to the branch where your account is held). Mention which period the statement is for.
Paragraph 2 (the possible error) – Indicate which item on the statement you are referring to. Give details such as a name or number for the item. Make it clear that it is a *possible* error.
Paragraph 3 (how the error might have occurred) – Possible ways include clerical error, computer error, typing error, human error. You don't need to be very detailed here, mainly because you can't know how the error might have occurred.
Paragraph 4 (what you want done) – If the error is in your favour, you might not want the bank to do anything! Assuming the error is in the bank's favour (or someone else's) you will want the error corrected. Use a phrase like "please credit my account".
Signing off - 'Yours faithfully' is most appropriate here. The situation is quite formal and you have probably never/rarely met the person you are writing to.

Model Answer 范文

Dear Sir or Madam,

This morning, I received my bank statement for the month of December and I believe that it may contain an error. For your reference, my account number 123 456 789 and is held at your branch.

I believe that the error is with regard to the thirteenth item on the statement, listed as a cheque payment for £49:95 to Black's Ltd. I am afraid I do not remember making any such payment. You will also notice that the cheque number (34-67-58-49-39) is unlike any of the other cheque numbers on the statement. Given that cheque numbers are in sequential order in cheque books, it would seem that there has been a mistake somewhere, and that this cheque has been added to my statement in error.

I would be grateful if you could check this for me and either inform me in writing or by telephone of the outcome. My mobile telephone number is 0909 326 753. Obviously, I would like my account to be credited with the sum of £49:95 should it be found that a mistake has been made.

Thank you in advance for dealing with this.

Yours faithfully,

Andrew Scott

(196 words)

4.4 Further Sample Questions with Model Answers 其他样题及范文

Here are a few more sample questions with model answers for you to look at and learn from.

Question and model Answer - Accommodation 样题及范文—住宿

You have been offered a place at a university and wish to find suitable accommodation. Write a letter to the accommodation officer including the following information:

- **the type of accommodation you wish to find**
- **some details about yourself**
- **any special requirements you may have**

and any other relevant information.

You should write at least 150 words.
You do not need to write your address.
Begin your letter as follows:
Dear Sir or Madam,

Dear Sir or Madam,

I recently received confirmation that I have gained a place on the M.Sc. Microbiology course at your university, starting this September, and am writing to you with regard to arranging for accommodation. My student registration number is 123456.

I understand that you offer accommodation both on and off campus, the latter costing between £15 and £30 per week. I would prefer to live off campus in a house with two or three other students, each student having his/her own room, ideally within a 30-minute walk of the university. I have budgeted for rent of £20 per week. If possible, I would like to remain in the same accommodation for the entire duration of my course, i.e. two academic years.

I do not have any special requirements, but would prefer to share the accommodation with students my age (I am 25) who are actively interested in sport. I myself am a keen rugby player. I do not mind whether the other students are on a similar course to me or not.

I would be grateful if you could send me details of two or three choices at your earliest convenience.

Yours faithfully,

Andrew Scott

(197 words)

Question and Model Amswer - Lost Property 样题及范文—财物丢失

You recently travelled by train and think that you left some of your possessions on the train. Write a letter to the lost property office of the main station and include the following information:

- **the details of your journey**
- **a description of the lost items**
- **what you would like the office to do**

and any other relevant information.

You should write at least 150 words.
You do not need to write your address.
Begin your letter as follows:
Dear Sir or Madam,

Dear Sir or Madam,

On Friday, 13th June of this year, I travelled on the overnight train (No. 275) from Glasgow to London, departing from Glasgow at 23:45. When I got off the train in London, I think I may have left my briefcase on the train. I am writing to you to see whether my briefcase happens to have been found and handed in to your office.
The briefcase itself is not particularly distinctive. It is black, made of leather, and scuffed from years of use. It has a small combination lock under the handle.
There is nothing of particular value in the suitcase apart from my passport. The passport number is W192837 and was issued in Glasgow in September 1998. Aside from the passport, there are only some papers related to my university studies, some items of stationary, and two letters.

I will not be returning to London in the foreseeable future. However, one of my housemates lives in London and would be happy to pick the briefcase up for me, assuming that it is at your office.

Would be so kind as to check if my briefcase has been handed in. Please let me know whether it has or has not by calling me on (0237) 657483.

Yours faithfully,

Andrew Scott

(214 words)

4.5 Types of Letters 信件类型

Complaints (e.g. about faulty products or poor service) 投诉（如对产品或者服务进行投诉）
Requests for Information (e.g. about courses) 咨询信息（如咨询课程信息）
Job Applications (cover letter) 申请工作（如求职信）
Customer Service (complaint, problem, enquiry) 客户服务（投诉，问题，询问）
Problems (e.g. with accommodation) 问题（如出现住宿问题）
Thank you (e.g. for a gift or special service) 感谢信（如感谢别人送的礼物或者感谢别人提供的服务）
Mistakes (e.g. bank statement, delivered wrong product) 错误声明（如银行账单，产品投递错误）
Change Course (due to dissatisfaction, circumstances, or preferences) 课程调换（如因不满、客观条件、个人偏好等等）
Conferences or Meetings (enquiries, conditions, accommodation) 会议（问讯，条件，食宿）
Lost Items (at airport or railway station) 寻物启事（在机场或火车站）

4.6 Useful Words and Phrases 有用的词汇及短语

I am writing to (complain about / enquire about / express my dissatisfaction with / inform you / advise you / draw your attention to / ask if / request / ask your permission / seek your assistance / apologise for / express my regret / say sorry / propose / suggest)

I trust you will / appreciate / would be happy if / would like / would be grateful if

I look forward to your immediate response / your reply / hearing from you / receiving your reply

Please accept my apologies / thanks / gratitude / best wishes

I feel that
I would like to suggest that
It may be beneficial if
I would like to suggest that
You may consider …ing
I'm sure you will agree that

… what can be done about …
apply
enclose
I am willing to
Don't hesitate (to contact me)
Report (something – loss / problem)
Trouble – as a verb

Chapter 5

Academic and General Training Task 2

学术类及普通培训类写作 Task 2

5.1 Sample Question 1 样题 1

Present a written argument or case to an educated reader with no specialist knowledge of the following topic.

Traffic jams are now a major problem in most cities. However, it seems that people are not prepared to give up their cars and use other forms of transport.

Discuss the reasons for these two situations and suggest how the situation might be improved or resolved.

You should write at least 250 words.
You should use your own ideas, knowledge and experience and support your arguments with examples and relevant evidence.

5.1.1 Understanding the Question and the Topic 理解问题和主题

The question has three parts. This actually makes the task easier, because you don't need to write so much on each question to reach the required minimum of 250 words. You need to:
1. give reasons why traffic jams are a major problem in many cities.
2. say why people are not prepared to give up their cars.
3. suggest solutions.
问题包括3个部分。事实上任务变得相对简单，因为你没有必要每个问题都回答很多，就可以达到250字的最低字数要求。你需要做的是：
1. 说明许多城市交通阻塞成为一个主要问题的原因。
2. 说明人们为什么不愿意放弃他们的汽车的原因。
3. 提出解决方案。

The question does not ask you to:
1. discuss problems that cities have.
2. say how big the traffic problem is.
3. judge whether people are right or wrong to want to drive.
4. discuss other forms of transport at length.
问题没有要求你做这些：
1. 讨论城市中存在的问题。
2. 说明交通问题的严重程度。
3. 判断人们选择驾车的对错。
4. 长篇大论地讨论其他交通方式。

5.1.2 Brainstorming 构思

Why traffic jams are a major problem.

This part of the question can be interpreted in two ways. First, it could mean the problems that traffic jams cause (delay people, burn more fuel, cause pollution). Second, it could mean the causes of traffic jams (too many cars, inefficient public transport, narrow streets, other road users, accidents).

交通阻塞为什么会成为一个主要问题。

问题的这一部分可以有两种解释。第一种，交通阻塞引起的种种问题（耽误人们的时间，浪费燃料，造成污染）。第二种，引起交通阻塞的种种原因（汽车过多，公交系统效率低，街道狭窄，使用公路的其他人，交通事故）。

Why people are not prepared to give up their cars.

Status symbol, freedom, 'right to drive'.

人们为什么不愿意放弃自己的汽车。

地位的象征，自由，驾驶权利。

Possible solutions.

Ban car use, limit car use, better public transport, increase cost of driving, education.

潜在的解决方案。

禁止使用小汽车，限制小汽车的使用，改进公交系统，增加驾驶成本，教育。

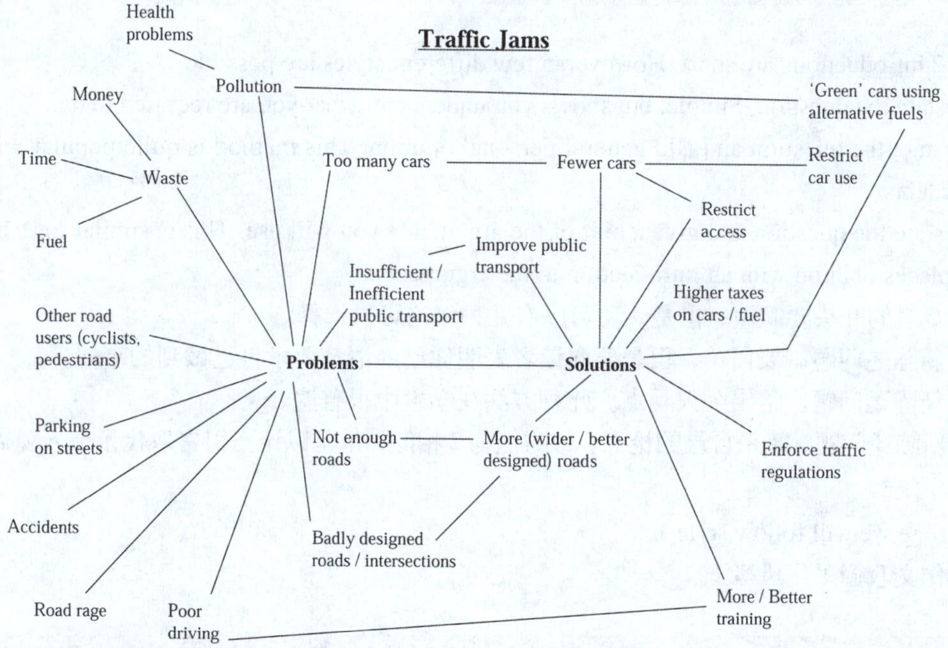

Vocabulary 词汇

more roads	fewer cars	higher taxes	waste fuel
waste time	'road rage'	police	parking on streets
other road users	restrictions	accidents	pollution
badly designed roads/junctions		enforce traffic regulations	

5.1.3 Organising the Essay 组织文章

The essay has really been organised for you by the way that the question is presented. Each part of the essay deals with a different aspect of the question. Of course, an introduction and conclusion are also required.

1. Introduction.
2. Why traffic jams are a major problem in many cities.
3. Why people are not prepared to give up their cars.
4. Solutions.
5. Conclusion.

文章是按照提出问题的先后来组织安排的。文章的每个部分涉及问题的一个不同侧面。当然，文章还需要开头和结论。

1. 开头。
2. 为什么交通阻塞成为许多城市的主要问题。
3. 为什么人们不愿意放弃自己的小汽车。
4. 解决方案。
5. 结论。

5.1.4 Writing the Introduction 开头写作

Task 2 introductions are short. However, a few different styles are possible.

1. Restate the question. Simple, but shows you understand what you are required to do.
2. Restate the question and add general personal opinion. This method is quite popular with students.
3. Restate the question and give a hint of the arguments you will use. This is similar to 2, but replaces opinion with an introduction to the arguments.

Task 2 里的开头要简短。但是，还可以有几种风格可供选择。

1. 重新陈述问题。要简单，但是要向读者表明你已经清楚要求自己做到的事情。
2. 重新陈述问题。给出个人观点。此种方法在学生中很普遍。
3. 重新陈述问题。暗示自己的论点。该方法与2相似，但是以论点引言取代了个人观点。

This time we will follow style 1.
这篇作文我们采用风格 1。

"Even people who live in the countryside know about the traffic jams that cause problems in cities around the world. In this essay, I would like to investigate why traffic jams have become such a problem and suggest how the problem could be resolved." (44 words)

5.1.5 Writing a Paragraph （主体）段落写作

Why traffic jams are a problem? 为什么交通是个问题？

You have probably already heard of the idea of a 'topic sentence' followed by 'supporting sentences'. This means that the first sentence for each paragraph introduces the subject of the paragraph and the sentences that follow it give support to the first sentence. This support is most often given through the use of arguments and examples.
你或许已经听说过"主题句"加"支持句"的提法：每一段的第一句话引入本段的主题，其他句子都给予第一句支持。这种支持通常是通过例证和例子的形式实现的。

First, let's deal with why traffic jams are a major problem. As was mentioned before, this part of the question can be interpreted in two ways. It could mean the problems that traffic jams cause or the causes of traffic jams. Therefore this part could be dealt with in two paragraphs. Which of these sentences do you think would be the best 'topic sentence' for the first paragraph?
首先，我们来处理交通阻塞成为主要问题的原因。如前所述，这一问题可以有两种解释：它既可以指交通阻塞引发的问题，也可以指引发交通阻塞的原因。因此，这部分可以分成两个段落。你认为下面的句子哪个最适合作为第一段的主题句。

1. "The three main problems with traffic jams are that they cause loss of time, extra expense, and damage the environment."
2. "Traffic jams cause many problems and are caused by several different factors."
3. "I think traffic jams cause pollution, which can be harmful to our bodies and the environment."

Sentence 3 gives the support in the topic sentence.
Sentence 2 is not specific enough and also introduces the first two paragraphs, not only the first one.
Sentence 1 is the most suitable because it clearly states the problems traffic jams cause and open the paragraph for an analysis of these points.
句子3给出了主题句需要的支持。
句子2不够具体，引入的是两个段落而不是一个段落。
句子1最为适合，该句明确地提出交通阻塞引发的问题，给分析这些问题的段落开了头。

Now, let's look at some possible supporting sentences.
现在我们来看一下一些可能的支持句。

Each individual who is stuck in a traffic jam may only waste 20 minutes and a few centilitres of fuel, but multiply those figures by the number of people in the jam, and then by the number of jams in the world, and you end up with a substantial waste of time, fuel, and money, every day. Think of what could be done with it all. Everyone is aware of the extra pollution caused, and it has been suggested by numerous medical experts that this pollution is linked to illnesses such as cancer and asthma. (95 words)

These sentences clearly cover the main thrust of the argument. Traffic jams cause problems because they waste substantial amounts of time, fuel, and money. That argument is undeniable, though the exact amount is hard to actually quantify. The fact that pollution is unhealthy is equally undeniable. If possible, always develop your arguments in this way – strong and simple! Try not to become 'emotional'. Don't use weak arguments where there is clearly a stronger one. Don't use long complex arguments, where there is a shorter, simpler one. When discussing pollution, in this essay for example, it is much better to focus on the effect on human health rather than the effect on wildlife, because there is not much wildlife in cities.

这些句子清楚地涵盖了论点的本质所在。交通阻塞会浪费大量的时间，燃料和金钱，所以会引发种种问题。虽然实际数量难以量化，这一论点还是无可否认的。污染有害健康也是毋庸置疑的。如果可能的话，这样展开你的论点——简单而有力！尽量不要情绪化。要尽量使你的论点强而有力，尽量让你的论述简短。在讨论污染问题的时候，如本文，最好聚焦于污染对人类健康的影响而不是其对野生动物的影响，因为城市中野生动物不多。

Why people are not prepared to give up cars 人们为什么不愿意放弃自己的小汽车

Someone once said that 'People are slaves to their cars'. I can understand why someone would say that. My sister uses her car even if she only has to drive 200 metres to the corner shop! The car is advertised as an expression of freedom. Look at the advertisements of cars on TV. Each car runs freely through the countryside, in stark contrast to the reality of driving in even a small city. To deny, or even restrict, the 'right to drive' could cause massive protests from drivers.

In addition, cars are very often status symbols. You don't buy a status symbol only to hide it away and never be used or shown. That contravenes the whole idea of a status symbol. Restricting car use would cause protests from those eager to show off their wealth. (136 words)

Suggested Solutions 提出解决方案

I think there are a few ways to try to deal with the problem. One that many people suggest is improved public transport. People use cars because they can use them to go where they want to go. If public transport served this purpose, people might protest less about giving up their cars. The problem is that public transport operates most efficiently on routes which people often use, not those less frequented. Therefore, people may keep cars for use when they travel on less-used routes or at times when they need to save time, such as in emergencies.

Another way is to introduce laws to restrict car use. This could be done by introducing time restrictions, i.e. not allowing cars in certain zones at given times, or by limiting the cars that can go into certain zones according to their licence plates.

A third way – one which I personally favour – is charging drivers to use their cars in designated areas at particular times. I am in favour of this solution as it uses the market mechanism of supply and demand. It also raises more money than it expends.

(186 words)

5.1.6 Complete Model Answer 完整的范文

Even people who live in the countryside know about the traffic jams that cause problems in cities around the world. In this essay, I would like to investigate why traffic jams have become such a problem and suggest how the problem could be resolved.

The three main problems with traffic jams are that they cause loss of time, extra expense, and damage the environment. Each individual who is stuck in a traffic jam may only waste 20 minutes and a few centilitres of fuel, but multiply those figures by the number of people in the jam, and then by the number of jams in the world, and you end up with a substantial waste of time, fuel, and money, every day. Think of what could be done with it all. Everyone is aware of the extra pollution caused, and it has been suggested by numerous medical experts that this pollution is linked to illnesses such as cancer and asthma.

Someone once said that 'People are slaves to their cars'. I can understand why someone would say that. My sister uses her car even if she only has to drive 200 metres to the corner shop! The car is advertised as an expression of freedom. Look at the advertisements of cars on TV. Each car runs freely through the countryside, in stark contrast to the reality of driving in even a small city. To deny, or even restrict, the 'right to drive' could cause massive protests from drivers.
In addition, cars are very often status symbols. You don't buy a status symbol only to hide it away and never be used or shown. That contravenes the whole idea of a status symbol. Restricting car use would cause protests from those eager to show off their wealth.

I think there are a few ways to try to deal with the problem. One that many people suggest is improved public transport. People use cars because they can use them to go where they want to go. If public transport served this purpose, people might protest less about giving up their cars. The problem is that public transport operates most efficiently on routes which people often use, not those less frequented. Therefore, people may keep cars for use when they travel on less-used routes or at times when they need to save time, such as in emergencies.

Another way is to introduce laws to restrict car use. This could be done by introducing time restrictions, i.e. not allowing cars in certain zones at given times, or by limiting the cars that can go into certain zones according to their licence plates.

A third way – one which I personally favour – is charging drivers to use their cars in designated areas at particular times. I am in favour of this solution as it uses the market mechanism of supply and demand. It also raises more money than it expends.

5.1.7 Sample Answer 1 学生答卷 1

With the development of economic, more and more people own a car themselves and drive to working, travelling and etc. It causes a majoy problem in most cities, that is traffic jams. But people don't plan to give up driving their cars instead of walking or other ways to working places.

Firstly, The cities are built to such a larger town that it is a long distance between the working place and home. and always the bus is so crowd that it is difficult for most of them to. catch it and arrive at the working place on time.

Secondly, The price of the car dramatic declined and after hard working, many people can afford a small car which is not so expensive. So more and more cars appear in the street. and more and more traffic jams happen on the road. Also, for these reasons, people don't prepared to change their ways to working. So that's a big problem.

However, anything can be improved and resolved if you make effort on it. For instance, take the following steps to have a try. first of all, make a humanity environment job for citizens, just like offering free buses, give the job near their house and anything else. for another, improving the traffic lines and developing new ways of travel. In other words, give more choice to people, so they can make a decision which is better for all of us.

(240 words)

Arguments, Ideas and Evidence: The student focuses a little too much on 'reasons' and not enough on 'solutions'. The result? The reasons are well explained, but the solutions are not. Notice that the essay is slightly underlength. Two of the solutions seem impractical. Free buses for employees sounds good, but employees don't usually live close to each other. For the same reason, moving companies near to where people live is also impractical.
论点、观点与论据：学生过多地注意了原因，没有对解决方案给予充分注意。结果如何呢？原因解释得很清楚，但是解决问题的办法却没有。值得注意的是文章的长度没有达到要求。有两个解决方案看上去不切实际。为员工提供免费的班车听上去很棒，但通常情况下员工们相互之间住得并不近。同样，将公司搬到员工居住的地方也不切实际。

Communicative Quality: The essay is easy to read and contains sufficient connectives.

论点、观点与论据：文章容易理解，连词使用比较充分。

Vocabulary and Sentence Structure: The student uses a good range of vocabulary, but often uses the wrong word (‘so crowd’, ‘dramatic declined’, ‘humanity job’). The grammar is limited in range and accuracy.

词汇与句子结构：学生的词汇量较大，但是经常出现用词错误（‘so crowd’, ‘dramatic declined’, ‘humanity job’）。语法从使用范围和精确度的角度都需提高。

5.1.8 Sample Answer 2 学生答卷 2

With the rapid development of people’s living standard, a dramatic increasing of cars which causes the daily traffic jams has become one of the biggest problem in social transportation. Everyday we trapped in a block of cars, even horribly. We have to endure the emmition of those ones which may do great harm to our health However. It seems that people who prefer their cars rather than other forms of transport. even in this crowded situation. In this essay, I’d like to talk about the reasons for this phenomenon and try to give some advise to resolve this problem.

There are numberous reasons for this and I’ll pick out three major ones of that. To begin with, Cars, which in the most times, are much more convenient than any other types of vehicles. They enable carry us to every places which are in the short distance, and also, we can bring or take many hugely heavy things along us without effort, moreover. Considered the extent of comfortable, most of us won’t wait a second to choose the car. Having soft sofa seat and cool air-conditioner, cars which have a dozen merits in driving circumstance have been attracting people all along. last but not least, Sometimes, as a result of the property and the prize of the cars, they have become a symbol of status, such as BMW, BENZ … etc lots of people just drive their cars around to show off.

In order to solve the heavy traffic situation currently, people think up varies solutions. As for me, the following are worth mentioning Firstly, more and wider roads should be laid down to relieve the traffic congestion Secondly, develop new types of pubic transportation, which are clean, huge capability, and energy saving.

To sum up, allthe above solutions are practical and reasonable. The only way to this end is that the civil citizens join hands with government together to make efforts for this situation. I wish that we can enjoy the fresh air and have free access to anywhere in sight.

(341 words)

Arguments, Ideas and Evidence: The student focuses on the use of cars and only gives two short and insufficient solutions. The argument is not very convincing. The essay, particularly the conclusion, contains several general meaningless statements. The introduction is far too long.

论点、观点与论据：学生将注意力集中在汽车的使用上，仅仅给出两个简短并且难以奏效的解决方案。论点说服力不强。文章，尤其是结论，包含着几个毫无意义的句子。导言过于冗长。

Communicative Quality: The essay flows reasonably well. The student uses several connectives and discourse markers well.

交流质量：文章行文比较流畅，较好地使用了几个连词和语篇标记。

Vocabulary and Sentence Structure: The vocabulary is sometimes inappropriate – "trapped in a block of cars", "give some advise", "the extent of comfortable". The grammar, however, is reasonably good.

词汇与句子结构：文章中有时出现用词不当的现象—trapped in a block of cars", give some advise", the extent of comfortable"。语法使用基本正确。

5.2 Sample Question 2 样题 2

Present a written argument or case to an educated reader with no specialist knowledge of the following topic.

Many people consider the death penalty to be an appropriate punishment in certain cases, whilst others think that there is never a reason for it to be used.

What is your opinion on the issue? Give reasons for your answer.

You should write at least 250 words.

You should use your own ideas, knowledge and experience and support your arguments with examples and relevant evidence.

Sample Answer 1 学生答卷 1

The death penalty is regarded as a controversial issue in many countries, and it sometimes will be assumed as a sensitive point which related to the human's right. Some people think it is a kind of efficient way to retain the decent law and social life order, while the others think it is a kind of attack to the human's right of living although he or she killed someone else.

Let's focus on the 1st point of view, which agrees with the death penalty. They believe that it will be helpful to keep social peace and reduce the violent crime. In fact, a large number of innocent people might feel safer with the protection of such strict law. They believe the death penalty must be a good threat method to those criminals, who will not be exist in the world as the punishment for rules breaking. I think it must be combined with the law education to gain the good results, otherwise, people will not be threatened for the unknown punishment of the death penalty. In China, there are some cases that illiterate people killed someone just for whom has stolen things. The thief was unfortunately killed together with the murder for the death penalty, which caused by the illiteracy not the death penalty.

On the other hand, some countries do not have death penalty at all, for example, The United States, which has accelerated the crime rate in the recent years, especially for the school violence or terror attack's hike. So we cannot simply disregard the effect of the strict law, such as the setting of the death penalty. However it doesn't mean death penalty is a kind of good solusions to our peaceful life and safe environments, and sometimes it may absorlutely not been corrected if the death penalty was wrong sentenced for any kind of reason. In that case, it was indeed a heavy attack to the human's life and the biggest tragedy to those relatives of the victim.

Conclusively, in order to maintain the fair of law and security of society, not only the government officers but also legislation designers should give a deep consideration for the death penalty issues. Otherwise, it will be difficult to gurantee the citizans normal life and basic human rights. In addition, the relative law administration procedures in the court should be published to the ordinary people.

(396 words)

Arguments, Ideas and Evidence: The candidate attempts to present both sides of the argument, but the ideas are confused and poorly developed. The candidate presents two examples. The Chinese one is confusing and the claim that the United States does not have the death penalty is simply untrue. The essay has no personal conclusion.

Communicative Quality: This is a mixed essay from this point of view. The introduction reads reasonably fluently, but the two main paragraphs are confusing.

Vocabulary and Sentence Structure: The sentence structures are sometimes confusing, e.g. "The United States, which has accelerated the crime rate in the recent years," and "I think it must be combined with the law education to gain the good results, otherwise, people will not be threatened for the unknown punishment of the death penalty." There are numerous cases of inappropriate use of vocabulary, e.g. "terror attack's hike", "wrong sentenced", "heavy attack", and "Conclusively". There are also several spelling mistakes, e.g. 'solusions', 'absorlutely', 'gurantee', and 'citizans'.

Sample Answer 2 学生答卷 2

Every community has its own rule. In our society, the rule is laid down in such a way that anyone who is not well-behaved should be punished. The death penalty, as a kind of punishment, deserves my total agreement.

Sentencing a criminal such as a murder to death could comfort victim's relative a lot. If a devil person killed or badly hurt another man, the latter's family or himself had good reason to demand the criminal to pay back his own life. This is natural for human beings When an old couple lost their dearest son, the death of the killer could make them fell the equality of the law.

On the contrary, if death penalty could be replaced by the endless imprisonment, criminal may not worry about losing their lives and do evil things as they wish. An imprisonment would cause many problems. Our country need to build a lot of prison to meet a great need. Too many prisoners are difficult to control, which would be a pressure for the society. So death penalty exists as a warning for those ill-behaved people, and it also do good to the society. It cannot be replaced by any other punishment.

The law guarantees the normal working of the society. A criminal who accused of great guilt should be punished by the death penalty. Not only can the penalty make the victim's family feel better, it also provide the society a rule of behavior. In a sentence, this kind of punishment is appropriate and cannot be replace by anything, today or future.

(261 words)

Arguments, Ideas and Evidence: The student clearly examines a few of the central arguments surrounding the death penalty. Paragraph 2 deserves special mention. Here the student takes the opposing argument and turns it to his/her advantage. Unfortunately, the student then ruins the argument by being too dogmatic – "It cannot be replaced by any other punishments", "cannot be replace by anything, today or future." As the student has not clearly defined when the death penalty should be used, the implication is that it could be used for every crime. Also, the death penalty has been replaced with other punishments, so what does 'cannot be replaced' mean?

Communicative Quality: The essay is very easy to read and understand. The student doesn't use too many connectives, but the sentences flow on nicely from one another.

Vocabulary and Sentence Structure: With regard to vocabulary, notice how the student often uses fairly basic words and phrases well. Sometimes the words are somewhat inappropriate ('dearest son', 'ill-behaved people'). The grammar is quite good, with only unintrusive mistakes. I think that it is well worth pointing out that dogmatism in an IELTS Task 2 essay can make the writer look foolish (or at least careless). Just put together the student's argument. "... anyone who is not well-behaved should be punished." (introduction) "It [The death penalty] cannot be replaced by any other punishments." (paragraph 2) Question: Would you like to live in such a society? If you agree with the death penalty, you need to define when it may be used.

Sample Answer 3 学生答卷 3

No matter what religion you believe in, the life of human being should not be deprive of by anybody. On the basis of this point, I completely disagree with the idea of death penalty. I'll list my reasons as follows.

On the one hand, death penalty is inhumane. The biggest difference between man and animal is that man is intelligent. If wee could kill each other, how can we differ from animals? And as we often say, there are not the two same leaves in the world. Everyone is special. It must own to some reason that he came to this world. Anyone could not deprive the right of living of him.

On the other hand, death penalty doesn't give people the Chance to do the Confession and begin a new life. The fact shows that many criminals in prison regret for their past life and they are determined to be a good citizen. But they just don't have time, like Jack in "21 gram". If we give them a second chance, it will benefit them as well as our society. And prisoners also work for the society, which is good for the economy.

In conclusion, being a human, we cannot kill our own people. And try to give the guilty people another chance, the life will get better. All this can be true if the death penalty disappears in this world. That's it.

(234 words)

Arguments, Ideas and Evidence: The student has a few good ideas, but they are not clearly explained or developed. Notice that the essay is underlength. The arguments are not well supported. Using an example from a film (fiction) that isn't even about the death penalty (21 Grams) is not a good idea. The student makes two references to religion, which is also probably not the best way to support her argument. What about the millions of people who are not religious? Besides, religious organisations do not legally invoke the death penalty – countries do. The student offers no evidence for the conclusion that "life will get better … if the death penalty disappears".

Communicative Quality: The essay is quite easy to read, but not so easy to understand. The student doesn't use too many connectives, but the sentences do flow on from one another.

Vocabulary and Sentence Structure: With regard to vocabulary, notice how the student often uses fairly basic words and phrases well. Sometimes the words are inappropriate ('the right of living', 'regret for their past'). The grammar is quite good, with only unintrusive mistakes.

This essay is ruined by a lack of appropriate support for the argument.

Sample answer 4 学生答卷 4

From the ancient times to the modern times, the death penalty is a proper punishment in particular cases, In the Middle Ages, Proper punishment had the function of defending the ruler's power, And now, It has the binding force to the people's ethics.

Nowadys, not only the despotic countries have the death penalty, but also the democratic ones use it. It illustrate that punish severely can submit the criminal, and can make them hardly to taking risks, Meanwhile, the death penalty restrain the people's evil nature. in other words, it will make people's behaviour conform the morality which already had been formed through thousands years.

On the contrary, the country which abolish this punishment undoubtedly decrease a significant weight what can stabilize the society. The binding force that people control themselves possibly cut down, and the fear to the societal security can be rised. After that, it will lead to societal upheaval and political chaos. The consequence is a extremely terrible thing.

For example, when the new china was set up, statesmen retained the death penalty, which submitted the criminals and reactionaries, and stabilize the new regime. Above all, the appropriate punishment protect the majority citizens right, and control the level of the offense.

In conclusion, the death penalty have advantage for the country, politics and citizen, It is the utter influential factor of the law, some countries conceivably abrogate the death penalty, in fact, they just used the long time imprisonment to supersede the name of death penalty. Hence the death penalty will always be retained from now to future.

(261 words)

Arguments, Ideas and Evidence: The main problem here is that the student's argument is so obviously wrong. The student's contention is that the death penalty creates social stability and countries that do not have the death penalty are doomed to chaos. Fact: countries that use the death penalty include Japan – very stable, Sudan – currently having a brutal civil war, Singapore – very stable, Zimbabwe – unstable. Fact: countries that do not use the death penalty include Britain – very stable, Nepal – unstable, Australia – very stable, Cambodia – not very stable.

Communicative Quality: The essay is clearly laid out and the student uses many connectives well. The problem is that the arguments in paragraphs 1 and 2 and the conclusion make little sense.

Vocabulary and Sentence Structure: The vocabulary is often inappropriate. "It [The death penalty] has the binding force to the people's ethics." "… punish severely can submit the criminal …" "… undoubtedly decrease a significant weight …" "The binding force that people control themselves possibly cut down." "… submitted the criminals …" Most of the conclusion is incomprehensible. Regarding grammar, the range is not bad, but there are many mistakes. In particular, the student fails to add an 's' to verbs when required – "It illustrate …", "The death penalty restrain …" The student has problems using commas, full stops, and capital letters.

Overall, this is a very interesting example to look at. Whilst Task 2 of the IELTS writing module is not a test of knowledge, it is expected that students will have a basic general knowledge and awareness. The student here clearly does not and it has an effect on the writing. Try to look at the situation like this. If you were at a university and presented this argument at a class, you would convince no-one to support your point of view. The aim of an IELTS Task 2 essay is to convince and persuade.

How to Answer Sample Question 2 怎样写好样题2

Understanding the Question

This question is quite simple. First, you need to decide which side you are on. Are you pro-death penalty or anti-death penalty? If you are pro-death penalty, you need to ask yourself another question – when should the death penalty be used? You may have noticed in the sample answers that students do not usually answer this question. This can create a problem, because it may lead the reader to assume that the writer believes the death penalty should be used for every single crime! Crimes that the death penalty is often used to punish include murder, spying, and terrorism.

Brainstorming and Vocabulary

See the brainstorming diagram for ideas on what to discuss, arguments, and useful vocabulary.

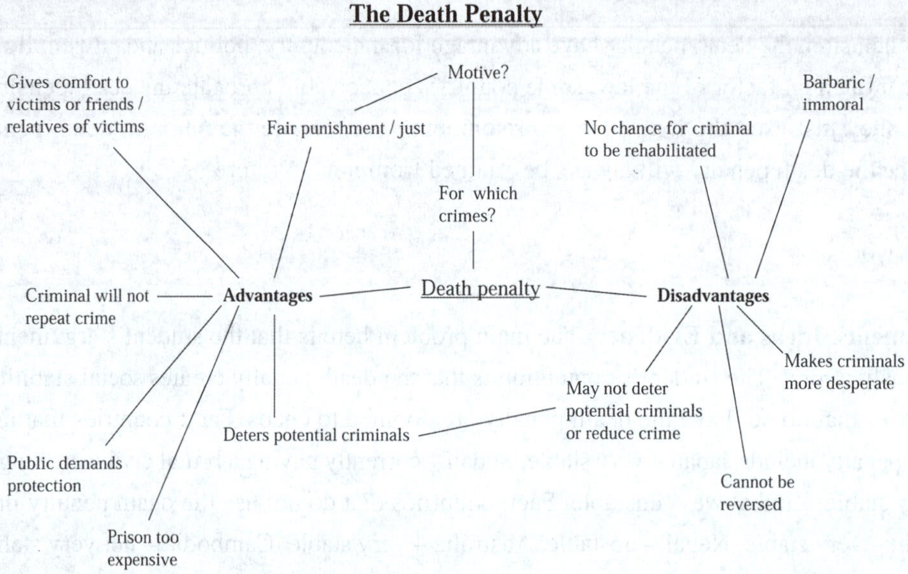

Organising the Essay

Introduction – The introduction should briefly restate the question, using the student's own words as far as possible. Many students like to place their opinion in the introduction, but this is not strictly necessary.

Body – It is best to use a separate paragraph for each argument. Several arguments are available to both supporters and opponents, so you can select the ones which you find it easiest to write about. Each paragraph needs a topic sentence and supporting sentences. Examples are desirable. These examples can be general (looking at countries which have or do not have the death penalty) or specific (looking at actual cases). You should point out opposition arguments and counter them where you can. This will prevent your essay from appearing too one-sided. Don't worry too much if you cannot counter a particular argument (see the third main paragraph of the model answer). If the issue was *totally* clear, there wouldn't be a debate about it!

Conclusion – In your conclusion you should clearly state your personal opinion on the issue. If you are pro-death penalty, you need to be very clear about when it should be used. In the conclusion should restate the main reasons for your standpoint. You shouldn't usually introduce new arguments at this point.

Model Answer 范文

The issue of the death penalty is an emotional one, with many people taking the attitude that it needs to be used both often and swiftly in order to deter crime and 'give criminals what they deserve'. Others believe that in a modern, so-called 'civilised' society, the death penalty is little more than barbarism.

The main reason usually given in support of the death penalty is that it deters crime. However, if we look at statistics from around the world the evidence is rather mixed. If we look at crime statistics from two of the countries which most frequently use the death penalty, China and the United States, we see that crime is more common per capita in the States than in Britain (which does not have the death penalty, except in times of war), but less common per person in China than in either Britain or the States. This is particularly true if we look at violent crime. Many Americans and non-Americans suggest that stricter gun control laws in the US would have a greater effect on reducing crime than the death penalty has.

A second argument used to justify capital punishment is that the criminal deserves such extreme punishment as a result of committing particular crimes. Whilst everyone would probably agree that the punishment should be proportionate to the crime, many argue that the death penalty is often a reaction to crimes that have caught the public attention. This, they say, contradicts the concept of equal justice for all.

Another argument used by advocates of capital punishment is that it prevents the criminal committing similar crimes in the future. This cannot be denied – it's pretty hard to commit a crime when you are dead. On the other hand, the criminal is not given the opportunity to make up for his/her crimes. Those who support capital punishment point out that the criminal has already used up his/her opportunities. Placing the criminal in prison is very costly. The time and money invested in rehabilitation may not have any effect. Why should we pay a fortune to keep a demonstrably dangerous person in prison for the rest of his/her life when our hospitals and schools are so short of cash?

Personally, I am an opponent of the death penalty. I believe that punishments should reflect the nature and effect of crimes, but that the ultimate penalty should not be used. Mistakes could be made which it is not possible to rectify. In addition, the death penalty is open to abuse by those who seek to use it for media or political reasons. Besides, there is no evidence that the death penalty has the effect of reducing crime, which is surely the aim of punishment.

(453 words)

5.3 Sample Question 3 样题 3

Present a written argument or case to an educated reader with no specialist knowledge of the following topic.

Some people say that it is not right for the government to spend so much money on artistic projects such as art galleries and sculptures.

What is your opinion on the issue? Give reasons for your answer.

You should write at least 250 words.

You should use your own ideas, knowledge and experience and support your arguments with examples and relevant evidence.

Sample Answer 1 学生答卷 1

For the purpose of beautification of cities, the government has offered lots of funds to the artistic project. The behaviour raises a sharp controversy as people stand on different positions. Some people inculding myself hold the opinion that the government ought to invest in the artistic project. Others, however, contradict it.

To begin with, construction of infrastructure should draw more attention from the government. As our country, which is a developing nation with limited funds, money collected from the taxpayers should be invested in the projects which are beneficial to majority of common people. The infrastructure such as transportation, communication and housing are the most essential framework of the development of our nation.

Further more, it is also important for the government to focus on education. According to the official statistics, there are nearly half of children in the rural regions are unable to finish their primary education, and some of them fail to go to school because of lack of money. Therefore, the authorities should provide a part of revenue to educational institutions, so that every children will have an opportunity of being educated.

Another point, it is necessary for the government to furnish the financial assistance to people who still live under the poverty line. Those people are suffered in which the food and cloth are still in short supply. So, the government should spend money and effort to set up a social pension system to meet the satisfaction of each person's essential demands for survival.

On the other hand, a sound conditioned environment will bring lots of enjoyments to people's daily life. But, due to the limitation of funds, it is more valuable to use those money on a position which is more needed.

In conclution, we hope that through effective and perfect operation of the government, the money of our nation will be used on those projects which will meet the demands of majority of our society.

(321 words)

Arguments, Ideas and Evidence: The candidate states at the beginning that (s)he agrees with the statement, then spends almost all of the essay agreeing with the opposing argument! The candidate's opinion is not clear to the reader.

Communicative Quality: The points made in the essay are quite clear, but the introduction, body, and conclusion simply do not match up.

Vocabulary and Sentence Structure: The sentence structures are reasonable, though there are mistakes, e.g. "As our country, which is a developing nation with limited funds, money collected from the taxpayers should be invested…" and "Those people are suffered in which the food and cloth are still in short supply." There are problems with inappropriate vocabulary, e.g. "sharp controversy", "limitation of funds", and also with spelling, e.g. 'inculding' and 'conclution'. There are also problems with plurals, e.g. "artistic project" and "children".

Sample Answer 2 学生答卷 2

In 2000, Guangzhou owned its first art gallery built by the government, before long, a new odeum was set up next to it, and nowadays, the National Opera, which is expected to cost the government a extremely expensive budget is under constructing in Beijing. Concerning such kind of phenomenon that reveals the government spends lots of money on artistic projects, I appreciate that whereas there are some opposed vioce.

For one thing, such behavior of the government attributes to satisfy public demand. Without worrying about shelter, food, clothes and other material things, people began to pursue a significant mental life. It showed that people in growthing number admit that listening concern, visiting painting exhibition and other activities relevant to art become one of the important parts of their life. According to this trend, more artistic places will gratify increasing requirement of people, as well as bring them convenient.

For another thing, art project seems like a symbol of a city or a country. Mentioned about the France, Palais du Louvre floats in one's mind; when someone saw the sculpture of mermaid, they may regard it as the mark of Denmark, also man always picture out Australia of the Sydney Opera. All these artistic projects combine mankind's wisdom and craft, reflect the culture and spirit of the nation, gaining its popularity around the world, and make its people proud of them.

All in all, in a long-term consideration, the government put a good deal of money on artistic projects is a wise decision, as time goes by, it will show more profound significant.

(262 words)

Arguments, Ideas and Evidence: The student presents a fairly clear argument with some very convincing examples. There are a few problems, e.g. it is not explained how artistic projects are "convenient".
Communicative Quality: The essay is easy to follow and well paragraphed. The student uses many connectives and discourse markers well.
Vocabulary and Sentence Structure: There are some vocabulary and grammar mistakes, but these do not prevent understanding. Vocabulary errors include – "extremely expensive budget", "under constructing", "opposed vioce [voice]", "attributes", "significant mental life", "growthing number", "profound significant". The range of grammatical structures is satisfactory, as is accuracy. An interesting problem is that the student uses too many commas, rather than dividing long sentences into short ones.

Sample Answer 3 学生答卷 3

Today, a picture in the newspaper attracted my attention, which showed a passerby stared at one strange painted sculpture with completely perplexity. He must have felt dizzy if he was told how much such "monster" costs.

It's true that human beings were born to eye for beauty. So art plays an indispensable role in our lifes. Espically while the living pace quickens. people ask more in the taste of life. Thus artistic projects are paid more and more attentions. But should the government spend so much money on them then? I think it needs to be considered carefully.

Though the economic is developing dramatically these years in our country, poverty is still a serious problem, in particular the gaps between the rich and the poor. The government should make sure the basic living standard first, then consider how to improve the life. Otherwise it is a waste of money, unless the government only works for the rich and regardless of the poor.

In my mind, spending too much money in the luxury artistic projects is unwise to a developing country with such a large population. According to President Mao's theory, we should judge everything by reality first. Everyone knows that what a hungry man need is food to meet his stomach but not art to satisfy his eyes.

However, I don't mean art is less important. On the contrary, art improves nature, as well as the quality of life. So certain amounts of artistic projects such as art galleries and sculptures are acceptable, and should be supported.

To sum up, as a creature in the world. It is wise to keep alive first, then try our best to improve the life and enjoy it.

(284 words)

Arguments, Ideas and Evidence: The essay presents a clear standpoint and reasonable arguments. The example of a hungry person is a little unlikely in modern China – people in China are often not rich, but hunger is not a problem now. The student could have noted that rich people can pay for art themselves, rather than relying on the government.

Communicative Quality: The essay is easy to understand and the student uses many connectives and discourse markers well.

Vocabulary and Sentence Structure: The student uses a lot of good vocabulary appropriately – 'attracted my attention', 'passer-by', 'perplexity', 'indispensable role', 'quickens', 'developing dramatically', 'regardless of the poor', 'quality of life'. There are many minor grammatical errors, which do not make the essay difficult to understand. The student uses a range of structures, including many complex sentences. The student uses modals, qualifiers, and connectives to express her exact meaning.

How to Answer Sample Question 3 怎样写好样题 3

Understanding the Question

This question is not quite as simple as the previous one on the death penalty. The death penalty is clearly 'yes' or 'no'. You cannot kill someone 'a little'! Here though, the question includes the words "so much money" (= as much money as now). The question does not ask you to decide whether the government should spend *all* its money on artistic projects, nor does it ask you to decide whether the government should spend *none* of its money on artistic projects. The question is asking 'how much'. It is asking you to decide whether to prioritise spending on artistic projects or not. The question also mentions "the government". This can be taken as a second part of the question. Should the *government* be responsible for spending money on artistic projects or should the costs be borne by individuals, private companies, or other organisations?

Brainstorming and Vocabulary

See the brainstorming diagram for ideas on what to discuss, arguments, and useful vocabulary.

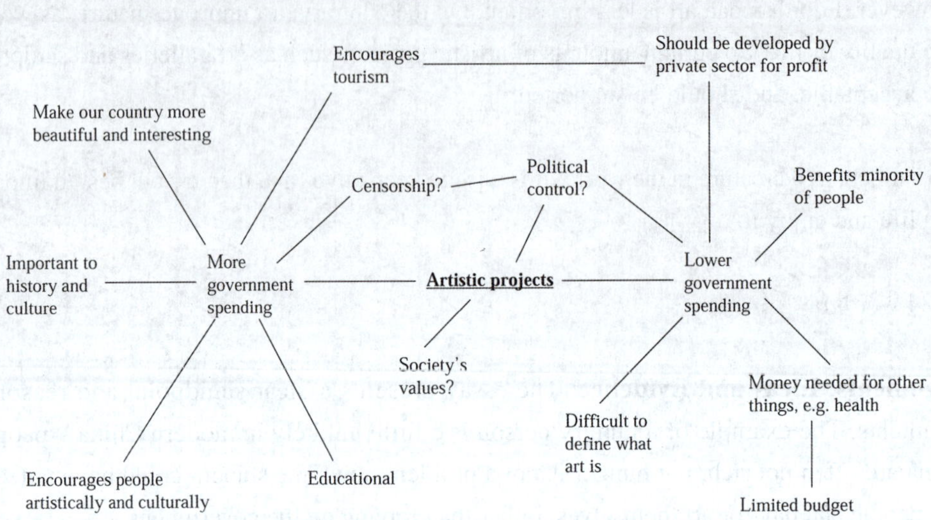

Organising the Essay

Introduction – The introduction should briefly restate the question, using the student's own words as far as possible. Many students like to place their opinion in the introduction, but this is not strictly necessary. You may like to point out the two different issues discussed in 'Understanding the Material' above.

Body – It is best to use a separate paragraph for each argument. Several arguments are available to both people who want the government to spend money on artistic projects and those who do not. Therefore, you can select the ones which you find it easiest to write about. Each paragraph needs a topic sentence and supporting sentences. Examples are desirable. These examples can be general (looking at your country or other countries you are familiar with) or specific (looking at specific artistic projects). You should point out opposition arguments and counter them where you can. This will prevent your essay from appearing too one-sided. Again, don't worry too much if you cannot counter a particular argument. If the issue was *totally* clear, there wouldn't be a debate about it!

Conclusion – In your conclusion you should clearly state your personal opinion on the issue. You will almost certainly need to express *to what extent* the government should fund artistic projects, since very few people will agree that the government should spend either all or none of its money on them.

Model Answer 范文

Governments do not have unlimited budgets. They need to prioritise spending and ensure that the money they spend is used wisely and efficiently. At a time when hospitals and schools seem to require more money than ever, many people question whether the government really needs to spend much money on the arts. Personally, I think that the government should concentrate on other issues.

People who support government funding of the arts claim that the arts are part of our culture. I am not entirely sure how much of the art that the government funds is part of our culture. Whilst some certainly is, much of the art on display in my country is not from Britain! Other items of art may be considered as such by experts and artists, but often ordinary people do not think they are artistic at all. Like the clothes we can see at top fashion shows, art is often all very nice, but not the kind of thing most people would have, even if they could afford it. If you asked ordinary British people to brainstorm about British culture, you would probably get responses like 'The Beatles', sarcastic comedies, football, and fish and chips. I doubt that many people would mention Damien Hirst or Benjamin Britten.

To claim that we should fund the arts because they are part of our heritage is a good argument. The government should certainly preserve some of our history for future generations. We need to ensure that a variety of art is preserved, not only traditional arts projects such as paintings in galleries. The government should not fund niche projects that very few people even regard as artistic, such as dead cows in formaldehyde, because the government needs to have the interests of the population at heart.

To reiterate, I believe that the government has higher priorities than art, though relatively small amounts of money should be spent on the arts in order to help preserve our cultural heritage. I believe that most funding for artistic projects should come from the people who go to see them and perhaps also from lottery money, as in done in Britain.

(358 words)

5.4 Sample Question 4 样题 4

Present a written argument or case to an educated reader with no specialist knowledge of the following topic.

Some people think that it is better for children to go to boarding school, whilst others think they should go to day schools.

What is your opinion on the issue? Give reasons for your answer.

You should write at least 250 words.

You should use your own ideas, knowledge and experience and support your arguments with examples and relevant evidence.

Sample Answer 学生答卷

Nowadays, as the competition in every field is much more intensive than ever before, parents pay more attention to their children's education for the purpose of a success life in future. Most parents believe that their children can receive great benefits in a boarding school, while others argue that a day school is more suitable for children.

The most important issue of attending boarding school is, that a boarding school is an ideal place for caltivating chilren's independence, which they seldom learn from their parents at home. Children who from a boarding school tend to come up with their own solutions to the problem they faced instead of turning to their parents for help. What is more, the experience of living with other children and taking care themselves will be a good lesson about how to behave properly. These children usually show a more cooperative attitude towards others than the childrens spoiled by their parents. Another point, they are more used to competing with others which will make it easier to adapt to modern society.

On the other hand, it can not be denied that going to a boarding school usually costs much higher than a ordinary day school. As a result, it tends to be that only children from rich families could afford to attend in a boarding shcool. and they may gradually develop a sense of superiority towards a ordingary day shcool children. Besides, chilren attending a boarding school seems to have less time to communicate with their parents, which may eventually creat a gap between them.

Weighing the two arguments, I am in support with the first one. For the point, it seems that a boarding school gives children not only the knowledges from teachers and books, but also the competitive ability which will help to creat a successful life in future.

(305 words)

Arguments, Ideas and Evidence: The candidate presents clear arguments, but these are occasionally dubious and require more support.

Communicative Quality: The points made in the essay are quite clear, making the essay reasonably easy to read.

Vocabulary and Sentence Structure: The sentence structures are reasonably good, though with minor (sometimes basic!) mistakes. There are very good examples of words and phrases used correctly, e.g. "tend to", "usually", "besides", "These children usually show a more cooperative attitude towards others than …", and "they may gradually develop a sense of superiority…"

Some complex sentences are almost grammatically perfect, e.g. "What is more, the experience of living with other children and taking care [of] themselves will be a good lesson about how to behave properly."

Unfortunately, there are numerous minor mistakes, e.g. "problem they faced", "the childrens spoiled", "costs much higher", and "knowledges". There are also several instances of poor spelling, e.g. 'caltivating', 'shcool', 'ordingary', 'chilren', and 'creat'.

How to Answer Sample Question 4 怎样写好样题 4

Understanding the Question

This question is not so easy, as few people will have direct experience of going to both types of school. Of course, only a small minority of children in any country go to a boarding school. As a result of these two factors, a lot of what you write will be based on what you have read, seen on TV, and heard from other people. Culturally, this question does have a slight Western bias. The idea of boarding schools is primarily a western concept. However, it is becoming more popular in China and Chinese people are very concerned with education, so it is a valid topic for IELTS.

Brainstorming and Vocabulary

See the brainstorming diagram for ideas on what to discuss, arguments, and useful vocabulary.

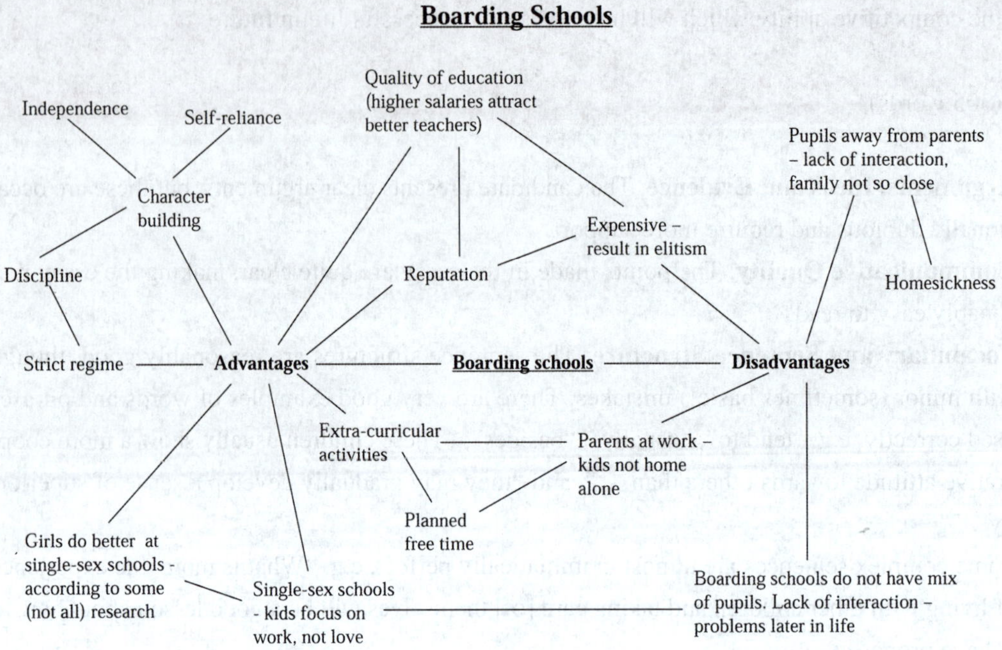

Organising the Essay

Introduction – The introduction should briefly restate the question, using the student's own words as far as possible. Many students like to place their opinion in the introduction, but this is not strictly necessary. If this topic is a little unfamiliar to you, I suggest that you could leave your opinion until the end of the essay. Many students have told me that they only form an opinion *while* they are writing an essay – there is nothing wrong with this approach!

Body – It is best to use a separate paragraph for each argument. Several arguments are available to both supporters and opponents, so you can select the ones which you find it easiest to write about. Each paragraph needs a topic sentence and supporting sentences. Examples are desirable. These examples can be general or specific, but be very careful about basing your entire argument on specific cases – someone will certainly be able to find specific cases which counter yours! It can be very misleading to claim 'I went to a boarding school and now I'm at Harvard. ' The two may be connected, but when someone points out another fact – 'Your father is a professor at Harvard' – your argument has been undermined. You should point out opposition arguments and counter them where you can. This will prevent your essay from appearing too one-sided. Don't worry too much if you cannot counter a particular argument (see the third main paragraph of the model answer). If the issue was *totally* clear, there wouldn't be a debate about it!

Conclusion – In your conclusion you should clearly state your personal opinion on the issue. If your answer is 'it depends', you should say what it depends on.

Model Answer 范文

Like most British children, I attended a day school. However, a minority of children do go to boarding schools, sometimes because parents believe the schools are better, sometimes because of their parents' occupations. Personally, I do not believe that either boarding schools or day schools offer a significant overall advantage to children. In this essay, I would like to look at the advantages that each system offers.

Boarding schools are ideal for parents whose work takes them abroad or who are otherwise unable to offer their children a 'normal' home life after school and at weekends. The children are looked after by professionals and the children learn to be independent of their parents from an early age. These same three reasons lead many parents to send their children to such schools even if they do not need to because of work.

Another reason that boarding schools are an attractive option is that they offer a more disciplined atmosphere, with children's time allotted to certain activities from the moment they rise in the morning until they rest at night. This is considered by the parents to be useful later in life.

Boarding schools are expensive, so demand for them is usually limited to high income families. As they have more money, they can provide better facilities and attract better teachers with higher salaries. This leads to greater opportunities for personal development for pupils.

However, this 'exclusivity' is often the basis of arguments against boarding schools. Some people feel that pupils from these schools will think themselves inherently superior to other pupils. This is one of the main benefits of going to a day school – the pupils are from various backgrounds. Day schools, unlike most boarding schools, are also mixed gender, giving boys and girls the chance to grow up together. Allowing children of different genders and backgrounds teaches them how to interact with various people, not just those similar to them. Obviously, this skill is useful later in life.

To conclude, I believe that both types of school have advantages in different areas. Families should decide for themselves which type they prefer to send their children to.

(356 words)

5.5 Sample Question 5 样题 5

Present a written argument or case to an educated reader with no specialist knowledge of the following topic.

People receive a lot of information from news reports presented by journalists. However, some people claim that we cannot believe the news that we are presented with.
What is your opinion on the issue?

In addition, what qualities do you think journalists should have?
Give reasons for your answer.

You should write at least 250 words.

You should use your own ideas, knowledge and experience and support your arguments with examples and relevant evidence.

Sample Answer 1 学生答卷 1

The responsibilites of the correspondences are to convey the objective and authentic informtation to the public. Stemming of the great impact to the audiences, media industry is regarded as the 4th power, the king without the crown. Shall we trust them or not is the question arrise among the people nowadays. There are several aspects should be considered to make a rational judgement:

Firstly and most importantly, to trust or to doubt the anthenticility is based on the reliabitily of the newspaper. If the newspaper constantly reports the facts of the events for a long period of time, then the newspaper is highly respected and trusted by the audiences. For instance, New York Times and Washington News are the most popular newspaper in US. On the contratry, some newspaper has little influence to the people because of the sustained fabricating news.

In the second place, on the other hand, some irresponsible news reporters have little pride of their social roles. Sometimes, they exaggerate things or make-up stories to draw public attentions. They are not the honored newspersons, they are the disgust rummor makers. They write stories based on hearsays, an example being the scandals of the celebrities private lives or the rummors of the government officials death. The truth is in the eyes of the beholders, people can make their own judgements. The upshot was that the ruined reputation of those journalists were inevitable.

Last but not least, some news stations excessively praise an enterprise or it's products to acquire their financial supports. The commercial motivation is apparent, their mutual benefits are prominent. As the result, people doubt their integrity, the good fame of one newspaper can be destroyed ever since then.

To conclude, we can not make our judgment by focusing on one judgement, that would lead us to an exem, public audiences should judge the different situations and to form or to adjust their own opinions from time to time.

(322 words)

Arguments, Ideas and Evidence: The arguments that the candidate presents are based on very dubious statements. The candidate writes, "The truth is in the eyes of the beholders, people can make their own judgements." The meaning of this statement is not at all clear. The idea is not developed. If different people hold different views, is there any way to know which is correct? Can people be relied upon to form correct judgements?

The candidate states that some journalists "write stories based on hearsays, an example being the scandals of the celebrities private lives or the rummors of the government officials death." However, those scandals and rumours may be true. The essay has no logical conclusion.

Communicative Quality: This essay is very difficult to follow. The meaning is usually not clear to the reader even after the reader has reread the passages carefully.

Vocabulary and Sentence Structure: The candidate has clearly memorized a string of words and phrases which (s)he cannot then use appropriately, e.g. "Stemming of the great impact to the audiences, media industry is regarded as the 4th power, the king without the crown.", "sustained fabricating news", "The truth is in the eyes of the beholders", "the upshot was that the ruined reputation of those journalists were inevitable."

The sentence structures are reasonable, but are ruined by poor spelling, e.g. "responsibilites", "infortmation", "arrise", "anthenticility", "reliabitily", "contratry", "rummor", "exem", and sometimes the inability of the candidate to distinguish between different forms of words, e.g. 'correspondences' rather than 'correspondents' and 'fabricating' rather than 'fabrication'.

Sample Answer 2 学生答卷 2

Nowadays, our lives are full of the massive news reports which are presented by journalists, and people aquire lots of information from them. However, some parts of people did not trust these news we received every day any more. As for me, I share their view, for the following reasons:

Firstly, some reporters make up news for attracting the people's eyes or just completing the work. Now the reporters are demanded to get the most explosive news in the highest speed, because of the drastic competition among different media and companies. However, at present, there're too many newspaper office, TV station, broadcasting station and cyber site to make exclusive news, so some of the journalists do some cheating things just like fabricating the news.

Secondly, some reporters make up news for lacking of responsibility. For instance, several media reported the same news at the same time, but the specific they said or wrote sometimes was quite different, especially numbers. These should be ascribed to some journalists who always made various mistakes in their reports. And then, how can we believe the news without the authenticity which considered as the most important characteristic in the news.

According to the reasons above, I am conviced that journalists should have qualities of honest and sense of responsibility. A person who have them could reports the news equitably and objectively, and recall the people's trust.

(230 words)

Arguments, Ideas and Evidence: The first paragraph nicely explains why some journalists might present news that is not entirely true. The second paragraph is a little more difficult to follow. If a journalist always makes mistakes, surely people will not trust him/her and cease reading his/her reports?

Communicative Quality: The introduction, the first boay paragraph and conclusion are clear and the student uses some connectives. The second paragraph is harder to understand, but still comprehensible.

Vocabulary and Sentence Structure: The vocabulary is reasonably good (acquire, fabricating, ascribed, authenticity, equitably, objectively), though there are some inappropriacies ("parts of people", "drastic competition", "recall the people's trust"). The grammar is quite poor. The student sometimes uses the past tense instead of the present tense ("did not trust these news we received", "reported the same news", "made various mistakes"). In the first paragraph, the student should have used the plural forms in his/her list.

How to Answer Sample Question 5 怎样写好样题5

Understanding the Question

This question clearly has two parts. First, whether we can we trust the news that we are presented with and, secondly, the qualities desirable in journalists. The first question is really a question of extent. It is impossible to believe all the news simply because some of it is contradictory. So, how much can we believe? Which news can we trust? The second question is a lot easier to answer. Think of some appropriate adjectives.

Brainstorming and Vocabulary

See the brainstorming diagram for ideas on what to discuss, arguments, and useful vocabulary.

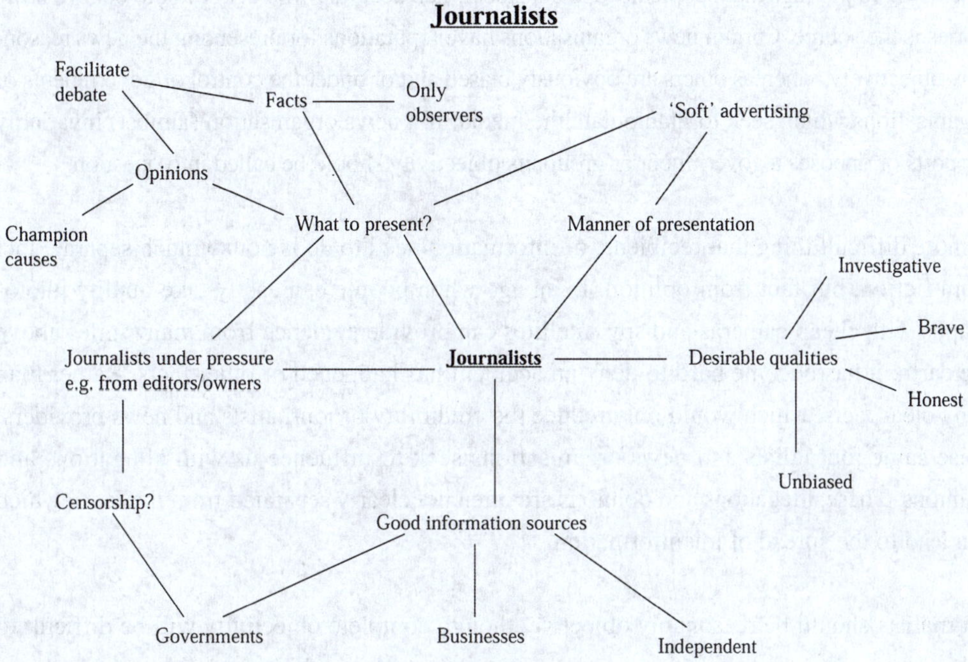

Organising the Essay

Introduction – The introduction should briefly restate the question, using the student's own words as far as possible. Many students like to place their opinion in the introduction, but this is not strictly necessary.

Body – It is best to use a separate paragraph for each argument. Several arguments are available to both people who think we can believe most of the news and those who think we cannot. Therefore, you can select the ones which you find it easiest to write about. Each paragraph needs a topic sentence and supporting sentences. Examples are desirable. These examples can be general (looking at media types) or specific (looking at specific examples and news reports). You should point out opposition arguments and counter them where you can. This will prevent your essay from appearing too one-sided. Again, don't worry too much if you cannot counter a particular argument. If the issue was *totally* clear, there wouldn't be a debate about it! One paragraph should be devoted to the qualities of journalists.

Conclusion – In your conclusion you should clearly state your personal opinion on the issue. You will almost certainly need to express *to what extent* you believe we can trust the news.

Model Answer 范文

It has often been said that we live in the information age. Most people in the world can receive information about events far from where they live, by radio, TV and the Internet. How much can we really trust this information and what qualities should the people who give us the information have?

One of the first things that people need to consider when deciding whether or not to believe news stories is the source. Certain news organisations have reputations for presenting the news reasonably objectively, whereas others are obviously biased and/or under the control of governments or organisations which seek to manipulate the media. If a news organisation (almost) invariably supports or opposes a government or group, its objectivity should be called into question.

A more difficult thing that recipients of information need to do is not so much separate fact from fiction, but fact from opinion. In an age when people can easily take quality photographs with cheap cameras and spy satellites can provide evidence from many miles above the earth, it has become hard to deny an accident has happened or other facts. Rather than deny clear facts, which would only reduce the credibility of journalists and news providers, these same journalists and news organisations seek to influence us with allegations and opinions. These allegations and opinions are often not clearly separated from the facts, which can lead to the spread of misinformation.

Journalists should be reasonably objective, though complete objectivity will be difficult to achieve, as everyone has their own opinions and standpoints. If a journalist clearly takes a side on an issue, but states this openly, people can decide whether to accept the ideas or not, knowing that the opinion is slanted. Journalists need to be investigative, seeking out information and opinions to present to readers, listeners, and viewers. They also need to be very good with words, expressing their exact meaning, often succinctly.

Generally, I think that we can believe the facts we are presented with, but the problem is when these facts become mixed with allegations and opinions, particularly when those allegations and opinions are not clearly identified as such but are presented as facts in themselves.

(364 words)

5.6 Sample Question 6 样题 6

Present a written argument or case to an educated reader with no specialist knowledge of the following topic.

It is often said that we are living in a world full of plastic bags and rubbish.

Discuss the reasons for this and suggest how the situation might be improved or resolved.

You should write at least 250 words.

You should use your own ideas, knowledge and experience and support your arguments with examples and relevant evidence.

Sample Answer 1 学生答卷 1

The main purpose to invend the throw-away products is to ensure the standard of hygiene. Insofaras, it is a breakthrough development, however, it has it's drawbacks. To some extent, it is the one of the resources of the pollution, the so-called while pollution. Furthermore, the waste of the materials and energy are enomours. The improvements of this situation is required, here are some possible solutions can be considered.

To begin with, to control the amount of the throw-away products. For instance, In US, some hotel room attendants would ask permissions of the guests to change their daily cleanning facilities. By this mean, the life of the throw-away products is extended, in other word, the amount of the throw-aways are deducted. The advantage is obvious, to cut the waste, meanwhile, to control the resource of the pollution.

Second, to avoid using the throw-away products. In Korea, people never use the throw-away chopsticks, instead, they use the steel made solid ones which is endured for the entire lifetime. The disavantage of it is that the standard of hygiene is not good enough compare to the throw-away products, but this can be improved by enhancing the sterilization technology.

Finally, to replace the polluted materials by the recycling ones, i.e. paper replace plastic, natrual gas replace petroleum to generate the vehicles, etc.

To sum up, it is not feasible to eliminate the white pollution, yet, we can always improve the situations on the regular basis by means of controlling, avoiding and replacing as we introduced above.

(252 words)

Arguments, Ideas and Evidence: The arguments that the candidate presents are based on very dubious statements and are not fully explained (notice the number of words). The candidate writes, "The main purpose to invend [invent] the throw-away products is to ensure the standard of hygiene." There is no evidence presented to support this statement. The candidate writes, "replace the polluted materials by the recycling [recycled] ones, i.e. paper replace plastic, natrual [natural] gas replace petroleum …". Plastic can be recycled. Natural gas cannot be recycled. Sterilised chopsticks are more hygienic than "throw away" ones kept in a dirty environment. The candidate does not present specific examples which clearly support his/her case. The essay has no logical conclusion, in that it does not relate to the body of the essay.

Communicative Quality: The essay is not entirely fluent in its communication, however the writing is not very difficult to understand.

Vocabulary and Sentence Structure: There is not a single correct sentence in the essay. Some sentences need to be divided for clarity. Words are often used inappropriately, e.g. "break-through development", "control the resource of the pollution", "which is endured", "generate the vehicles". There are several examples of poor spelling, e.g. "Insofaras", "enomours", "cleanning", "disavantage", and perhaps most significantly, "while pollution".

Sample Answer 2 学生答卷 2

There is much discussion nowadays as to why we are living in a world full of plastic bags and rubbish. Diverse contributing factors can be identified. In the following, I would like to present my point of view.

In modern society, especially in big cities, people have more and more consumption in different areas such as shopping, entertainment and tour, for which more and more plastic bags and rubbish are produced.

We can see that in some of the developing areas where environmental protection is not realized broadly by the public, plastic bags are used frequently in shops. Most of them will seldom be used more than twice, and will be thrown away after use. Made by a kind of light and un-dissolvable material, plastic bags therefore remain in rubbish, float in water or pile on the ground, they are so called "white pollution".

The modern society is not only producing "white pollution", but also more rubbish at the same time. For example, for some business purposes, more and more packages are used in production. Most of them are used for sale, transport or store. When the product are finally consumed or used, those packages mostly cannot be used again. New rubbishes are consequently produced for business activities.

One more reason is that, in some developing areas, rubbish-disposed systems are not as good as those in developed areas. Backward technique and disposed procedure cause the rubbish to become another kind of environment pollution. It was reported that in some countries, rubbish was simply covered up or burned away. As time went on, the soil situation near the rubbish-disposed places was getting worse, the relevant underground water and air quality were even affected seriously.

In view of these reasons, I suggest that urgent steps must be taken. First of all, more relevant environment protection ideas should be introduced to public by medias and educations, such as advertising propaganda about using less plastic bags and product packages. Second, more practical and effective laws and regulations should be set up to limit and punish illegal polluted activities. Finally, it's the best to pay more attention to develop and use advanced rubbish-disposed technique, so that our current living environment can be improved as early as possible.

(372 words)

Arguments, Ideas and Evidence: The candidate presents reasonably clear arguments with regard to reasons for the situation, but these require more support. The statements about solutions are not developed.

Communicative Quality: The points made in the essay are fairly clear and often expressed logically. The candidate makes use of connectives, usually correctly, making the essay easy to read. The essay is quite well laid out and sequenced, apart from the last paragraph.

Vocabulary and Sentence Structure: The sentence structures are reasonably good, though with many (sometimes basic!) mistakes. The candidate made many mistakes with plurals and uncountable nouns, such as 'rubbish', 'media' and 'education'.

Some complex sentences are used, which can usually be understood, even though they are not grammatically perfect. Some sentences are unclear, e.g. "New rubbishes are consequently produced for business activities."

There are some instances of incorrect vocabulary, e.g. 'propaganda', and also many cases where the candidate uses the wrong form of the word, e.g. "illegal polluted activities" ('illegal polluting activities') and "rubbish disposed technique" ('rubbish disposal techniques').

Sample Answer 3 学生答卷3

The earth is indeed faced with a serious problem which concern about litter and waste. Some pessimist even say that the world is now filled with rubbish while the technology and economics grow in such a high speed. In my opinion, the original reason for the problem should be discussed carefully and moreover, solutions are more important.

Everyone knows that all the litter and waste come from human beings. As the sharply increase of the population, more and more waste from everyday life are produced. For instance, in China, a country with a huge population of more than 1.3 billion, the rubbish come from everyday life is really countless, it is even hardly to be evaluate. This phenomena appears in many developing countries, not all over the world. However, the waste and litter which come from industry exist very widely on the earth, especially the smelting, paper-making and chemical industry. These industry provide a lot of profit and they are truly necessary to human beings' development, but the waste come from them is really a threat to our environment. Besides, the fellings of the forest and the abuse of chemical fertilizer make the fertile land into desert, so the self-recover ability of environment declines sharply so that the huge amount of rubbish cannot be assimilated by the surroundings.

Many scientist and countries has now realized the importance of solving this serious problem. Profitable city-program and build rational waste-processing system can reduce the everyday life rubbish's pollution. Recycling is also an effective method which is now in use all over the world. As for individual waste and pollution, the human has a long way to find the solution. Yet in many place in the world, some effective device such as recycling, deal with the waste concentrately, etc has work wonders.

We have only one earth, to prevent it from being filled with litter and waste and to keep the environment wonderful is the responsibilities of every person. I believe all the human beings should be alerted and adopt more and more effective solutions to this problem.

(345 words)

Arguments, Ideas and Evidence: The student focuses a lot on the causes and less on solutions (even though (s)he says in the introduction "solutions are more important"). The result is that the solutions are not developed.

Communicative Quality: The essay is quite easy to follow and the student uses connectives appropriately.

Vocabulary and Sentence Structure: The vocabulary is quite good and is usually used appropriately. There are some mistakes regarding using the correct form of words ("sharply increase", "hardly to be evaluate", "self-recover ability", "human beings should be alerted"). There is a fair range of grammar and most mistakes do not prevent understanding of the argument. However, there are many minor mistakes ("waste … are produced", "rubbish come from", "in many place").

Sample Answer 4 学生答卷 4

As we know, in present days people is living in Earth which is full of litter and waste. People pipe waste water to the sea, bury litter and trash under the land. As the population growing up the amount of the litter is increasing rapidly.

One of the reasons is the human activity. Tons of rabish ais produce by people's everyday life, such as waste paper, broken furniture, the goods we left. Another is the industrial production. The industrial waste is producted with the other productions at the same time. As a matter of fact, the industrial waste is different from the normal rabish. They are fatel sometime. The water which is polluted by the water waste come from factories could make people sick even kill people. The nuclear waste which comes from nuclear plants sent out radiation all the time. In one word, the litter and waste is threaten our world.

Although we can't get rid of all the waste, we can still try our best to improve the situation. first of all we should develop the new technology to reduce the production of the waste. second of all we should limimit the development of the industry, which could also make the amount of waste decline. The last but not the least, we should control the steady rising of our population, to control the waste we make.

It is reported now the people in the world are doing their best to fight against the litter and waste. Although It is not an easy task, people still need to make the waste promblem out.

(264 words)

Arguments, Ideas and Evidence: The student introduces solutions, but doesn't really develop them. Notice that the number of words is only a little over the minimum requirement. Two of the solutions do not appear realistic. One says we should limit the development of industry. It's not clear that any government would agree to do that. The student also suggests population control. Well, China already does that with the one child policy. Western industrial countries (the biggest polluters) already have the lowest birth rates in the world. It's hard to see what else could be done in that area. A 'no child' policy?

Communicative Quality: The essay is fairly easy to read and contains sufficient connectives.

Vocabulary and Sentence Structure: The student sometimes uses the wrong form of words and there are several spelling mistakes (rabish, ais, producted, fatel, limimit, promblem). The grammar is reasonable, though it is limited in range.

How to Answer Sample Question 6 怎样写好样题6

Understanding the Question

This question is clearly divided into two parts – reasons for the problem and solutions to the problem. The reasons should be fairly evident and factual. Any ideas about solutions need to be supported with evidence. Generalisations such as 'We should care for the environment' and 'The government needs to take some measures' are unacceptable. The essay requires specific solutions. These need to be practical (reasonably easy to introduce and broadly acceptable to the average citizen) and cost-effective (worth the money, or even money-making). The question does not specifically mention who should solve the problem, so bear in mind that there is plenty of scope for discussion there. In classes, I have often asked students how to solve environmental problems. They always say that the government should do something, but few realise that individual people can also do a lot!

Brainstorming and Vocabulary

See the brainstorming diagram for ideas on what to discuss, arguments, and useful vocabulary.

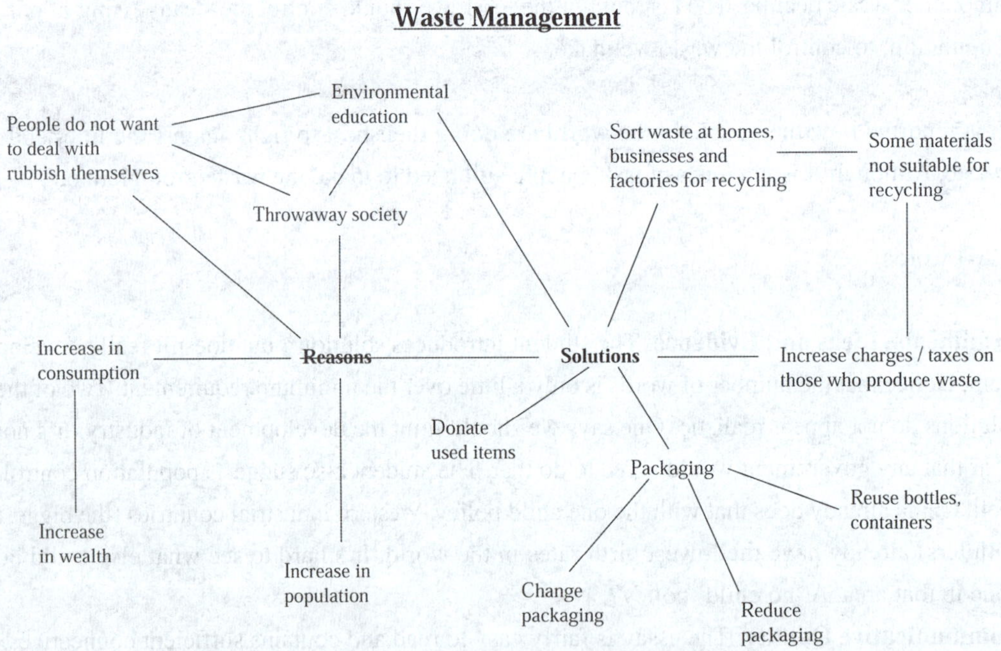

Organising the Essay

Introduction – The introduction should briefly restate the question, using the student's own words as far as possible. Many students like to place their opinion in the introduction, but this is not strictly necessary. Point out that there are two separate questions to be answered.

Body – It is best to use a separate paragraph for each point. There are two ways to write the essay. The 'classic' approach is to deal with the causes and then deal with the solutions. Another way (see the model answer) is to look at the causes and deal with the solutions in the same paragraph. Each paragraph needs a topic sentence and supporting sentences. Examples are desirable. These examples can be general (looking at your country or other countries you are familiar with) or specific (looking at specific cases of waste management). Remember that you are not dealing with *whether* we should deal with our waste better, but *how* to deal with it.

Conclusion – In your conclusion you should clearly state your personal opinion on the best way (s) to resolve this issue. Restate your opinion and make it clear why you believe this particular method to be the most effective.

Model Answer 范文

'Economic development' is nowadays clearly associated with consumerism. We consider Zaire to be less developed, not simply because of a lack of clean drinking water, but because the people there do not generally possess mobile phones. We consider the USA to be developed, not because of the relatively high number of people who die in violent crime, but because most Americans have cars. One of the negative aspects of consumerism is that it helps create a lot of waste material, which needs to be dealt with increasingly urgently.

As we buy more products, we inevitably throw out old ones, because we don't need them any more. The problem of what to do with old refrigerators (and the environmentally dangerous CFC's in them) became a big issue several years ago in Europe. Many old items can be recycled or refurbished and used again. A company in the USA, GreenDisk, recycles computer discs, whilst a British charity repairs and sends used bicycles to developing countries.

We also use substantial amounts of packaging. This can often be reduced or recycled materials can be used. Consumer pressure can have an effect. Years ago, McDonalds (in the UK) used plastic to package hamburgers. Now, as a result of consumer pressure and bad publicity, they use recycled paper.

Some countries, Germany in particular, have advanced recycling schemes. These help reduce the effects of waste, though they do not really affect the amount of waste produced. One aspect of this scheme is that people who separate materials for recycling are not charged for their removal. However, they are charged for waste that cannot be recycled or is not prepared for recycling.

I believe that this is the real key to waste reduction and better waste management. If people have to pay directly for the cost of waste materials, they will think more about the issue. If companies have to do the same, they will also think harder about waste management and the materials they use.

(328 words)

5.7 Sample Question 7 样题 7

Present a written argument or case to an educated reader with no specialist knowledge of the following topic.

Some people think that it is necessary to punish children in order to teach them the difference between right and wrong.

Do you agree or disagree? Give reasons for your answer.

If you agree, what kind of punishment do you think should be given to children by parents and teachers? Give reasons for your answer.

You should write at least 250 words.

You should use your own ideas, knowledge and experience and support your arguments with examples and relevant evidence.

Sample Answer 1 学生答卷 1

Nowadays more and more people notice the importance of the method of educating children, and argue that if the punishment is necessary when they do something wrong. The advantages and the disadvantages of punishment to children are analyzed as following.

It is easy to think out there are some advantages to do some punishment to children when they do wrong things. Firstly, it is helpful for children to distinguish and remember the right and the wrong while they may be confused if only be told something. Secondly, it can make children realize the responsibility in some degree for the wrong things have been done that also the adults who do anything wrong will be punished by the government or the society. However, it should be noticed that these benefits must be conditional on the right judge by their parents and teachers that if the children did do something wrong, or the results would be worse, and these advantages would turn to disadvantages.

On the other hand, the disadvantages should not be ignored if the children are punished because of having done wrong things. Firstly, punishment might damage the children's confidence or self-respection. Some parents or teachers disregard the occasion when they punish children. And the research shows that the self-respection of the children will be hurt when they are punished in the public. Therefore, they will have the antagonized moods. Secondly, some kinds of punishments may be harmful to the physical healthy of the children. For instance, make the children starve or kneel on the stone. So the ways of punishment should be pay more attention to.

To sum up the above, I claim that parents and teachers should punish children cautiously. When the children do something wrong, the initial proper step is that explain them the reason and what they should do. If they cannot remember that and do the same thing again or they will not listen to you, punishment is needed. Still the ways of punishments should be chosen carefully. Personally, I prefer to apart the children from their hobbies for a certain time. Anyway, we must help the children to learn to think.

(357 words)

Arguments, Ideas and Evidence: The candidate presents reasonably clear arguments, but these are occasionally dubious and require more support. There are no specific examples of the effects of punishment. The candidate misses the opportunity to distinguish between punishments delivered by parents and those given by teachers. The candidate also only provides one example of what (s)he considers to be appropriate punishment.
Communicative Quality: The points made in the essay are quite clear, making the essay reasonably easy to read.
Vocabulary and Sentence Structure: The sentence structures are reasonably good, though with minor (sometimes basic!) mistakes. Some complex sentences are almost grammatically perfect, e.g. "If they cannot remember that and do the same thing again or they will not listen to you, punishment is needed." Unfortunately, there are several instances of inappropriate vocabulary, e.g. 'judge', 'self-respection', 'antagonized', 'healthy', and 'starve'.

Sample Answer 2 学生答卷 2

When you have a child, and he/she do something you think it's not right, what do you do? Do you consider that it's necessary to punish them? The problem is always boring the parents and teachers. In fact, I think we shouldn't punish the children. My personal opinion disagree with it.

First of all, the children themselves are don't have mistakes. They could do it in a wrong way because they don't know. If you punish the immediately, they will be very worried about it. And they will be very depress or have a lot of stress. I suppose if you do it for a long time, it's not quite good for them.

In addition to the reason, I believe every children has the curiosity. And you will discover that sometimes they will always do something you tell them that is wrong after you punish them.

In other words, the children have the rebellious psychology. They may do the opposite and it's wrong.

None the less though, everything is not absolute. We don't punish the children but it's not mean that we don't preach them, or we spoil them. We should preach them to do the right way softly and tell the difference between right and wrong. At last, they will do it in the right way because they know why it is right. Conversely, if you punish them or treat them very rudely, I think the result isn't good.

In conclusion, in my opinion the patient preachment is better than the punishment. And in this way, it's good for children to grow up.

(264 words)

Arguments, Ideas and Evidence: The student presents a good basic argument, but doesn't provide enough support. Notice that the number of words only just exceeds the minimum requirement! The student often makes assumptions without providing evidence for them. "They [Children] do it in a wrong way because they don't know." "… the children have the rebellious psychology." Notice that these two sentences actually contradict each other!

Communicative Quality: The essay is sometimes hard to follow. "… sometimes they will always do something you tell them that is wrong after you punish them." The student's arguments do not quite follow in a logical pattern. See AIE. On the other hand, the student uses many connectives and discourse markers correctly.

Vocabulary and Sentence Structure: The vocabulary and sentence structures can be confusing. "The problem is always boring the parents and teachers." "… children themselves do not have mistakes." "… we don't preach them, or we spoil them." The student repeats unnecessarily – "I think we shouldn't punish the children. My personal opinion disagree with it." 'Preach' is an inappropriate word. 'Talk to' or perhaps 'persuade' could be used instead. Do not begin sentences with 'And' in formal essays.

How to Answer Sample Question 7 怎样写好样题7

Understanding the Question

This question is clearly divided in to two parts. The first question is whether or not to punish children (as opposed to talking with them, as suggested in Sample Answer 2). The second is how to punish children, if you believe they should be punished. There is also a possible third question about the difference between parents and teachers punishing children – should these situations be treated the same or differently?

Brainstorming and Vocabulary

See the brainstorming diagram for ideas on what to discuss, arguments, and useful vocabulary.

Punishment

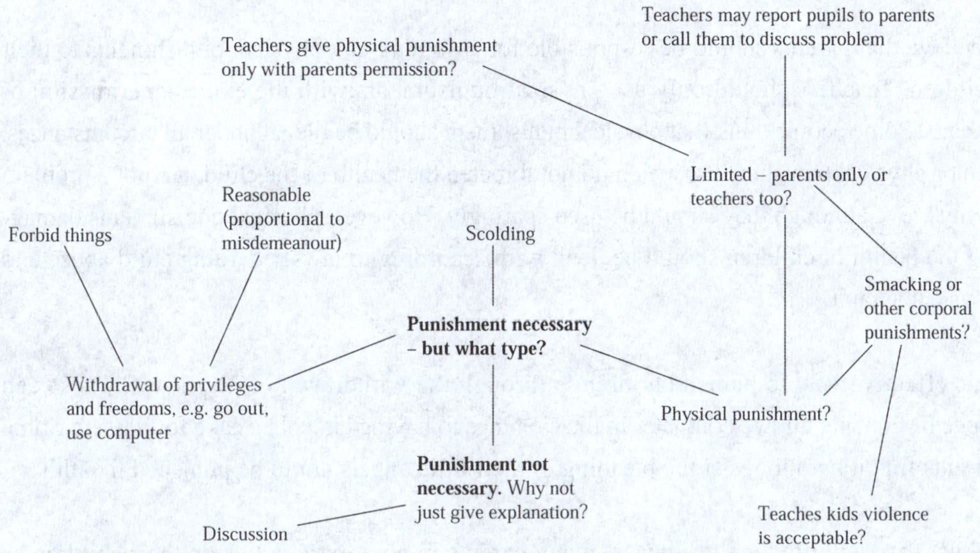

Organising the Essay

Introduction – The introduction should briefly restate the question, using the student's own words as far as possible. Many students like to place their opinion in the introduction, but this is not strictly necessary.

Body – It is best to use a separate paragraph for each point. Deal with whether to punish children and then deal with the situations if you agree (see model answer). The first paragraph should deal with whether to punish children because the remainder of the essay will follow from this point. However, if you are unsure, you can deal with examples as you go through the essay. Each paragraph needs a topic sentence and supporting sentences. Examples are desirable. These examples can be general (looking at how children are punished generally) or specific (looking at specific cases where children are punished).

Conclusion – In your conclusion you should clearly state your personal opinion on punishing children. Restate your key reason(s) and make it clear why you believe this to be the most effective.

Model Answer 范文

Personally, I think it is evident that children sometimes need to be punished when they do something wrong. I believe that this helps them grow up, not only learn the difference between right and wrong. However, I do not believe that punishment is always the only alternative.

Some people believe that punishment is not necessary. They hold the view that if situations are explained to children, they will comprehend and act accordingly. There are certainly times when this works, particularly when the child is mature enough to understand the mistake and not repeat the misdemeanour. However, if this condition is not met, punishment may prove necessary in order to reduce the chance of repetition.

I believe that parents should be responsible for assigning any physical punishments to their children. Teachers should only use physical punishments with the express permission of parents. Some people think that physical punishment should be illegal under all circumstances. Minor physical punishments, which do not threaten the health of the child, are not a problem in my view, although they should be used sparingly. However, physical punishments damaging the health of children should be dealt with according to laws regarding child abuse and physical assault.

One effective way to punish children is through the withdrawal of privileges. These can range from being allowed out later in the evenings to having chocolate cake for dessert. Some parents find it hard to resist the pleading of their little angels not to be punished like this!

Rather than withdrawing privileges, many parents impose extra duties on their children as punishments. These extra duties can range from washing the car to taking out the trash. Some parents don't like to do this, because it implies that household chores are a punishment, rather than things people need to do as part of everyday life.

As I mentioned before, I believe that teachers should only have the right to use physical punishments with the permission of parents, whereas parents should be permitted to use them within reason. I believe that non-physical punishments can be effective. They should be proportionate to the misdemeanour. Not punishing a child is always an option if it is clear that the child understands the error and can demonstrate that the incident is unlikely to reoccur.

(378 words)

5.8 Sample Question 8 样题 8

Present a written argument or case to an educated reader with no specialist knowledge of the following topic.

Some people argue that using animals in scientific experiments is cruel and unnecessary, whilst other insist that such experiments are necessary and have many advantages.

What is your opinion on the issue? Give reasons for your answer.

You should write at least 250 words.

You should use your own ideas, knowledge and experience and support your arguments with examples and relevant evidence.

Sample Answer 1 学生答卷 1

One is the most challenging problem of today's society question is of whether it is necessary that human beings need to use animals to make experimentations. Some people argue that the action is so cruel, oppositely, many insist on taking animal to evident science that have more advantages than harms.

First of all, people who disagree on making experimentations through using animals, believe that the experimentations such like this is so cruel, and extremely unfair, because of the equal of the life. What's more, animals can still help us to balance the nature, even though the breeds of them are reducing more and more. From the points, the fact, given the knowledge meaning through using animals, is terrible worry.

Is it really cruel? Supporters say "no". On the one hand, they think that it is required to use animals for vastly improving of sciences. For instance, in the area of medicine, if we do not use the animals, there is no way of knowing if the drugs are effective and fast, even if it has harmful to people. In addition, scientists also study some drugs, which can fight out the bacteria on the livestock. In the view of the fact, the people disagreed ought to look at the active impact. Whereas should not only consider animals experimentations as sacrifices.

On the anther, scientists who, engaging to study the reasons of the extinction of the rare animals, spend all their energy and time in this life, just for protection the rare animals, meanwhile they go on to point out and insist, the researches of science are on a marvelous terms with nature.

In short, the truth is, we really get a lot of benefits from the experimentations, using the animal to make, and more achievements then even the cost of the input of the animals, further more it is not any cruel at all.

(313 words)

Arguments, Ideas and Evidence: The arguments that the candidate presents are not entirely clear, though the candidate does give reasonable examples in support of them. The essay has no clear, personal conclusion.
Communicative Quality: The essay is not entirely fluent in its communication and much of the essay needs to be read very carefully in order to be understood.
Vocabulary and Sentence Structure: The only two correct sentences in the essay are both very short. Several long, complex sentences need to be divided for clarity. Some sentences make no sense, e.g. "From the points, the fact, given the knowledge meaning through using animals, is terrible worry." Words are often used inappropriately, e.g. "evident", "the equal of the life", "breeds", "the active impact" and "on a marvelous terms with nature". There are several examples of poor spelling, e.g. "oppositely", "anther".

Sample Answer 2 学生答卷 2

When we come to talk about scientific experiments, It is clear lots of experiments have chosen animals as models, such as monkeys, mice and so on, in order to make out whether there are somethings similar to human beings. Maybe some people take the side with this action. First of all, there is so large an amount of animals that they are not worthy. They think using a few of animals as model will not make any sense for the world. Secondly, the structures of some animals' body are similar to our human beings. To research and make experiments on animals can be benefit for our people. For example, some unknown or dangerous medicines can be taken by animals firstly. Just the only medicines being demonstrated to be safe can be used for people.

On the contrary, others claim that choosing animals in scientific experiments is useless and unecessary at all. They think that human beings are the most complex animal around the world, compared with others. The behaviors and structures indicated by animals can not reflect any significant evidence. What's more, we have lived with animals for when the history of human beings began. we lived correspondingly with each other, so we should take actions to protect them otherwise we will be punished in future.

In my mind, scientific experiments with animals can be seen as the method to protect animals as well as protect ourselves. The reason is that some diseases always break out in animals firstly, and that is followed by the man. For example, SARS was found at Guozili first and then transplanted to human beings. So if we do deeply research and experiments on animals, we can prevent some diseases from being swung away. Of course, when we do it, we should take it seriously and treat animals with love and care. We'd better build a system to protect animals who have been chosen in experiment.

In conclusion, as technology makes a rapid progress, it is inevitable to do lots of scientific experiments. When we benefit from it, we should also take responsibility for it. I think we can get along with animals.

(358 words)

Arguments, Ideas and Evidence: Most of the arguments are not expressed clearly. In the introductory paragraph, the student suggests that people who support animal experiments think it does "not make any sense", which doesn't make sense! The student does not support ideas with evidence, e.g. "We have lived with animals … so we should … protect them." The conclusion that we can get along with animals and do experiments on them seems quite strange.

Communicative Quality: The student uses plenty of appropriate connectives, but the sentences are not always sequenced logically. A few sentences should be taken out as they are meaningless and interrupt the flow of the essay, e.g. "The behaviors and structures indicated by animals can not reflect any significant evidence." The introductory paragraph should be a lot shorter, or written as the introduction and first paragraph.

Vocabulary and Sentence Structure: The grammar is quite good, though the range of structures is not very wide. The vocabulary is sometimes inappropriate, e.g. 'models', 'choosing', 'at all', 'transplanted', 'deeply'.

How to Answer Sample Question 8 怎样写好样题8

Understanding the Question

This question is fairly clear. If you agree with using animals in experiments, you may need to explain *to what extent* you think it's acceptable. Opinions need to be supported with appropriate evidence. People who are pro-vivisection need to make a case that it is (sometimes/often) necessary to use animals in experiments. They should be fairly specific. The argument that such experiments save human lives is the most common. Those people who are anti-vivisection need to demonstrate that alternative methods are available and practical. Recent advances in biotechnology have strengthened their side of the argument. Generalisations such as 'Animals are our friends' are insufficient. Humans have not been very friendly towards animals, certain animals will attack humans without provocation, and most animals are afraid of humans.

Brainstorming and Vocabulary

See the brainstorming diagram for ideas on what to discuss, arguments, and useful vocabulary.

Animal Experiments

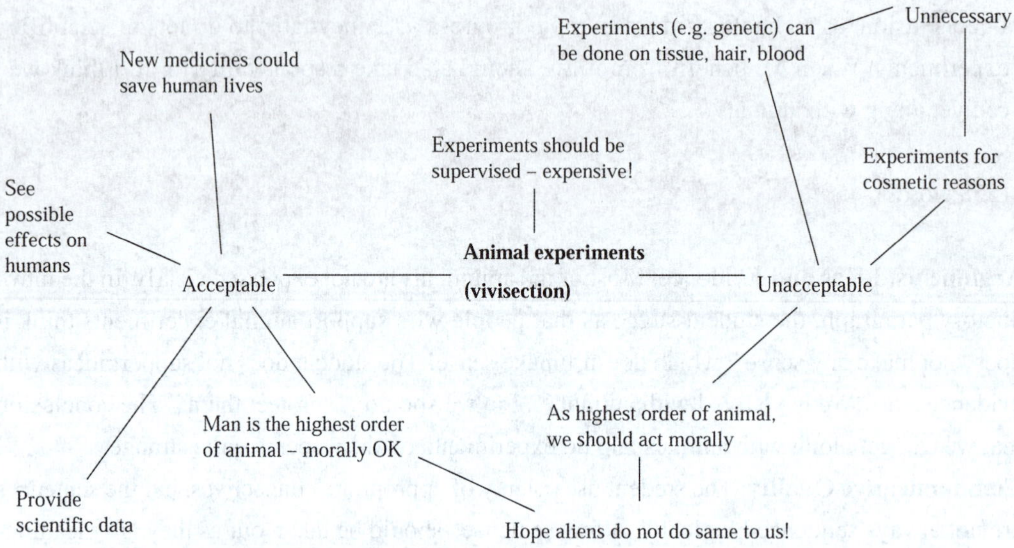

Organising the Essay

Introduction – The introduction should briefly restate the question, using the student's own words as far as possible. Many students like to place their opinion in the introduction, but this is not strictly necessary.

Body – It is best to use a separate paragraph for each argument. There are two ways to write the essay. The 'classic' approach is to have two or three arguments which illustrate your point of view. Afterwards, write one or two paragraphs dealing with the opposing point of view. Another way of approaching an essay of this type is to look at each of the arguments supporting your opinion in turn and, within the same paragraph, deal with the counter-arguments to this point. In other words, deal with the supporting and opposing arguments together. This is a little tricky, so practise it first and have your essays checked by a native speaker or a non-native speaker with a high level of English. Each paragraph needs a topic sentence and supporting sentences. Examples are desirable. These examples can be general or specific. Of course, few of us have had personal experience of experimenting on live animals, though you may have dissected dead animals at school.

Conclusion – In your conclusion you should clearly state your personal opinion on the issue. Summarise your main reason(s) for taking that viewpoint.

Model Answer 范文

Discussions about humans and their relationship with animals occur on several different levels. One debate concerns the use of animals in scientific experiments. The animals are sometimes used in order to assess the effect of medicines and cosmetics on humans, but to what extent are they necessary?

The most common argument against such experiments is that they are cruel. Cruelty suggests that the animals used in the experiments undergo some kind of pain, discomfort or deformity. This is understandably upsetting to many, who imagine the rabbit, mouse or frog that they had and cared for as a child having to endure such things. Most experiments that were carried out on animals do not now require a live animal for realistic results. Results and conclusions can be arrived at using tissue grown from cells or, in the case of genetic experiments, using hair or blood samples, which can be gained with little or no discomfort.

Another argument used by opponents of animal experiments relates to the type of experiment. I find myself in complete agreement with them with regard to experiments for cosmetic purposes. I cannot think of a single item of toiletry which would justify pain or death to an animal. However, there are some medical experiments which need to be done on animals prior to being introduced for humans. In such cases, I do believe that the life of the human is more valuable than the life of a lab rat.

Personally, I am for experiments on animals only for medical reasons where alternative sources of material for the experiments are inappropriate or useless. Scientists should take care to conduct experiments with due care and regard for the animals they are using. Ideally, there should be a body to monitor such experiments, paid for by the companies and organizations conducting them.

(302 words)

5.9 Sample Question 9 样题 9

Present a written argument or case to an educated reader with no specialist knowledge of the following topic.

Many people consider nuclear technology to be beneficial whilst others consider that its disadvantages far outweigh any of its advantages.

What is your opinion on the issue? Give reasons for your answer.

You should write at least 250 words.

You should use your own ideas, knowledge and experience and support your arguments with examples and relevant evidence.

Sample Answer 1 学生答卷 1

Nowadays nuclear technology has been more and more popular in some countries. However, as a coin has two sides, it has many advantages, and some disadvantages as well.

To begin with the advantages, there are two main aspects. Firstly, with the development of society, nuclear technology already applied to nuclear weapons. Undoubtedly, it is a huge progress of nuclear technology. It can defend the country as fairly strong equipment, especially an outbreak of war. Therefore in some extent it can be represented how strong a country is.

Secondly, there is a trend that nuclear energy is used to many kinds of sphere, even for space. It is no doubt that nuclear energy which produces less waste is cleaner and more efficient than most materials such as coal. According to the reports, nuclear energy has been utilized in more and more areas.

Although it has advantages mentioned above, there are some disadvantages opposite. First of all, it costs much for the nuclear technology, especially the first expenditure. Consequently, few countries can apply to nuclear technology. Undoubtedly, the more it is used to the research, the more benefits it can be made.

In addition, nuclear weapon is very dangerous. It can easily destroy the whole country and all of lives around, so how to use it in an appropriate way is really a serious problem.

In conclusion, in my opinion, I think it is good to develop nuclear technology in the world, in particular for those countries which are rich. It is probably a trend to use high technologies to replace the old ones. If people use nuclear technology by the appropriate way, meanwhile, make it safety enough to prevent it from exposing, it can bring us more benefits and push our society forward.

(292 words)

Arguments, Ideas and Evidence: The candidate presents reasonably clear arguments, but these require support. There are no specific examples of the use of nuclear technology or its effects. In other words, the candidate has arguments and ideas, but no evidence.

Communicative Quality: The points made in the essay are quite clear, although sometimes they are expressed in rather basic and dubious ways. The candidate makes wide use of connectives, usually correctly, making the essay reasonably easy to read. The essay is reasonably well laid out.

Vocabulary and Sentence Structure: The sentence structures are reasonably good, though with many (sometimes basic!) mistakes. The candidates attempts many complex sentences which can usually be understood, even though they are not grammatically perfect, e.g. "In conclusion, in my opinion, I think it is good to develop nuclear technology in the world, in particular for those countries which are rich." There are some instances of incorrect vocabulary, e.g. 'disadvantages opposite', 'first expenditure', 'apply', and 'exposing'.

Sample Answer 2 学生答卷 2

Nowadays, nuclear technology is used in many fields widely, such as the military affairs, scientific searching, industrial working and so on. When the nuclear technology has been used, it would release a large quantity energy. I am of the opinion that the nuclear technology has its own benefits. and its advantages far outweigh any of its disadvantages.

First of all, the nuclear technology will improve our life. The resources is limitary, not only we should protect it, but also we should exploit and use it in a good way I think the nuclear technology will give us more resources. It is usually used in the military affairs, making the military stronger, and keeping the nation's safty. When it has been used in industrial working, people will get more new things and make our life colourful and modern, like the nuclear television, nuclear wave machine and nuclear system to defend the stealing.

For instance, there is a hospital that use the nuclear technology to cure the patient some people think that the nuclear's wave is bad for human's body, and we called it the nuclear radiation. In fact, this radiation has a cutting across ability, the doctors use the machine to change the radiation's table or reduce the radiation, and use the nuclear ray in an operation. cutting somethings conveniently and saving the human's life.

In conclusion, the nuclear technology is widely used in different fields, and giving more improvement to our life. we should protect it and use it better. however, it is also necessary for keeping the radiation and avoiding the radiation that make people weakness and death.

(269 words)

Arguments, Ideas and Evidence: The essay has a few good ideas, but they are not developed. The student obviously supports the use of nuclear technology, yet does appreciate its drawbacks. A few examples are 'made up' – nuclear TV, nuclear rays cutting people – and therefore pointless.
Communicative Quality: The essay isn't laid out very well. The second paragraph begins "For instance", which is probably not a good idea. However, the meaning of most of the sentences is clear (despite errors) and several connectives are used well.
Vocabulary and Sentence Structure: The vocabulary is fairly simple, but effective. Some of the vocabulary is unsuitable, e.g. 'colorful'. There are many grammatical errors, but these do not usually prevent the reader from understanding the essay. A few sentences, particularly in the last paragraph and conclusion, are meaningless or very confusing.

Sample Answer 3 学生答卷 3

Considering the benefit of that modern technology has brought to us, nuclear technology can't be neglected. Although, like any kind of new things, it has disadvantages, I doubt that nobody could deny its enormous benefit.

Nuclear technology is certainly a breakthrough in the history of power using. Nuclear, as a new kind of power, proves its superior to others in many fields such as electricity supply. Moreover, it has advantages not only in the extraordinary large amount of power supply, but also in the environment-protecting strategy, which is said to be the most attracting character. For example, in some European countries, especially those close to Britain, the problem of acid rain is becoming worse as a result of the effect of British rich coal deposit. But France, on the other hand, derives three quarters of its electricity from nuclear power so that it can release such problem.

It is true that nuclear may cause eviable accidents. Some people always have such nightmare. Similarly, planes are said to be more dangerous than other ways of transportation such as bus, train or even bicycle. Actually, the percentage of air accident every year is obviously smaller than others. In other words, it happens only occasionally. Commonly, people are afraid of new things because they don't know it, have never heard or seen such things before. Nevertheless, modern technology like nuclear technology shouldn't be denied or refused because of its disadvantage.

To sum up, nuclear technology has revolutionized our life and will be in more widely use from my view. Occasion accidents indicate that there are still some problem in this new technology to be resolved, which is scientists' future mission.

(277 words)

Arguments, Ideas and Evidence: The student only mentions nuclear power, not the other uses of nuclear technology. However, this doesn't matter too much. Recent laws have reduced (though not eliminated) the problem of acid rain in Britain. Besides, coal deposits do not cause pollution at all. Coal causes pollution when it is burnt. The fact that France uses nuclear power for much of its energy needs does not make it immune to acid rain, as acid rain does not respect borders. Whilst the student does mention nuclear accidents, it is not clear whether (s)he understands how severe they can be. Overall, the argument is not entirely clear, often because the student uses weak example and very general statements.

Communicative Quality: The student uses many connectives correctly. The problem is that many sentences are not clear or are virtually meaningless.

Vocabulary and Sentence Structure: Several sentences do not make sense. "It has disadvantages, I doubt nobody could deny its enormous benefit." "Nuclear, as a new kind of power, proves its superior …" "… nuclear may cause e[n]viable accidents." "… nuclear technology shouldn't be denied or refused because of its disadvantage." This is mainly due to inappropriate vocabulary. On the other hand, the grammar is good and there are several good complex sentences.

How to Answer Sample Question 9 怎样写好样题9

Understanding the Question

At first glance, this question is fairly clear, but be careful about *how* you answer it. The question refers to nuclear *technology*, *not* nuclear power or nuclear weapons (although clearly these will figure prominently in your essay). Opinions need to be supported with appropriate evidence. You might agree with the use of nuclear technology in some areas but not in others. One thing to be careful of here is the use of 'will'. 'Will' implies that something is fairly certain. Phrases like "Nuclear technology will destroy the earth" and "Nuclear technology will solve all our energy problems" do not have concrete evidence to support them.

Brainstorming and Vocabulary

See the brainstorming diagram for ideas on what to discuss, arguments, and useful vocabulary.

Organising the Essay

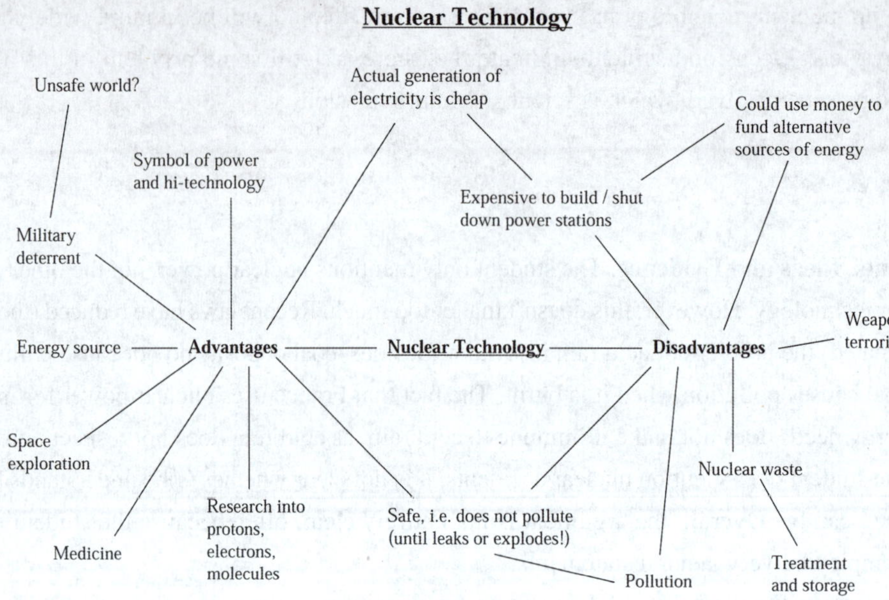

Introduction – The introduction should briefly restate the question, using the student's own words as far as possible. Many students like to place their opinion in the introduction, but this is not strictly necessary.

Body – There are three main ways of writing this essay. The first is the 'classic' approach, having arguments which illustrate your point of view (one paragraph for each) followed by counterarguments (one paragraph for each). The second way is to look at each individual use of nuclear technology (each use in a separate paragraph), putting the 'for' and 'against' arguments in the same paragraphs. A third method is to look at each of the arguments supporting your opinion in turn and, within the same paragraph, deal with the counter-arguments to this point. In other words, deal with the supporting and opposing arguments together. Each paragraph needs a topic sentence and supporting sentences. Examples are desirable. These examples can be general or specific. This is a good example of a 'general knowledge' topic – it is something which you can find out about very easily from newspapers or the Internet.

Conclusion – In your conclusion you should clearly state your personal opinion on the issue. Summarise your main reason(s) for taking that viewpoint.

Model Answer 范文

The advent of nuclear technology is one of the most important developments in modern history. It was originally conceived as a source of energy and military might. Since the end of World War II, there has been a debate as to whether the advantages of this technology outweigh its disadvantages.

Nuclear weapons formed the backbone of military power during the Cold War and helped prevent direct conflict between the two groups. Since the end of this ideological conflict, the numbers of such weapons has been greatly reduced. However, there is a fear of indiscriminate use of nuclear weapons by so-called 'rogue states' or terrorists. Most of the world's states have voluntarily agreed not to develop them or to help other countries to do so, through signing the Nuclear Non-Proliferation Treaty. Government agencies around the world monitor nuclear weapons and the special materials (e.g. uranium) needed to make them in order to prevent them being acquired.

The second area where nuclear technology has been used is in energy generation. It is cheap to generate and causes little damage to the environment. However, there are three main objections to this energy source. Firstly, though the cost of actual generation is lower, the cost grows enormously once you include the cost of constructing, safeguarding and decommissioning the power station. Secondly, if radioactive material leaks, it can cause irreparable damage. The accident at Chernobyl is the most obvious example. Thirdly, the waste radioactive material, including not only the uranium, but also water and even the clothes used by power station personnel, must be disposed of. Many people suggest that we should shift the money we spend on nuclear energy to other, cleaner and renewable energy sources, such as wave power and wind power.

The development of nuclear technology has led to related developments in other scientific areas, the most obvious example being medicine. For example, radiation treatments are used in the fight against cancer. In the future, we may need to rely on nuclear power for space exploration, as solar power may not be sufficient. Nuclear technology has also led to research into electrons, protons and molecules, which we are only just beginning to understand.

Personally, I am optimistic that the days of a global nuclear war have passed. The use of individual nuclear weapons by dictator or fanatics remains a threat and we must trust the major countries of the world to ensure that such incidents do not occur. This leaves the peaceful use of nuclear technology. I think that as an energy source it has proven too expensive, too risky, and indeed too controversial. Having said that, there may be situations where nuclear energy is the appropriate energy source, so a limited number of power stations may be necessary. We cannot guess at what applications nuclear technology may have in the future, so I do not believe we should stop its development.

(480 words)

5.10 Sample Question 10 样题 10

Present a written argument or case to an educated reader with no specialist knowledge of the following topic.

Modern educational institutions do not offer all the ingredients that are needed for success.

To what extent do you agree with the above statement?

Give reasons for your answer.

You should write at least 250 words.

You should use your own ideas, knowledge and experience and support your arguments with examples and relevant evidence.

Sample Answer 学生答卷

With the development of modern education, more and more people have chances to study in schools, even in universities. Can the educational institutions offer all the ingredients that needed for success? My answer is “no”.

In modern society, ingredients of success are including not only abundant knowledge, but also good creativeness, good psychology quality and communication capability, which are just lack of some educational institutions.

Firstly, modern educational institutions can’t develop creativeness obviously. In fact many institutions pay much attention to examinations. For example, while I was in university, my main task is to pass the continuous examinations. I often was praised for getting high scores, which meaned success as a students. Now I really feel it is an obstacle for my future development that refusing creativeness.

Secondly, psychology education should be an important part of college life. We often find some excellent persons failed for their weak psychology quality. They can’t face the pressure correctly while they can grasp knowledge well. So psychology quality is becoming more important factors for companies to choose employees.

Finally, communication capability of students in schools is still in the less important place.

This ability can be trained in society practices, such as lecture, sales, debate. However, more and more curriculums are shouldered by students, they communicate more with books than with persons.

As a result, a really talent is booming from a totally education, including wisdom and psychology. Most institutions have to improve their educational ideas to strengthen the ability for students to succeed in the future. Moreover, every persons should catch opportunities in your daily life to progress, studying is not completed in schools.

(272 words)

Arguments, Ideas and Evidence: The arguments that the candidate presents are reasonably clear, though some more evidence could have been presented to support them.

Communicative Quality: The essay is not very fluent in its communication, but the ideas are presented fairly clearly.

Vocabulary and Sentence Structure: The candidate clearly has many problems in this area. Words are often used inappropriately, e.g. "psychology quality", "communication quality", "refusing", "psychology quality", "society practices", "a really talent", and "communicate more with books". The past tense of 'mean' is 'meant'.

The candidate also has more basic problems, such as with plurals – "persons", "a students", and "psychology quality is becoming more important factors". There are numerous basic grammatical errors, e.g. "ingredients of success are including", and "while I was in university, my main task is". The second sentence of the introduction indicates that the candidate cannot even copy correctly!

How to Answer Sample Question 10 怎样写好样题 10

Understanding the Question

At first glance, this question is fairly clear. Do universities provide all the necessary ingredients for success or not? However, the unwritten question asks 'What are the ingredients for success?' You have to answer this before you can decide whether or not universities provide them. This question is more philosophical than other questions we have examined. If a person is kind, where does that kindness come from? Parents? School? Friends? Society? Genes? It seems almost impossible to reach a conclusion! Providing evidence for any opinion will be difficult.

Brainstorming and Vocabulary

See the brainstorming diagram for ideas on what to discuss, arguments, and useful vocabulary.

Universities and the Ingredients for Success

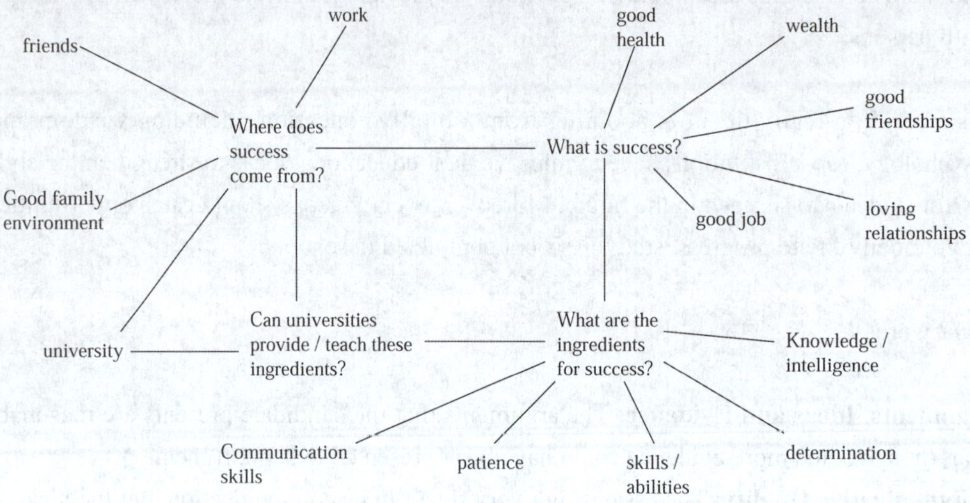

Organising the Essay

Introduction – The introduction should briefly restate the question, using the student's own words as far as possible. Many students like to place their opinion in the introduction, but this is not strictly necessary.

Body – It is best to use a separate paragraph for each argument. The first paragraph should at least provide a rough definition of what you think 'the ingredients of success' are. The following paragraph(s) should argue your point of view, according to what you have said in paragraph one. It should be possible to deal with opposing positions within these paragraphs rather than separately. Note that you may find it difficult to think of an opposing position. In that case, just continue with your own ideas. It is certainly worth considering whether success is actually inhibited by a university education, though it is doubtful that many people would reach this conclusion.

Conclusion – In your conclusion you should clearly state your personal opinion on the issue. Summarise your main reason(s) for taking that viewpoint.

Model Answer 范文

The question of what should be taught at educational institutions is as old as the institutions themselves. There are clearly certain things that are considered essential for success, but do they coincide with what is taught at schools and universities?

There is considerable disagreement on what the ingredients for success actually are, but most people would probably include such things as a good job, happy family life, good emotional state, healthy life, and good friendships. It is not *only* the responsibility of educational establishments to provide these ingredients. Families and society in general help provide the ingredients for success. Educational establishments do provide a basis for these things. The basis for good employment is provided directly through education on a variety of subjects. Most curricula provide health education. One of the most important things pupils 'learn' at school is how to get along with people.

Schools and universities are often criticised because they do not appear to provide much 'practical' education. The evidence is that this situation has improved considerably in recent years. Many courses now include practical elements designed to allow students to apply their knowledge in the 'real' world. The subjects that are taught have evolved to take into account new technologies, situations, and approaches. When I was at school, we didn't learn about computers. Now, even young children have computer classes. Latin was commonly taught at British schools. Now, Chinese teachers are going to Britain to teach. A sound knowledge of technology and foreign languages can certainly give people an edge in the modern world.

Those who suggest that schools and universities do not provide all the ingredients for success point to people like Bill Gates who quit university, but is undoubtedly successful. However, I would suggest that this demonstrates that a high standard of education is not *necessary* for success. It does *not* mean that attending schools and universities is detrimental to your chances of success. The ingredients of success can be found outside educational establishments, of course, but it seems to me that schools and universities can provide the ingredients, and often do.

(348 words)

5.11 Sample Question 11 样题 11

Present a written argument or case to an educated reader with no specialist knowledge of the following topic.

"Free health care is a basic right that should be provided by the state to all citizens."
"There is simply not enough money in the state budget to provide free health care."
Discuss these two points of view. What is your opinion on the provision of free health care by the state?

You should write at least 250 words.

You should use your own ideas, knowledge and experience and support your arguments with examples and relevant evidence.

Sample Answer 学生答卷

In today's world, the life steps are on edge every day and people usually work at high pressure. Free health care is very important for all citizens. In my view, their health should be ensured with physical checked-up by the state termly, for the following reasons.

The health of citizens indicates the strength of state. People in good conditions can work energetically. They can create much wealth and turn in more duties for nation. These duties can be used to re-construction and citizens' welfare. They benefied society and should be gainer. The good reputation would be formed here when they get free health care.

In addition, the health of citizens is related to the quality of unborn children. They are the future of Nation. Free health care will supply health guarantee for their parent, at the same time, serve them well-regulated checking up to ensure prepotency and high grade. The children can grow up soundly.

In sum, free health care as a basic right should be provided by the state to all citizens. But the money in the state budget to provide free health care is far from need.

It just can cover 30% town population. Some officeholder thought that it sinks money consumedly. They prefer to use the money to build new underground stations, new theatres or new cinemas, so much as hospitals. These behaviors were shortage foresight and go against benign development of our Nation. We should show them some scientific study reports to persuade them to change their old ideas.

Arguments, Ideas and Evidence: The student's argument is not entirely clear. The first paragraph is irrelevant, because the issue of whether good health is desirable is not the topic. The second paragraph contains sentences that are clearly untrue ("Free health care will supply health guarantee …") or outside current scientific possibilities ("… ensure prepotency and high grade"). The writer should say why the state should provide health care, not citizens themselves or their employers.

Communicative Quality: The student uses few connectives, but the sentences usually follow on from each other in a logical order.

Vocabulary and Sentence Structure: There are numerous minor grammatical mistakes, but only a few intrusive ones ("They benefied society and should be gainer" and "Some office holders thought that it sinks money consumedly."). However, use of inappropriate vocabulary is considerable, for example 'life steps', 'on edge', 'checked-up', 'termly', 'repetition', 'sinks', 'consumedly', 'behaviors', 'benign'.

How to Answer Sample Question 11 怎样写好样题 11

Understanding the Question

This issue is very topical and it is very easy to find information about it in newspapers and on the Internet. The situation varies considerably for each country, so my first suggestion is that you clearly state that you are writing about China (unless you are very familiar with the situation in another country). Most students will go for the 'auto-response' that "China has a large population, so …" You should realise that this is often a false argument. According to this argument, Britain (60 million people) has a *worse* health care system than Botswana (1.5 million people)! In your essay, remember to look at both points of view as presented in the question – the question specifically asks you to discuss both viewpoints.

Brainstorming and Vocabulary

See the brainstorming diagram for ideas on what to discuss, arguments, and useful vocabulary.

Free Health Care

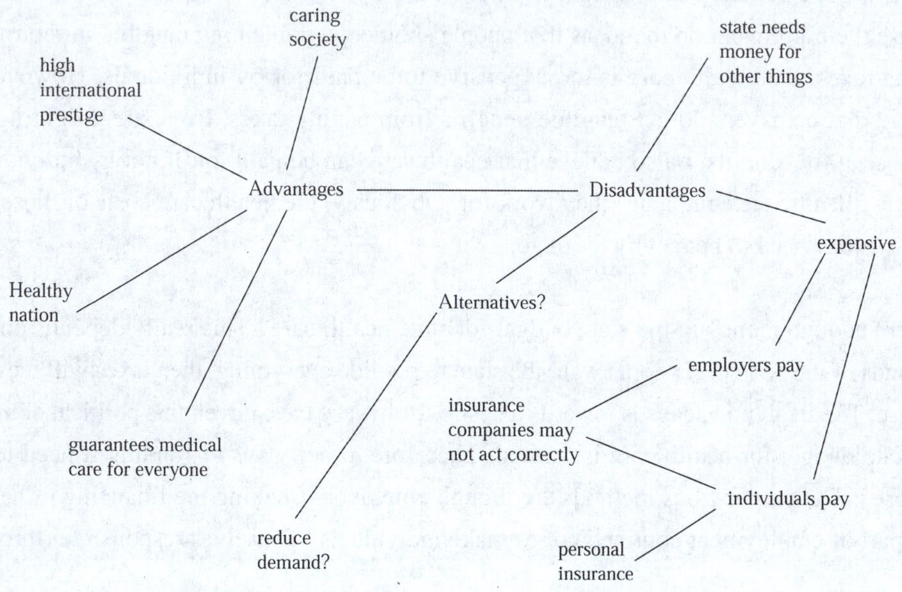

Organising the Essay

Introduction – The introduction should briefly restate the question, using the student's own words as far as possible. Many students like to place their opinion in the introduction, but this is not strictly necessary.

Body – There are three main ways of writing this essay. They are the same as for answering topic 9. The first is the 'classic' approach, having arguments which illustrate your point of view (one paragraph for each) followed by counterarguments (one paragraph for each). The second way is to look at each viewpoint separately, putting the 'for' and 'against' arguments in the same paragraphs. A third method is to look at each of the arguments supporting your opinion in turn and, within the same paragraph, deal with the counter-arguments to this point. In other words, deal with the supporting and opposing arguments together. Each paragraph needs a topic sentence and supporting sentences. Examples are desirable. These examples can be general or specific. You are recommended to choose examples from China, as you know the situation here best. Note that you can also look at other ways of financing health care, such as through employers or through personal insurance. You may choose to support a combination of methods.

Conclusion – In your conclusion you should clearly state your personal opinion on the issue. You may need to suggest the *extent* to which the government should supply free health care. Remember that this question is as much about money as anything else!

Model Answer 范文

In the past, many countries decided to introduce free state health care for citizens. Recently, however, it has become increasingly difficult for governments to find sufficient funding for increasingly expensive state health systems. Even though it would be wonderful if free health care could be provided by the state, I am also aware that the state budget is finite.

Is free health care really a basic right to be provided by the state? People who believe that it is, base their argument on the ideas that people should get something tangible in return for paying taxes, that health care is too expensive to be paid for by individuals. However, I believe that taxpayers do get tangible benefits from paying taxes, from street lighting, to social security benefits. I also believe that health care can be paid for, if not by individuals directly, then by the companies they work for. Obviously, the health care costs of those not working may need to be met by the state.

Is there enough money in the state budget for state health care? This really depends on the demands of the people. If people want the state to provide everything, then taxes will inevitably rise. The trend nowadays is towards a desire for lower taxes. Given this political climate, the state budget for health care is limited. Therefore, other ways of funding it need to be explored. The two obvious methods are though employers (making the financing of health care part of employment contracts) or to make individuals themselves responsible (through personal health plans).

Personally, I believe that the provision of free health care by the state would be marvellous, but that rising costs and demands make this almost impossible. Taking the weight of this responsibility from the state would lead to people taking more responsibility themselves and allow for tax reductions.

(307 words)

5.12 Sample Question 12 样题 12

Present a written argument or case to an educated reader with no specialist knowledge of the following topic.

Many people believe that migration across national borders promotes development and international understanding. Others suggest that more often it causes severe problems for the countries that people migrate from and the countries that they migrate to.

Discuss these opinions and state your own conclusion on the issue.

You should write at least 250 words.
You should use your own ideas, knowledge and experience and support your arguments with examples and relevant evidence.

Sample Answer 学生答卷

As differ opinion from different people think that migration across national develop and improve international understanding or it causes severe problems for the migrate own country and the countries that they migrate to, I absolutely agree with the first opinion.

One of the reason we can see from the example: A chinese businessman who migrate to UK.

Firstly, the person can bring capital fund for UK and then help the GND running well.

Secondly, the business can community with British friend and learn experience for each other and improve international understanding.

The most important point is the businessman can use the first language community with the chinese friend teach the new technology and help china develop soon

To sum up, from the example. I believe that migration across national borders promotes development and international understanding.

(135 words)

Arguments, Ideas and Evidence: There are only a few ideas and they are not developed. The essay is far too short as a result. Notice that the student always says 'can' – there is *no* mention of what *actually* happens when international migration occurs. The student's example is not very clear. Why does the Chinese businessman have to *migrate* to achieve his aims?

Communicative Quality: The words are quite clear, but the sentences are not well connected.

Vocabulary and Sentence Structure: The student only uses the present tense. Accuracy is high, but the range is very, very limited. The vocabulary is very simple and sometimes incorrect – 'As differ opinion', 'the migrate', 'help the GND running well', 'community'. The student doesn't use capital letters when required (Chinese, China).

How to Answer Sample Question 12 怎样写好样题 12

Understanding the Question

This issue is also very topical and it is very easy to find information about it in newspapers and on the Internet. If you are taking the General Training module, this question should be very familiar to you. Many academic students stay in the countries where they have studied, even after they complete the study program, so all IELTS candidates should have ideas about this topic. The situation varies considerably for each country, depending largely on whether it is a country people tend to migrate to (e.g. USA, Australia, Canada) or a country people tend to migrate from (e.g. China, India, Mexico). You should certainly take China as your main focus, but try to look at the issue from the standpoint of recipient countries too. One way to do this is simply to imagine several hundred thousand foreigners coming to China and taking jobs in more sectors of society. At the moment, there are proportionately few foreigners living and working in China and they tend to take jobs in certain sectors (business and teaching).

Brainstorming and Vocabulary

See the brainstorming diagram for ideas on what to discuss, arguments, and useful vocabulary.

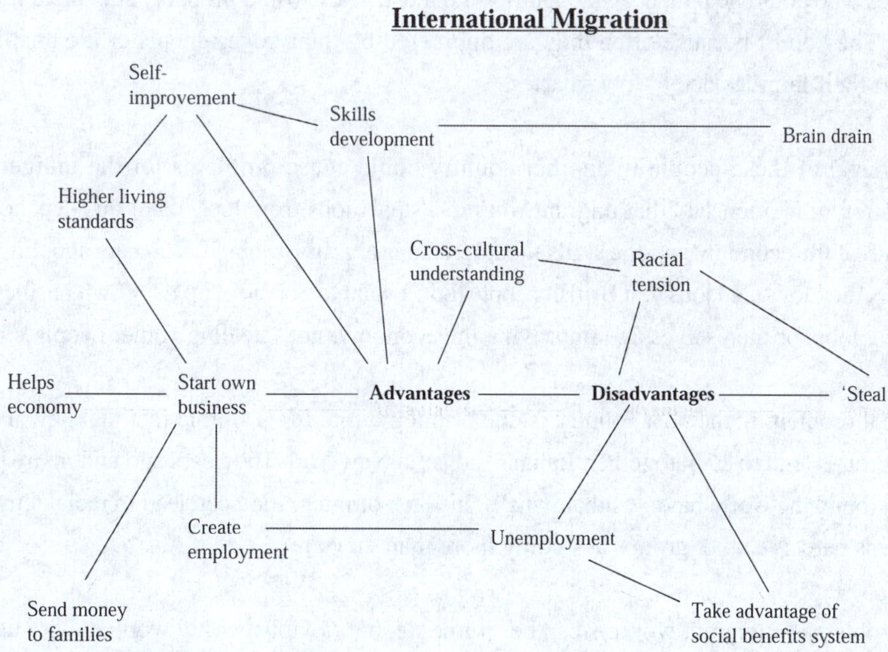

Organising the Essay

Introduction – The introduction should briefly restate the question, using the student's own words as far as possible. Many students like to place their opinion in the introduction, but this is not strictly necessary.

Body – There are several ways of approaching this essay, depending mainly on your personal focus. You can choose to focus mainly on the countries people migrate to, the ones they migrate from, or balance the two. The advantage of this is that you can mainly stay with areas where you know the situation and also the necessary vocabulary. The question does not specifically ask you to consider whether international migration is 'good' or 'bad', but you can certainly include your opinion. To keep your essay clear, you should try to divide arguments into separate paragraphs depending on whether they are about the countries people go to, or come from, or whether they are about the people who migrate.

Conclusion – In your conclusion you should clearly state your personal opinion on the issue. You may need to suggest the *extent* to which international migration should be permitted and what controls may need to be placed on it.

Model Answer 范文

Migration across national borders has existed for centuries, so it cannot be called a new phenomenon. However, does it have more costs than benefits?

The costs of migration are most often felt in the countries that people leave. The people who leave are likely to be those who either have skills that can be used abroad or those who lack skills but are prepared to take risks and work hard in order to succeed. These people are often the ones who could help their own countries the most. They would probably stay there if they could. They don't because often they are oppressed by their governments or are unable to support their families due to low salaries.

The arrival of these people in another country could cause problems for the indigenous population. It is often said that migrant workers "steal" jobs from locals, but this depends on the state of the economy and the skills the migrants bring. In Britain 30-40 years ago, migrant workers took low-paid jobs that British people didn't want to do, or set up their own businesses, creating jobs for themselves and improving the economy, not "stealing" other people's jobs.

The real problem in the host country is one of integration. It's a simple fact that new immigrant groups tend to stick together. Italians did so in New York 100 years ago and many large cities around the world have 'Chinatowns'. This lack of integration can lead to racial tensions if groups perceive other groups as getting more than they are.

The problems of migrant workers can be overcome, but obviously only workers with useful skills and some who are prepared to undergo training should be accepted. The host country needs to make every effort to integrate new migrants into society. However, it is almost inevitable that migrants will cluster together, so migrants need to be aware of their duty to integrate, too.

(317 words)

5.13 Sample Question 13 样题 13

Present a written argument or case to an educated reader with no specialist knowledge of the following topic.

Very few women hold key positions in politics and business. How could society help more women achieve such positions?

You should write at least 250 words.
You should use your own ideas, knowledge and experience and support your arguments with examples and relevant evidence.

Sample answer 1 学生答卷 1

The view has been threw away by people in growing numbers that the Women were not fit for the key position in politics and business. In fact, Women's achievement in those positions were as excellent as men's. However, in another side, we have to admit that the opportunities achieve the positions in politics and economy women have gotten were much less'than men have. The proportional devel0opment with male and female likes two legs of the continued advance of society. Thus, it is an important task more women must get help to hold such key positions.

Firstly, Women should get as many as possible educated and trained chances. So they could have enough abilities to fit for the challenges in key roles when the opportunities coming.

Secondly, The society must assure to provide equal developing chances for women and men without any sexism in the selection of key positions.

Last but not least, The society must change many traditional concepts, for example, when a woman just held key position in politics or business. Because hasn't enough experiences in this position, she may be make some mistakes. We must prevent the view then likes women are less intelligent than men in key roles. and so forth. There should are more tolerances and encouragements to female-leaders in our society.

Although there are also many impediments at the road women get key positions presently. I believe the public will think it's natural more and more women held those key positions as men one day after all kinds of help by whole society.

(259 words)

Arguments, Ideas and Evidence: The student introduces three ideas (all good ones), but really only develops the third one. Notice that the word count only just exceeds the minimum requirement. The student indicates *what* should be done, but doesn't *really* tackle the issue of *how* to achieve the objectives. For example, why have women had fewer opportunities than men? Once this question is answered, solutions should appear.

Communicative Quality: The essay is generally easy to read and contains sufficient connectives. However, some of the sentences are hard to understand due to poor sentence structure.

Vocabulary and Sentence Structure: The student tries to use good vocabulary, but is let down by inappropriacy and poor grammar. Look at these sentences. "Firstly, women should get as many as possible educated and trained chances." "Because hasn't enough experiences in this position, she may be make some mistakes." The sentences are clear, but the student cannot distinguish well between different forms of words, has problems with word order, and problems with uncountable nouns.

Sample Answer 2 学生答卷 2

At present, it is obvious that women don't get fair treatment in their work career. No matter when they apply for jobs, or are in the work, they often frustrate more than men. Most of time, they are not be concerned. Even if they have the ability and perform perfectly, very few of them can hold key positions in the field they work at. This has been a serious issue in our society. In my opinion, it should be attributed to prejudice against women.

We must admit that for a long time in the history, women devoted themselves to their family. So people were given a deep impression that the only thing women can do is taking care of their husbands and children. However, it is not true. Women are intelligent and they have the ability to do what men can do, in some field even better than men. Therefore, people in the society should correct their thought about women. They are not only housewives, but also can be outstanding workers, they shouldn't be the symbol of weakness, because they are ability to overcome every difficulties.

Moreover, our society should give women more chances. Firstly, leaders should give more training chances to their female employees. As we know, most of time, leaders prefer to give the chance to men, even if the women employee has the same ability as the man. If women have the training to improve their knowledge and work skills, they will be more competitive and do much better in their work. Secondly, in my view, government should enact some policy to deal with this problem if it is possible. For example, to force the corporation to leave some key positions for women, such as some special partment in which women do better than men.

To sum up, it is high time we put an end to the undesirable phenomen of prejudice against women. And the society should help women get fair treatment as men, and achieve key positions in politics and business.

(336 words)

Arguments, Ideas and Evidence: The ideas presented in the essay are good ones, but need a little more development and support. For example, in the second paragraph, the student mentions 'training' but what kind of training?

Communicative Quality: The essay is easy to follow and the student uses many connectives and discourse markers well.

Vocabulary and Sentence Structure: There is some good vocabulary and collocation ("attributed to prejudice", "symbol of weakness", "enact [a] policy", "fair treatment") in this essay. Unfortunately, the grammar is quite poor. Basic mistakes are common and the student occasionally uses the wrong form of a word ("they often frustrate", "they are not be concerned", "they are ability"). There are some spelling mistakes (husbents, competetive, partment, phenomen).

Sample Answer 3 学生答卷 3

With the development of society, women are allowed to work outside their families. However, there is still some discrimination: very few women have the chance to hold key positions in politics and business. It's a social problem and our society should take some measures to help more women achieve such positions.

On the one hand, the prevalent attitude towards women working should be changed. At present, quite a number of people believe that women's ability are not so good as men. As a result, most employer wouldn't choose women to be charge of the important project. As far as I'm concerned, such view is very ridiculous. Everyone is born equally and the ability is cultivated later, through education, social actions and communication. Therefore, whether men or women is more suitable for key position, it all depends. To help, Our government could bravely promote capable women for key position to give an example to all the society.

On the other hand, well educated women should continuely improve themselves to quanlify key positions in Politics and business. As we all know, in this rapidly changing world, competition is here and there, especially in high position. For the reason that it is crucial for those who operate the company or manage the city, town and so on to make decisions, so the work itself needs high quality people to make things better and better.

In a word, the problem is difficult to solve. Both the average people and women have to make great effort.

(251 words)

Arguments, Ideas and Evidence: The student has missed the point of the question. The student mainly talks about *equality*, but the question is about how to *improve* the status of women. One method is mentioned (the government should set an example), but it is not given sufficient supporting evidence or ideas. The last four sentences make little sense in relation to the topic.

Communicative Quality: The essay is easy to read and the student uses many connectives well.

Vocabulary and Sentence Structure: The vocabulary actually used in the essay is reasonably good, but is not used to answer the question. There are a few inappropriacies. The grammar is also reasonably good, but there is a limited range of structures.

How to Answer – Sample Question 13 怎样写好样题 13

Understanding the Question

This issue is yet another very topical one and it is very easy to find information about it in newspapers and on the Internet. Almost every girl / woman reading this book will know something about this issue! And every man *should*! The situation varies considerably for each country, so my first suggestion is that you clearly state that you are writing about China (unless you are very familiar with the situation in another country). The differences between China and countries such as the USA, Britain, and Australia are fairly widely known, so you might wish to refer to them. Most students will go for the 'auto-response' that "China is a traditional country …" Whilst this is true in some ways, remember that one of the key principles of "New" China after the 1949 revolution has been sex equality. The focus of the question is forward-looking – what can be done to improve the situation. You may disagree with the question and argue that the position of women does not need to be improved, though it is doubtful that many people will argue that.

Brainstorming and Vocabulary

See the brainstorming diagram for ideas on what to discuss, arguments, and useful vocabulary.

Status of Women

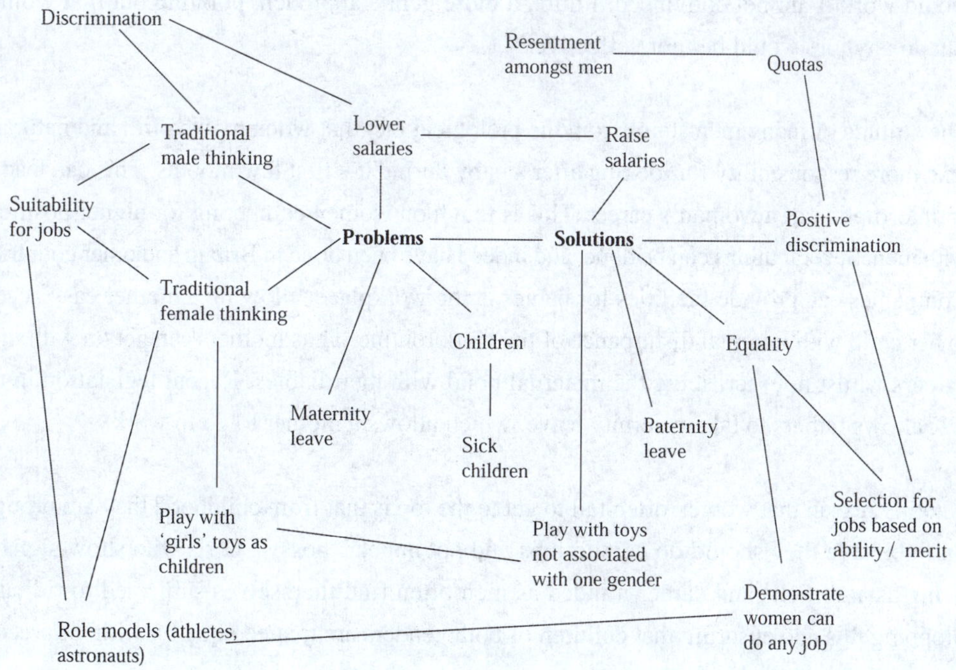

Organising the Essay

Introduction – The introduction should briefly restate the question, using the student's own words as far as possible. Many students like to place their opinion in the introduction, but this is not strictly necessary.

Body – The best way to deal with this essay is probably to look at why women are disadvantaged in society. Once you have these reasons, one per paragraph would probably be best, you can consider how the situation could be changed to give women a better chance. You can deal with counter-arguments as they appear in each paragraph or at the end of the essay.

Conclusion – In your conclusion you should clearly state your personal opinion on the best solutions. You may need to suggest the extent to which the government, companies, and individuals should take responsibility for creating sex equality. If your conclusion is that women should not have equality with men or that they do not need any help in any form, try to be diplomatic about it!

Model Answer 范文

It is still unusual for many women to hold high positions in politics and business despite the fact that most societies believe that sex equality is correct. I would like to suggest a few ways in which the situation could be improved.

To do this, we need to look at why women do not already reach high positions. One clear reason is that many men have sexist attitudes towards women, believing them to do be inferior. To be fair, most men are hardly aware that they hold such attitudes. They blurt out sentences like "That job isn't really suitable for a woman", without realising they are being sexist. Some people think that punishing men, or embarrassing them, for making such statements would work. I am not convinced. I think a more gentle approach, pointing out that women can do any job, would be more effective.

The attitude of many men stems from the biological fact that women give birth and naturally take more responsibility for looking after a baby during it's first few months. This can lead to an interruption of a woman's career. This is tough on women competing for higher positions with men. Several things can be done, and indeed have been done in Britain and other countries. Companies can provide facilities for babies at the workplace, allowing a mother easy access to her child with minimal disturbance of the work routine. Thus mothers can get on with their careers whilst not sacrificing the maternal bond with their babies. Recent legislation in the UK allows fathers to take paternity leave, which allows a mother to go to work.

Another reason that women often fail to get to the top is that from childhood they are brought up to believe they should do certain jobs and not appear 'bossy'. Girls who show signs of being as ambitious and career-minded as men often find themselves subjected to ridicule. Stopping this and ensuring that children of both genders are treated equally, without preconceived ideas of what a 'woman' should be, will help a lot.

Many people believe that one way forward is to have quotas for women in top positions. This, however, has met with opposition from men (who claim that the best person should get the top jobs) and by women (who do not want to be part of a quota, but want to be promoted on their merits). I think that the measures I have outlined above can succeed, though admittedly only in the long-term. It will be a while until women rise through the ranks to take a much higher proportion of top jobs in politics and business.

(440 words)

答案

Exercise 1　Present simple and present continuous

1. points　2. prefers　3. watches　4. am doing
5. visit　6. doesn't boil　7. am not watching　8. say … feel
9. am reading　10. don't understand

Exercise 2　Present and past tenses

1. have been writing　2. was not (wasn't)　3. has been watching / has watched
4. have done … want　5. have been used　6. has not boiled
7. go　8. have been walking　9. read / have been reading
10. do not read

Exercise 3　Past tense forms

1. had been playing … started　2. had not heard … mentioned
3. was snowing … arrived　4. rang … was cooking
5. was watching / watched … went

Exercise 4　Future tense forms

1. will probably visit　2. will not have slept　3. will not be sleeping
4. will have built　5. will have worked

Exercise 5　Verbs – Antonyms and Synonyms

Set A. agree – contradict, challenge – accept, compare – contrast, criticise – praise, divide – join, increase – decrease, strengthen – weaken, succeed – fail.

Set B. admit – deny, damage – heal, extend – reduce, lend – borrow, permit – prohibit, present – receive, produce – use, tire – wake.

Set C. double – halve, expand – contract, free – limit, heat – cool, move – stop, leave – remain, rise – fall, support – oppose.

Set D. continue – stop, inform – mislead, interfere – leave, notice – miss, retain – reform, show – hide, specify – generalise, volunteer – force.

Set E. choose – select, decrease – lower, divide – split, emphasise – stress, increase – raise, justify – defend, occur – happen, suggest – recommend.

Set F. abandon – leave, accelerate – hasten, answer – respond, assume – think, criticise – attack, exchange – trade, facilitate – permit, pursue – follow.

Exercise 6 Practise your linking words!

1. after
2. Before
3. until
4. as soon as
5. After
6. just as
7. while
8. Meanwhile
9. as
10. whilst
11. Moreover
12. As well as
13. In addition
14. also
15. too
16. even though
17. Although
18. In spite of that
19. despite
20. though
21. whereas
22. On the other hand
23. In contrast
24. yet
25. Nonetheless
26. unless
27. in case
28. Otherwise
29. rains
30. depending on
31. because of
32. due to
33. since
34. as
35. because
36. For example
37. In conclusion
38. instead of
39. eventually
40. as
41. Besides
42. Although
43. Whereas
44. to
45. whether
46. due to
47. to
48. Therefore
49. except
50. while

Exercise 10 Clauses

1

1. which/that	2. who/that	3. whose	4. where	5. who/that
6. when	7. when	8. which/that	9. who/that	10. that + when

3

Phrases of purpose / Infinitive clauses

1. A person needs to be strong in order to succeed in the world.
2. You need good people working for you to operate a successful business.
3. An athlete must train hard for success in the Olympics.
4. People should eat the right food to maintain good health.
5. A bar requires something special in order to attract customers.
6. In order for the police to check your identity, they may take your fingerprints.
7. In order to ensure security, there should be some cameras.
8. To keep children happy at a party, make sure there is entertainment.

9. For success in IELTS, you need to prepare well.
10. In order for us to contact you anytime, you need a mobile phone.

Exercise 11 Adjectives – Antonyms and Synonyms

Set A. active – passive, brave – cowardly, changeable – constant, destructive – constructive, enticing – repulsive, foreseeable – unpredictable, grandiose – modest, icy – warm, judicious – imprudent.

Set B. mainstream – marginal, novel – common, omnipotent – powerless, potent – weak, reliable – uncertain, skilful – incompetent, tedious – interesting, unjust – fair, worthy – unsuitable, young – mature.

Set C. acceptable – agreeable, blunt – outspoken, clumsy – awkward, decent – appropriate, economical – thrifty, fictitious – imaginary, grave – serious, heated – passionate, illicit – forbidden, keen – sagacious.

Set D. ludicrous – absurd, mistaken – misinformed, necessary – indispensable, organised – coordinated, permanent – lasting, rapid – swift, sensible – rational, transparent – clear, unsuitable – inappropriate, whole – entire.

附录 1 Bloopers 洋相百出

Illogical Arguments

You must have specialised knowledge to enjoy classical music.
('Knowledge' is not required to enjoy any kind of music!)

I don't have time to read, because I must study.
(Studying usually involves reading!)

I shared it by myself.
(You cannot share things with yourself!)

It has some disadvantages, because it's good for their future.
('Disadvantages' are bad by definition!)

I like animals, because there are many animals in the countryside.
I like panda, because it is the most protected animal in China.
I like cats, because I can see them on the streets.
(We like things because of their attributes!)

China is a big country, so we have four seasons.
(Small countries can have four seasons too!)

She is a good person, because I know her father.
(The fact that you know her father doesn't mean she is a good person!)

Poetic Statements

… enlarge your eyesight.
('broaden your horizons')

… absorbed in her kindness and reliability.
('impressed by her kindness and reliability')

It was an ocean of drought.
(An ocean is water. A drought means no water.)

It gives me a deep impression.
(It made an impression on me.)

Really?

I am writing to express that I am going to receive the aid from you.
(Are you *sure* I'm going to help you?)

I need some hands from you.
(I think you mean 'a hand'!)

More and more people are getting older.
(Really? I thought we were getting younger?)

In my opinion, I'm a student.
(You're not sure?)

Pandas can give us the development.
(Sounds unlikely!)

Disco logic is a Western danger.
(I'm not sure what 'disco logic' is!)

My ability make me couldn't study.
(?)

The Chinese government will put a one-child policy.
(The Chinese government *has* a one-child policy!)

To have the same job as yourself has it's own advantages.
(It certainly does!)

… especially in developing and developed countries.
(And what about countries that are not developing or developed?)

My friend must be like animal.
(Which one? 'Like' and 'be like' are quite different!)

It is not as important as it is now.
(?)

I will graduated from the university next year, so I want to go to Australia.
('Will' is for the future. 'Graduated' is in the past!)

I seldom like to visit that place sometimes.
(Confusing!)

People who like dark colours are special, because they can make bright colours.
(Hmmm …)

I go shopping for sports equipment. For example, I bought a cat yesterday.
(you use a cat as sports equipment?!)

In my country, animals are used to telephone.
(New technology?)

Vocabulary Problems

You need some skills, such as a partner, to play table tennis.
(A 'partner' is not a skill.)

People often watch sports on TV, because they are friends.
(You mean they watch sport on TV *together*.)

When we heard the news, we hungered together.
(?)

We share the same things – even the same boyfriend!
(This is possible, but you might mean 'friend' not 'boyfriend'.)

Wuhan has many lakes, so it has another name – the city of rivers.
('Lakes' and 'rivers' are different.)

My major is violence.
(I don't think so!)

Spelling Mistakes

… watching dishes.
('washing')

I don't worry about the cost, because my boss gave me a nice celery.
('salary')

I like dumplings with a salary inside.
('celery')

I often go to the loo to see wild animals.
('zoo')

In Shanghai there is marry university.
('many')

Modesty is Important

My city has a bright future, because of me.
The Olympic Games in China is a big success for me.

附录 2 Useful Websites 有用的网站

www.ielts.org

The official IELTS website. Contains lots of useful advice about taking the test and some sample materials.

www.britishcouncil.org.cn

The British Council administers the IELTS test in China. A visit to this website is essential before you even apply to take the IELTS test.

www.ielts-test.com

A website by and for IELTS candidates. Some useful advice.

www.international.holmesglan.vic.edu.au

Contains information and materials you can use online or download.

www.eslcafe.com

Excellent website for general English. Great for teachers and students. Some IELTS related resources.

www.usingenglish.com

Very useful for grammar explanations.

www.51ielts.com

Information and lots of sample questions. Don't take the advice on this site too seriously! And do NOT copy the sample answers (because they're not very good!). In Chinese.

www.englishclub.com

Lots of useful help for students who seriously want to improve their English.

www.in2english.com.cn

An excellent interactive website offering plenty of help with learning English.

www.timesonline.co.uk

The Sunday Times Good University Guide. Great resource for those wishing to attend British universities.

